Conquistador in Chains

Conquistador in Chains

Cabeza de Vaca
and the
Indians of the Americas

DAVID A. HOWARD

The University of Alabama Press
TUSCALOOSA AND LONDON

Copyright © 1997

The University of Alabama Press

Tuscaloosa, Alabama 35487-0380

designed by erin toppin bradley

The paper on which this book is printed
meets the minimum requirements
of American National Standard
for Information Science–Permanence of Paper
for Printed Library Materials, ANSI Z39.48-1984.

Acknowledgment is made
to Oxford University Press
for permission to quote
a passage from Samuel Eliot Morison,
The European Discovery of America: The Southern Voyages,
copyright © 1994 Oxford University Press.

Library of Congress Cataloging-in-Publication Data

Howard, David A.

Conquistador in chains : Cabeza de Vaca
and the Indians of the Americas / David A. Howard.

p.   cm.

Includes bibliographical references and index.

ISBN 0-8173-0828-8 (pbk. : alk. paper)

1. Núñez Cabeza de Vaca, Alvar, 16th cent. 2. Explorers—America—Biography.
3. Explorers—Spain—Biography. 4. Indians of North America—First contact with Europeans.
5. America—Discovery and exploration—Spanish. I. Title.

E125.N9H68   1997

970.01′6′092—dc20

[B]   96-10629

British Library Cataloguing-in-Publication Data available

Contents

Maps

Preface

No longer do the Spanish conquerors of the New World stand in a flattering light. Generations of celebration and romance have given way to a focus on cruelty, violence, tyranny and brutality. Yet such a viewpoint is too narrow, especially for a unique conquistador named Alvar Núñez Cabeza de Vaca. A life-changing adventure led Cabeza de Vaca to a vision of a different kind of conquest, one that would safeguard liberty and justice for the Indians of the New World. Although this Spanish soldier and official understood the goal of conquest as did the other soldiers of his era, he differed in his beliefs about the means used to gain that goal. He sought a conquest that was just and humane, true to Spanish religion and law.

His ideas of liberty or justice were entirely Spanish. The Indians of America, he assumed, would be better off under Spanish and Christian civilization than under their own political and social systems. Thus, Cabeza de Vaca was an imperialist who imagined that the policies of the government of Spain might be achieved in America by just and humane means and under Spanish law. The model for such a conquest came from his reaction to the abuses by other conquistadores in bringing Indians under Spanish authority. To try to hold him to the values of the post- and anti-imperialist outlook of the late twentieth century would be to miss the vital differences between him and the others of his generation.

This account of Cabeza de Vaca's career is based on published primary sources. During the past century many works have been published in Spain, Argentina, and Paraguay relating to the era of conquest and colonization in the Río de la Plata province (see bibliography). An index of relevant unpublished sources in the Archivo General de Indias in Seville, Spain, appears in Raúl Molina, *Misiones Argentinas en los archivos europeos,* 378–435. The titles of documents there show that little of significance remains unpublished.

Other lists of titles in that archive give the same result: Luis Alberto Musso Ambrosi, *El Río de la Plata en el archivo general de Indias de Sevilla, guía para investigadores;* and Victor Tau Anzoátegui, ed., *Libros registros-cedularios del Río de la Plata (1534–1717): Catálogo I.* The same situation exists for the Archivo Nacional in Asunción, Paraguay: see *Guía de los documentos microfotografiados por la unidad móvil de microfilm de la UNESCO* and Francisco Sevillano Colom, "Lista del contenido de los volúmenes microfilmados del archivo nacional de Asunción."

This narrative focuses on Cabeza de Vaca himself but also, as necessary, on those Europeans and Indians on two continents who were part of his ordeals and successes.

Acknowledgments

Many people have helped me in this study of Alvar Núñez Cabeza de Vaca. The first thoughts that led to my research came at a National Endowment for the Humanities Summer Seminar at Harvard University, directed by the late J. H. Parry. Although a number of college and university libraries and librarians provided a variety of sources, particular thanks must go to those at Harvard University, Duke University, Cornell University, the State University of New York at Buffalo, and my own institution, Houghton College. Also at Houghton College, my colleagues in the History Department gave encouragement and support: Drs. Katherine Lindley, William Doezema, and A. Cameron Airhart. Much of the research was done during Sabbaticals supported by Houghton College. Thanks also are due to those readers, people unknown to me, who have reviewed and commented on this text during its evaluation, and to Dr. Eugene Lyon for recommending The University of Alabama Press for publication. The University of Alabama Press has provided much help and encouragement. I am thankful to its editor, Malcolm M. MacDonald, manuscript editor Ellen Goldlust, and the staff of the Press. Finally, my family has helped me in many ways directly connected to my research, including the maps. My dear wife, Dr. Irmgard K. Howard, has read almost as many versions as I have. I thank her most of all.

Conquistador in Chains

Introduction

The great tale of adventure by Spanish conquistador Alvar Núñez Cabeza de Vaca in North America begins abruptly indeed. "On the 17th day of the month of June of 1527, Governor Pánfilo de Narváez left from the Port of San Lúcar de Barrameda, with power and command from your majesty to conquer and govern the provinces which are from the River of Las Palmas to the Cape of Florida." So opens his famous book, first published in 1542 with the title *La relación*. As treasurer and chief constable, Cabeza de Vaca was one of the royal officials with Narváez. Yet not until the end of the book do readers learn about Cabeza de Vaca's background, and even then he provides merely the names of his father, Francisco de Vera, his grandfather, Pedro de Vera (conqueror of the Canary Islands), and his mother, Doña Tereza Cabeza de Vaca.[1]

One might expect to see him called Vera, or even Núñez, as many Latin American writers now favor. He himself used his mother's name, Cabeza de Vaca, possibly to mark the honor of her family, although his father's family name, Vera, did not lack standing either. In 1212, as legend had it, during the Spanish reconquest of the Muslims, a peasant ancestor of his mother, Martín Alhaja, gave aid to the Christians by using a cow's skull to point out a mountain pass north of Seville. As a reward after the victory, King Sancho of Navarre renamed him Cabeza de Vaca—cow's head.

The early life of Cabeza de Vaca must be derived from sources other than his own books. What little is known about his activities before he first set out for America in 1527 may be read in the works of two authors, Morris Bishop and Enrique de Gandía. Gandía determined that Cabeza de Vaca was born in Jerez de la Frontera, Spain, in 1500. That date is found in testimony given by Cabeza de Vaca in Valladolid in September 1548, when he stated on oath that he was about forty-eight years old.[2] Other historians have put his birth at around 1490. The eldest of four children, he lived with an uncle and aunt after his parents died. While he was still young he entered into his first career as a soldier. Gandía quoted testimony from legal records in the Archives of the Indies of Seville which gives brief reports about his military duty in Italy. He was enlisted under Don Alonso de Caravajal as a page or drummer and was in Italy by late 1511 or early 1512, participating in a famous battle and siege at Bologna. In April 1512 he was seriously injured at the battle of Ravenna, which the Spaniards lost. His last post was as a lieutenant in the city of Gaeta, near Naples.

Bishop placed Cabeza de Vaca back in Seville by 1513, in the service of the Duke of Medina Sidonia. In 1520 a civil war broke out in Castile, the revolt of the *comuneros,* and the duke took the side of Charles I, the king of Spain (1516–56), who as Charles V was also Holy Roman emperor (1519–56). Cabeza de Vaca helped the duke and served the king in battles from Seville to Valladolid, Tordesillas, and Villalar. In addition to his valorous deeds in opposing the comuneros, he fought against the French in Navarre. Nothing is known of him between 1522 and 1527, just before he left for America.[3]

Seeing the Poorness of the Land

For eight years a bleak and perilous wilderness held Alvar Núñez Cabeza de Vaca captive.[1] Such hardship and misery would have a great effect on anyone. His long ordeal, "so savage and so remote from the service of God and all good reason," changed him profoundly.[2] A typical conquistador who had come to the New World for riches, for power, and to make a name, he emerged from years of captivity with a new goal: to bring the Indians of America into the Spanish empire with justice and liberty.

This drastic change raised Cabeza de Vaca to a position of singular importance in American history. He became a champion and protector of the Indians, seeking a humane conquest which by kindness, justice, and good treatment would civilize (or Hispanize) and make Christians of them. The questions that came from that undertaking were also singularly important. What happened to Cabeza de Vaca in the wilderness of North America? What prompted him to defend the Indians? Was a humane conquest even possible?

Cabeza de Vaca first came to America in a company led by the conquistador Pánfilo de Narváez. A veteran of warfare in America, Narváez had fought Indians in the Greater Antilles and Spaniards (Hernán Cortés) in Mexico, where he lost an eye. On December 11, 1527, he got the capitulations (a contract with the crown) that he needed for a conquest of "Florida."[3] Like so many others, he dreamed of another Mexico. To look after royal interests, the king of Spain, Charles I, sent along Cabeza de Vaca as royal treasurer and chief constable (*alguacil mayor*).[4]

In June 1527 Governor Narváez sailed for America. His fleet of five ships carried some six hundred people, but more than 145 of them decided to stay at Santo Domingo. Later, at Cuba, sixty others were lost in a hurricane. When Narváez finally sailed to Florida in April 1528, he had only four hundred men and eighty horses. Such conquistadores were adventurers of varied backgrounds, some more desperate than others, and they often proved quite effective in battle. Discipline and the methods of warfare were more customary than formal, and the key to control over such a company was its leadership. On Good Friday Narváez's ships landed on Florida's west coast, although the exact site remains open to debate. The next day, at an Indian village deserted by its wary people, Narváez claimed the land in the name of Charles I.[5]

Ten years later, Cabeza de Vaca wrote a report for the king about the experiences that followed. It was published in 1542 (at Zamora) as *La relación* (Relation), and a second edition appeared in 1555 (at Valladolid) under the title *Naufragios* (Shipwrecks).[6] This classic story of conquest, written in part to win another royal office, tells of his many adventures and reveals his changing ideas about the native people of America. This book says little about the Indians in Florida—a few sentences about what he did and saw provide the only evidence of his ideas.[7] Naturally, he wrote mostly about his own work and the problems of survival. The Indians at the town on the coast where he landed were hostile, a warning of troubles to come.[8] The Spaniards, who had their own reasons to go onward, forced the Indians to act as guides and took their stores of corn.

Cabeza de Vaca's legal responsibilities did include the Indians. While the main duties were financial, he was instructed to "take care of and be diligent to look after anything that may tend to our royal service," including telling the king "how the natives are treated, our instructions observed, and other

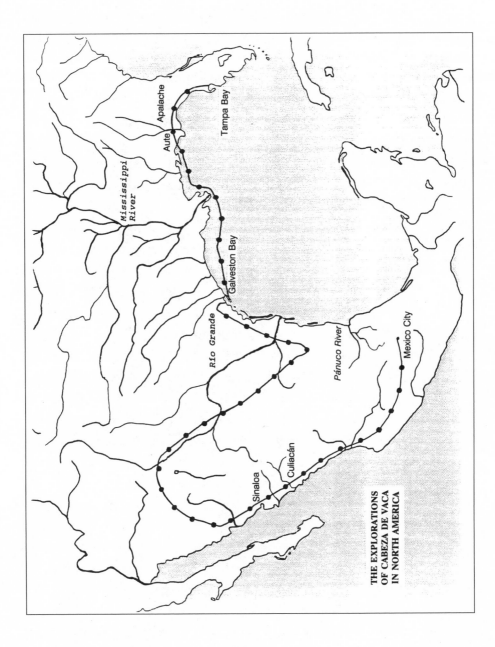

THE EXPLORATIONS
OF CABEZA DE VACA
IN NORTH AMERICA

of the things respecting their liberties that we have commanded; especially the matters touching the service of our Lord and divine worship, the teachings of the Indians in the Holy Faith."[9] As alguacil mayor, Cabeza de Vaca's duties included watching over the Spaniards to keep them from harming the Indians.[10] Yet he appeared to be no more upset about how the Indians were treated than were his companions and showed no more regret about ignoring their "liberties."

The Spaniards had come to America for gold. When they saw that the Indians had small quantities of it (probably salvaged from wrecked Spanish ships), they asked where it was found. By good luck or wisdom, the Indians said that very far away was a province called Apalache, where there was much gold.[11] Surely no answer was more likely to get rid of such an army of invaders.[12] Narváez, taking a gamble, decided to go inland, while his ships carried supplies up the coast. Cabeza de Vaca strongly opposed taking such a risk; he wanted to wait until the Spaniards had a secure port and more supplies. Narváez had made up his mind, however, and he said that if Cabeza de Vaca was afraid to go inland on the *entrada* (armed expedition), he could take charge of the ships. That scorn, of course, bound Cabeza de Vaca by honor to go with the governor, however rash the plan. The thought of gold was also a strong lure, for his remarks show that he shared in its enchantment.

The expedition inland caused great suffering. Three hundred soldiers, forty on horseback, crossed the rough countryside with immense effort. After much arduous travel they met another group of about two hundred Indians, whose actions caused the intruders to seize five or six of them. Such strife was to mark the rest of that journey.[13] Nearly starving, the Spaniards came at last to the town of Apalache. (The site of that town has been determined to be Ivitachuco, and the land attached to it covered some forty miles east to west and north to south.)[14] Reaching their goal, where food and gold were expected, revived the men. To take the town, Narváez put fifty infantry and nine cavalry under Cabeza de Vaca, an experienced officer, who did not question attacking unsuspecting people. In Florida he was merely another conquistador, one of many willing to use force without question, a soldier following orders.

Apalache was not another Mexico. Narváez found only women and children there, for the men had fled. One can imagine the shock of finding that this town of forty small, thatched huts was the largest in the area. In two hours the Indian men came to ask for their families and peace. Narváez agreed but upset the Indians by holding a chief hostage. A day later they began trying to drive out the invaders, attacking suddenly and from ambush, but the Spaniards could not force a battle with foes who were so quick to retreat.

For almost a month the Spaniards stayed in the area. Three scouting trips showed that the nearby people were poor and the traveling was bad. They asked the hostage chief and the Indians who came with them from beyond Apalache about the people, the land, and its supplies. All of them agreed that Apalache was the largest town—farther away, the people became fewer and much poorer. It was a region of large lakes, dense forest, and great wilderness, but no people. To the south, however, the land had towns and food. Nine days' journey toward the sea was the town of Aute, they explained. There the Indians had maize, beans, squash, and fish.

The Spaniards were ready to quit. Cabeza de Vaca recalled their deep gloom. "Seeing the poorness of the land, the bad reports that [the Indians] gave us of the people and all the rest, and how the Indians made constant war upon us, wounding men and horses at the places where we went to get water, attacking from the lakes in so much safety that we could not harm them," the invaders decided to go to the sea.

These Indians excited little feeling in Cabeza de Vaca. Only their military qualities struck him. Writing about a furious attack, for example, he said that "all the Indians we saw from Florida are archers, and because they are naked and so tall, from a distance they seem gigantic. They are a people admirably well-formed, very slender, and with great strength and quickness."[15] In fact, they wounded him in one of their assaults. In America Cabeza de Vaca was merely a spectator. The humanity of the Indians and their way of life did not interest him very much. He did not try to change or Christianize them, in spite of his royal orders. The Indians had value only as they were useful to the Spaniards. Taking their food or property and making them act as hostages or guides drew no blame. These steps were necessary for the Spaniards to survive, even though the Indians might thereby starve. According to historian José B. Fernández, Cabeza de Vaca left out of his book Narváez's atrocities in Florida because the failure to prevent them probably would make it hard to get another royal grant.[16] It is just as likely that if Cabeza de Vaca saw such misdeeds, he did not yet care very much about what was happening to the Indians.

Back to the sea went the Spaniards. Nine days from Apalache they came to Aute, burnt and deserted already, but with much corn, squash, and beans left behind.[17] After two days rest, Cabeza de Vaca took some men to the coast. His scouts found that it was very hard to travel along the shoreline, and there was no sign of the ships. Reporting to Narváez at Aute, he learned that Indians had attacked and that the men were becoming sick. Only one choice was left. As impossible as it must have seemed because they lacked skills, tools, and materials, they needed to get to the sea and make boats. An extremely hard, daylong journey brought them to the shore at a place that they named the Bay of Horses. The number of sick grew by the hour, and more than forty died of hunger and illness. The desperate survivors used whatever was at hand and put together five boats or barges. On September 22 they were able to cast off. Each of the unsound vessels carried about fifty men, heading along the coast toward New Spain.[18]

For weeks the Spaniards sailed and drifted, often through storms. They fought off Indian attacks and survived with little food. Finally, came the coast of Texas, where they were shipwrecked on an island. The date, noted by Cabeza de Vaca, was November 6, 1528.[19] A few of the men survived, fed and sheltered thanks to the pity of the Indians. Those who went back out to sea were never again seen; among them was Narváez, who abandoned the rest to their fate.[20]

So Miserable an Existence

The shipwreck led to a great change in Cabeza de Vaca. He and the others knew that they would soon die without help, which had to come from the people who lived there—the Indians.[1] For the first time since coming to North America, these Spaniards had a need to learn something about the humanity of the Indians. The island held two peoples, named the Capoques and the Han, who were part of a somewhat diverse Indian population, speaking different languages but labeled for convenience the Karankawa. Each group had about four hundred members. As nonsedentary Indians, they moved from the island to the mainland when seasonal food supplies required. By the twentieth century the Karankawa had become extinct.[2]

For Cabeza de Vaca these Indians became the key to life. He and the other mariners slowly recovered from their hard landing. After they had eaten, rested, and explored the island, they tried to launch their boat, but an enormous wave immediately crashed over them. The battered craft tipped and sank, and three men drowned. Seeing the disaster, the Indians began crying aloud; their concern touched Cabeza de Vaca. "Truly, finding that these men, so crude and lacking reason like brutes, were grieving so much for us, increased for me and the rest of the company our anxiety and concern for our misfortune."

This hint of human sympathy helped him decide what to do. He begged the Indians to take the Spaniards to their camp. His men were terrified. They knew that earlier in Mexico the Aztecs had sacrificed Spanish captives before their idols. However, these Indians seemed so agreeable that by the next morning that worry faded for the warmed and fed survivors.[3]

The Spaniards named the island *Malhado,* meaning evil fate or doom. By withholding food, the Indians eventually forced some of the unwilling Spaniards to practice medicine, "without examining us or demanding our licenses." The Spanish cures came about by "making the sign of the cross, blowing on them, reciting a Pater Noster and an Ave Maria, and praying the best that we could that God our Lord would give them health." An added plea was that God would inspire the Indians to treat them well. As God willed, said Cabeza de Vaca, their patients at once told the other Indians that they were healthy and sound. Such cures, reflecting both Spanish and Indian ideas about medical treatment, would be vital to his eventual escape.[4] Ironically, half of the Indians soon died of a stomach sickness, which some of them guessed was of Spanish origin.[5]

The six years that followed were harsh. The Spaniards traveled to and from the mainland to find food, often living as slaves or captives of different groups. Until his escape in 1534, Cabeza de Vaca stayed with several Indian peoples. The hunters and gatherers who lived away from the coast survived for part of the year mainly on prickly pear fruits or pecan nuts. As these foods grew in two widely separated areas and ripened at different times of the summer or fall, those Indians ranged over some five thousand square miles.[6]

Most of the Spaniards soon died, and Cabeza de Vaca gave this part of his story only a few pages. He wrote with some relief about getting freedom to travel and to carry on trade as a merchant for the Charruco Indians, acting as a neutral stranger who could exchange goods between hostile peoples. Cabeza de Vaca stayed as aloof from the Indians as his way of life allowed. His book shows how far he kept himself from them emotionally during the years on Malhado Island and the mainland. Often he thought them to be peculiar. The end of one passage makes clear his view of how they lived: "They have other strange customs, but I have related the most important and notable."[7] He often commented about Indians in a general way, so it is not always possible to link his remarks with specific peoples.[8] The bonds that grew later, during the long walk to New Spain, were not yet evident. He still admired their war skills and valor, but from the time of the shipwreck until the escape began, his book portrays him as ready to attack Indian villages and loot Indian food. The difference, of course, was that now he had to work and beg for food. If a passing ship had taken him off the coast of Texas, he would have missed the experiences that made him one of the chief supporters and defenders of the Indians. After six years in the wilderness, he looked upon them just as he had in the beginning. They still had value only for his own survival. Not until he began the journey to New Spain did his view of the Indians change.

The time spent with the Indians on Malhado Island was not happy. The perils of starvation, overwork, illness, hard winters, and death fueled his desire to escape. He believed that the Spanish settlement at Pánuco, located to the south on the Pánuco River, was nearby. The bad treatment and forced labor finally caused him to flee to the mainland, where he was able to do the trading that so pleased him. With freedom to come and go as he wanted and not as a slave, he explored the countryside to look for a way out. This urge to escape was not shared by all the Spaniards. For several years he tried to get Lope de Oviedo to go with him. Oviedo finally agreed but then turned back when some Indians terrorized them. Three other men joined him: Andrés Dorantes of Béjar, his "Arabian" black slave, Estebanico of Azamor, and Alonso del Castillo Maldonado of Salamanca. If they had refused to flee, said Cabeza de Vaca, he was ready to go without them. His desire was at its peak, for he had recently eluded Indians who had tried to kill him three times.[9] During 1533 and 1534 he and Dorantes were captured by a group of two hundred Mariames Indians and learned to speak their language. Estebanico and Castillo were held by the nearby Iguases Indians, and the four men escaped from these two groups in late September or early October 1534. The Spaniards planned to head south at summer's end, when the Mariames Indians went north to their winter living area.[10]

Once they had passed the point of recapture, their treatment changed radically. People met them who were eager to help. After years of living with erratic Indian behavior—friendship and violence, respect and bondage, pity and cruelty—they were treated with awe and reverence. Cabeza de Vaca, in turn, began to learn sympathy and understanding for the Indians. He also came to see the hand of God leading him out of the wilderness. Several times since coming to Florida he had been aware of divine protection and aid, but only now was he assured that God would use these adventures for some purpose. Cabeza de Vaca's much happier relations with the Indians on the road to New Spain and his growing sense of Providence led him to the values that made him a friend and helper to the Indians.

That flight began in great fear. The fugitives went as far as they could go, and the sun had set before they stopped among the Avavares Indians.[11] According to sixteenth-century historian Gonzalo Fernández de Oviedo y Valdés, the Avavares knew about the Spaniards but not how badly the other Indians had treated them, "which was very good for these sinners."[12] They were welcomed, for their fame as healers and miracle workers had gone on before them, and they stayed for eight months. Soon Castillo was asked for healing, and a sign of the cross and prayer entrusting them to God again brought success. The result was food—and more Indians asking for help. Cabeza de Vaca began to see this kindness from the Indians as a spiritual help. "We gave many thanks to God, because each day His mercy and grace were increasing."

While they were among these Indians, five very sick people were brought to Castillo. Prayers again seemed to cure them, encouraging Cabeza de Vaca's hopes for help to escape from "so miserable an existence." Yet, healing began to mean more to him than self-interest. "For ourselves it brought to mind that we give many thanks to our Lord, in order that we know more fully His goodness and have firm hope that He was delivering us and leading us to where we might be able to serve Him." He saw that God would spare them for a reason. Besides escaping from captivity to a Spanish area, he was becoming aware of a divine purpose for his life, which was to be of service to God.

Early in the journey, the most amazing cure took place. Castillo was an unwilling physician, afraid that his sins would make him fail in serious cases, so when a call came from an Indian camp for help, Dorantes and Cabeza de Vaca answered. They arrived to find the man dead, "his eyes turned up, without any pulse, and with all the signs of death." Still, Cabeza de Vaca prayed for help. That night the Indians came to his lodging and told him in great wonder that the dead man was alive. Others he had cared for were also well and happy. The Indians offered him food and other things of value. He had found the way to get help, friendship, or whatever else might be desired from them. Thus far Dorantes and Estebanico had not made any cures, but with so many asking for help, "we all came to be physicians." The Indians began to say that the Spaniards were "truly sons of the Sun." They were sure enough of healing to believe that if the men were there, none of them would die. Cabeza de Vaca boasted that for daring and boldness in undertaking a cure, he was the most noted of all.[13] Nevertheless, in his report to the king it was important not to imply miraculous powers or the skills to practice medicine, for any hint of that activity could mean trouble in Spain.[14]

Among the Avavares the Spaniards healed more than physical maladies; they also treated spiritual illness. Indians spoke of a strange being called Mala-Cosa (Evil Thing) that in the past had harmed and terrified them. The four Spaniards laughed—until they saw the scarred bodies. "We told them that it was an evil being, and in the best way we could we explained that if they believed in God our Lord and were Christians like ourselves, they would not be afraid of that thing, nor would it dare come again to do such things to them."

For the first time Cabeza de Vaca taught the Indians about the Christian religion. This Evil Thing, he believed, meant demonic attacks, and for that kind of suffering the only cure was Christianity. The Indians needed safety from demons, and they might have it from the Christian faith. Soon, teaching about Christianity became one of his goals. Wherever they went, the four men spoke of religion. Cabeza de Vaca included an example of their teaching. "We indicated to them through signs by which they understood us, that in Heaven there was a Man that we called God, Who had created Heaven and earth. We worshipped Him and held Him as Lord. We did what He commanded, and from His hand came all good things. If they did likewise, it would go very well with them." This sermon is found somewhat later in his book and shows growing skill in teaching, including the use of signs. As José de Acosta (ca. 1539–1600) noted, "compelled by necessity, they became evangelical physicians."[15]

Oviedo also wrote about their teaching. "Those Christians admonished and instructed all these people to have reverence for Heaven and raise their eyes to it. When they had some need, they were to commend themselves to Almighty God, their hands placed together, kneeling. And so they did. They believed that these Christians came from Heaven, and they enjoyed greatly when they told them anything about there." Had there been a better way to teach besides sign language, added Oviedo, then "according to the faith and zeal with which they listened to the Christians, and according to the few errors and idolatries which those people held, the Christians who escaped said that they thought without doubt that they would be good Christians."[16]

Tales of Cabeza de Vaca's influence on the Indians show up in unlikely places. Garcilaso de la Vega, "The Inca," gave an example in his book, *La Florida*, about Hernando de Soto's conquest in North America. In one area many crosses of wood were found on the dwellings. It was learned that the Indians "had news about the kindness and wonders that Alvar Núñez Cabeza de Vaca and Andrés Dorantes and their friends, by virtue of Jesus Christ our Lord, had done in the provinces of Florida which they walked over in the years the Indians held them as slaves, as the same Alvar Núñez left it in writing in his *Comentarios*." Vega made it clear that Cabeza de Vaca had not actually visited these specific Indians, but word of his great deeds had spread from one region to another.[17]

A second account is more directly tied to Cabeza de Vaca. In 1582 Antonio de Espejo led a company to explore what is now New Mexico. He reported being met by Indians (the Jumanos) who seemed to know Christian practices and teaching, for "they point at God our Lord, facing Heaven, and name Him Apalito in their language. He it is whom they know as Lord, and He gives them whatever they possess. Many men, women and children came in order that we, the friar and the Spaniards, might bless them, and they clearly got much satisfaction from it." When asked where such knowledge came from, the Indians declared that "three Christians and a black man had passed through there, and by the indications that they gave, it appeared to have been [Alvaro] Núñez Cabeza de Vaca, Dorantes, Castillo Maldonado and a black man." [18]

Finally, their work evidently passed on in legend among Indians even into the early seventeenth century. Diego de Guzmán, a missionary in the province of Sinaloa, wrote in 1629 of meeting some Indians led in prayer by a man who many decades ago had been with Cabeza de Vaca and the others on their march toward New Spain. [19]

We Left the Whole Land in Peace

Those months with the Avavares were extremely hard. While the Indians helped the four men in many ways, bad weather and the unending search for food delayed the escape, and everyone had to struggle to survive. All went naked, but the Spaniards were less hardened. "We sloughed off our leathery skins in the manner of snakes twice in the year." Yet, bodily pain could help spiritual healing. For Cabeza de Vaca, suffering led to a sense of religious kinship with Jesus Christ. In places where brush and thorns were rough and dense, gathering firewood left his body torn and streaming blood. At times, after shedding much blood, he could not carry or drag out the wood. "When I thought about this misery, I had no other help or comfort but to reflect on the passion of Jesus Christ our Saviour, and on the blood that He shed for me, and to think how much more would be the torment that He suffered from the thorns than anything I then endured."[1]

His discovery of the humanity of the Indians had several causes. For years he used them to exist, but their demand for medical cures led him to see a need for God. He came to see that God, while healing the Indians who sheltered and fed him, was also giving him strength beyond human power to survive. Then it became clear that the Indians needed spiritual as well as physical healing. His awareness of that need enabled him to see the likeness of their humanity to his own. The threat from the Evil Thing, which he believed could be cured only by Christianity, showed him for the first time that Indians were like him spiritually as well as physically. They had value as human beings, not merely because they were helpful to him.

This new outlook was formed not by a single event or sudden religious crisis. Utter helplessness and a growing vision of religious purpose were its basis. As he beheld his need for God, he saw that same need among the Indians as well, opening his eyes to their shared humanity. After he left the Avavares Indians, the journey to New Spain renewed his sense of divine care and guidance again and again, for when new Indians on the way heard about the cures, they became friendly, helpful, and even worshipful. Healing was vital in gaining their favor and in assuring Cabeza de Vaca that God had a purpose in his ordeal.

Respect for the Indians did not cause him to romanticize or idealize them and how they lived. The coastal Texas people who had enslaved him were "very evil," and he avoided them entirely after his escape. Much better were the inland dwellers, but even they were "liars" for telling others that "we were children of the Sun and that we had power to heal the sick and to kill them, and other lies even greater than these." The Indians who listened to such "lies" passed them on to the people in the next village, and "said about us everything that the others had taught them and added much more, because all these Indian people are great friends of falsehood and very deceitful, all the more when they seek some advantage."[2]

His book has many similar reports about Indians, most of them sounding straightforward and fair.[3] "I wanted to tell all this," he wrote "because all mankind wishes to know the manners and practices of others, besides which, those who sometime may come exploring might be informed of their customs and courage, which is likely to be useful on similar occasions."[4] In various chapters, for example, he spoke of their sexual roles and relations, marriages, child rearing, quarrels, and ties with neighbors.[5] He especially admired the Indian warriors. They had as much craftiness against enemies, he thought, as if they had been trained in Italy and in regular warfare. They were tough and sturdily built. "Often they are pierced with arrows from one side to the other, and yet they do not die from the wounds if the intestines or heart are not struck; rather, they heal quickly." Their eyesight and hearing were the best in the world, and their way of life made them able to withstand hunger, thirst, and cold.[6] As he lived among them, he found that they had qualities he valued, in spite of the violence, wretchedness, and savagery that he pictured.

The four men left the Avavares Indians about June 1535. Heading southwest at first, they visited the Maliacones, the Arbadaos, and, apparently, the Cuchendados Indians.[7] Then they crossed the Rio Grande into what now is Mexico. Instead of going south toward Pánuco, they turned northwest to avoid the Indians of the coast. In addition, their guides were using known paths that skirted mountains and went where friendly Indians with food could be found. Also, the Spaniards wanted to explore and report on that region, and they believed the Pacific coast of New Spain to be much closer than it actually was. Altogether, this detour covered a distance of more than two thousand miles.[8] After crossing the Rio Grande, they continued traveling among nomadic hunters and gatherers. These bands of twenty to fifty people, often related by marriage, culture, and dialect, can be identified as the Toboso and Concho, who lived along the way passed by Cabeza de Vaca.[9]

As new Indians were encountered, they in turn guided the Spaniards forward. Thus their names spread, gaining them a welcome in the villages along the way. In each one they were offered gifts amidst great excitement and then they touched and were touched by the inhabitants, made the sign of the cross and prayed, and healed those in need. Again and again there was healing, or, equally important, when there was not, the Indians retained their belief in the Spaniards' power to cure.[10]

Cabeza de Vaca went beyond the sign of the cross and prayer to practice surgery. He learned cautery from the Indians, and it worked well for him.[11] His early career as a Spanish soldier, wounded at the battle of Ravenna, would have exposed him to battlefield medicine. Later, in an operation that won him much honor, he removed an arrow that long ago had pierced a man in the back and lodged near his heart. With a knife Cabeza de Vaca opened the man's chest, carefully cut out the arrow, and stitched the incision. Later, when he took out the stitches, the man told him that the pain was gone.[12] These healings amazed the Indians, and their confidence in the Spaniards grew day by day.

The explorers' fame became so great that many Indians were happy to guide or escort them. Once, getting lost in a pathless region, they were rescued by some women who had followed them. In each village they received more presents and food than they could use or carry, so they kept only what they needed and gave the rest to the Indians in their company. In effect, the villages were looted by the Indians who accompanied the four men. The victims, however, later made up their losses by going along to the next village. Cabeza de Vaca was troubled about taking goods from Indians who treated them so well but could not put a stop to it. "We had not the influence to remedy it, or to dare to punish those who were doing this, and at that time we had to forbear until we might have more authority among them."[13]

The phrase "we might have more authority" is significant. The Indians willingly gave up whatever they had, so he did not lack personal influence. Already, it appears, he was thinking of the future, about coming back to this land and its people with legal authority from Charles I for a conquest that would be peaceful and humane. The Indians would accept an authority that would benefit them and end such plundering. These words are the first hint that growing in his mind was the idea of a conquest that was not destructive but was peaceful and just and that might serve not only the Spaniard but the Indian as well. Another hint about bringing that area under the rule of Spain came when it was time to decide which way to go, into the interior or toward the coast. One reason for going inland was to examine the land to be able to report on it.[14] Apparently something there was worth telling the Spanish government. The question of what Cabeza de Vaca did see in America was to come up again later.

As the journey went on, Cabeza de Vaca's interest in the Indians grew. From the start he found their customs strange, but he did not meddle with them, even those that were "diabolical."[15] As his prestige and power grew, however, he became more willing to try to change things. One example was of parents who injured a child by inflicting long scratches. When he saw "this cruelty," it angered him, and he demanded to know why they were doing it. The scratches turned out to be for crying in Cabeza de Vaca's presence. That anger and the attempt to find out the reason for such harm were new. He had not acted that way before. Even so, the Indians in that village found favor as well. "They are the most governable people that we met in this region, of better quality, and they are generally very alert."[16]

Other Indians won even higher praise. After walking for a few days the four men came to a town of well-made houses and settled farmers, located where the Río Conchos met the Rio Grande. They were the first houses the party had seen since Florida. Following a festive and respectful welcome, he found the inhabitants "the best-formed people that we saw, more lively and clever, and they understood and responded best to whatever we asked."[17] In 1582, Antonio de Espejo called these Indians the Jumanos, and they still recalled this visit after half a century.[18]

The esteem that the four men enjoyed can be seen in a visit to a town that they well remembered. There the Indians gave Dorantes more than six hundred deer hearts, whereupon the Spaniards named it *El Pueblo de los Corazones,* the Town of Hearts. The date was near Christmas 1535. Getting a rare hint of possible riches, the explorers received some beads, pieces of coral, and turquoise from the north. For Cabeza de Vaca there were five "emeralds" made into arrowheads that also came from the north.[19]

The four men used careful staging to enhance their standing among the Indians. With one group, for example, they walked all day, not eating until night. They ate so little that the Indians were astonished. Strength was only part of their image. To enhance their authority and importance they rarely talked to Indians. Estebanico asked them whatever the Spaniards needed to know—a hint, perhaps, of his position with regard to the other three.

Cabeza de Vaca wrote about two ways that his party used its "authority" over the Indians. "Through all these regions, those having wars with each other immediately became friendly in order to come and meet us and bring

everything they had, and by this manner we left the whole land in peace."[20]
Also, besides bringing peace to the Indians, the explorers started to teach the
Christian faith, as already discussed. A few months had brought striking new
ideas to Cabeza de Vaca, with greater awareness, much more respect for the
Indians, and a sense of higher values for his own life.

To Lead All These Peoples to Be Christians

The thought of reaching other Spaniards helped to drive the men forward. There was joy, then, when they saw the first sign of their countrymen. One day Castillo spotted a small belt buckle with a horseshoe nail hanging from the neck of an Indian. It was an ornament from heaven, he explained, from men who had beards like the explorers. From out of the sea they had come and killed two Indians and then sailed away on their ships. The four men were thankful, for they had almost given up hope of seeing other Spaniards, as well as uneasy that the ships might not come back. They were also afraid; the Indians might want revenge for having been attacked. They told the Indians that they would look for those people and stop them from killing or catching slaves.

Suddenly, it was clear that the Indians needed to be kept safe from such Spaniards. As Cabeza de Vaca walked over a land where his own people had passed, he became upset. With sadness he wrote of the tragedy then taking place on the frontier between Spanish and Indian regions. No reader, especially not Charles I, could miss the point of his words. Cabeza de Vaca reported that he and his companions had crossed much of the area and found it to be empty, the people fleeing to the mountains, too afraid of the Spaniards to have dwellings or to farm. Spanish historian Gonzalo Fernández de Oviedo y Valdés lamented the tragedy as well. There had been three Spanish raids there, he noted, to take the people and destroy their villages. Those who were left were in such terror that they did not dare to be seen.

Cabeza de Vaca knew poverty. He had lived in it for years. Yet seeing Spaniards bring it about in a rich land by looting and war grieved him. "It was something for which we had very great pity, seeing the land very fertile and beautiful, full of water and streams, and to look at villages deserted and burned and the people so weak and sickly, all running away and hiding." The inhabitants dared not plant crops and ate only the bark and roots of trees. In their wretched state, "it seemed that they wanted to die." His anguish is striking. The Spaniards who made such a waste of the land were surely no different from Cabeza de Vaca and his conquistadores when they landed in Florida. He was the one who had changed. Years earlier he had set out to do what these destroyers were about to finish. How much, indeed, had living in that land changed his understanding and purpose.

That journey exposed great damage and famine. The Indians told how the land had been invaded and destroyed; towns burned; and men, women, and children taken away. Anyone who could do so had fled. Sometimes Cabeza de Vaca worried that the Indians might punish him for the sins of the slave hunters, but their respect for his good works—or magic—kept him and his companions safe. Where the Spaniards imagined harm, Oviedo wrote, the people instead revered and honored them. Despite the natives' fear of the other Spaniards, they welcomed the four men "because they thought them to be something holy and god-like, or men come from Heaven." It caused Cabeza de Vaca to pause in his story and remark to the king, "One sees clearly that to lead all these peoples to be Christians and to submission to the imperial majesty, they have to be brought with good treatment. This way is very certain. Any other way is not."[1] As a royal official, he had come to the point of acting from a sense of responsibility.

A striking parallel links this new understanding with the ideas of a Dominican friar, Bartolomé de Las Casas. Like Cabeza de Vaca, Las Casas had experienced over time a dramatic and life-changing religious awakening by facing directly a challenge to his relationship with Indians.[2] While Cabeza de Vaca was escaping the wilderness, Las Casas, famous as the "Protector of the Indians," was devising principles for Christian missions based on his own work in America. During the 1530s Las Casas argued in a Latin treatise the point that Cabeza de Vaca was just learning: Christian faith must be spread by gentleness and good treatment, not by force.[3] Although both men were in Spain on visits that overlapped from June 1540 until December 1541, there is no evidence that they ever met to discuss these matters.[4]

Another important parallel was their ideas regarding Indian slavery. In European tradition lawful slavery might be imposed on captives of just warfare, and persons justly enslaved might be purchased. The conquest in America added such other causes as cannibalism, obstructing the preaching of Christianity, or violently opposing the creation of Spanish settlements or mines. Owing to the great abuses of these grounds for enslavement (as Cabeza de Vaca described), a debate resulted in Spain and America during the early sixteenth century, leading to antislavery arguments and legislation. They had little effect, and for the Indians the encomienda system was replacing slavery as a means of exploiting their labor. Las Casas concluded that the wars against the Indians were so unjust as to prevent any enslavement of them.[5] Even Cabeza de Vaca's experiences in North America became useful for Las Casas. His *Apologética historia sumaria,* written during the 1550s, refers a number of times to Cabeza de Vaca's *Relación* for proof that North American Indians did not engage in idolatry or human sacrifice. Both men were in Spain during this time also, but evidence of personal contact is once again lacking.[6]

The instructions that Charles I gave to Cabeza de Vaca in 1527 as royal treasurer had specific duties, one of which was to see how the Indians were treated.[7] That duty had at last become clear to him. Even his report to the government was part of that charge, so he often pointed out in its pages his ideas about how to manage the Indians. When that account became a book about his adventures in the wilderness of North America, his message went out to a wider group of influential Spaniards. His sense of the wrong being done to the injured and abused Indians was much stronger than it had been at first, but he still had to find a way to help them. One useful step was to get some food. Many Indians were hiding in the mountains to get away from the Spanish slave hunters. The four and the large number of Indians with them were welcomed warmly. These villagers gave the men all their corn, which they used to help the starving people who had led them there.[8] It was only a start, perhaps, but it was risky to take a gift of food from unknown Indians who had good reason to hate Spaniards and give it to strangers. In the days that followed, Cabeza de Vaca found other ways to help the people. In addition to his legal responsibility to Charles I and to the Spaniards and Indians under his authority by order of the king, he acquired a Christian responsibility for others. This dual responsibility was to God as well as to the king. Caring for the Indians was not based on sentiment alone; it was responsibility in its essence.

Guided by Pima Indians, the company of travelers came to the Spanish zone. More and more terrified people joined them for safety as signs of the slave hunters became clearer. The four men told the Indians not to be afraid, Oviedo wrote, for they would send the other Spaniards "back to their own settlements, and not cause harm." Although the Indians had great fear, their defenders rejoiced as they got closer to fellow Spaniards. "We gave many thanks to God our Lord," remembered Cabeza de Vaca, "for causing us to be removed from such sorrowful and miserable captivity." When they drew near to the slave hunters, he and Estebanico took eleven Indians to find them. A day later they caught up with Captain Diego de Alcaraz and three other men on horseback. Seeing Cabeza de Vaca dressed so strangely and in the company of Indians, they were shocked: "They stared at me for a long time, so astonished that they neither spoke to me nor could answer me." This meeting was on the western coast of New Spain, the province of New Galicia, at Río Petatlán (now Río Sinaloa), probably in late January 1536.

Cabeza de Vaca clearly had been thinking about this event for some time. He knew what he wanted—a signed statement of the year, month, and day that they had arrived and of the way in which they came. Curiously, he forgot to put the date in his own report of the event. Oviedo added that the document also referred to the Indians; the four men "brought those people of peace and good will who were following them."[9] Perhaps Cabeza de Vaca imagined that he could save the Indians from slavery by getting the slave hunters to admit on paper that these people were friendly. If so, he was wrong.

The wilderness had been overcome. Liberation, however, released the stresses that had been building for a long time. When Dorantes and Castillo joined the other two, five days later, they were followed by more than six hundred Indians who had fled the slave hunters. The Spanish captain, Diego de Alcaraz, asked them to call out other Indians who were hiding nearby. Six hundred more appeared, with food and other gifts. So many Indians were a prize not to be lost by the slave hunters, and much quarreling among the Spaniards ensued. The four men were so angry that when they finally resumed their journey, they forgot to take many of the gifts collected along the way.

The slave hunters tried to frighten the Indians into leaving their friends by asserting that Cabeza de Vaca and his party were the same as the slave hunters but were "people of little luck or valor. [The slave hunters] were the lords of that land whom they had to obey and serve." The Indians agreed among themselves that the slave hunters were lying about the four explorers: Cabeza de Vaca and his men "came from where the sun rose, and [the slave hunters] came from where it set. We healed the sick, and they killed those who were well. We came naked and shoeless; they came on horseback, clothed and with lances." The contrast expanded: "We were not greedy for anything; on the contrary, we immediately gave everything back, whatever they gave to us, to be shared, and we kept nothing. The other Spaniards had no other purpose but to plunder everything, whatever they found, and they never gave anything to anybody." The Indians could see clearly how unlike the two groups of Spaniards were and even magnified the merits of their friends.

Indeed, added Cabeza de Vaca, he never could make the Indians believe that the two groups of Spaniards were connected.

Cabeza de Vaca defended the Indians to bring them "by good treatment" into the Christian faith and under Spanish sovereignty. He argued that this method was "very certain," whereas "any other way is not." When the Indians were with their protectors, "they did not fear the Christians or their lances." Yet the question remained about what would happen when the explorers could no longer shield the Indians. At present they could only be sent back to their villages to till the land and plant seed. The Indians agreed to follow that plan if the slave hunters let them. "I say and assert it very surely," Cabeza de Vaca wrote, "that if they did not do so, it will be the Christians' fault."

The outcome was not good. The slave hunters sent the four travelers on their journey by way of mountains and deserts to separate them from their Indians; thus, Cabeza de Vaca's men would not discover what was done with the Indians. "Wherein it appears how much the plans of men are mocked, that we were going to look for liberty for them, and when we thought that we had it, so much happened to the contrary." The slave hunters plotted to seize the Indians, and Cabeza de Vaca soon learned that they had fled again to the mountains.[10]

Then, about mid-February 1536, Cabeza de Vaca's party met Melchior Díaz at Culiazan (Culiacán).[11] A man of good repute and the mayor and captain of the province of New Galicia, Díaz was eager to help the Indians. As the local people had fled and their labor was lost, the land seemed to him to be wasted. The four men could do much service to God and the king, he believed, by calling the Indians out of hiding to settle as farmers on the empty land. He begged them to stay there to help with the Indians, and for over two months they did so. It was hard to know how to begin. Although their Indian followers were no longer with them, two Indians who were there as captives of the slave hunters knew of the "great authority" they had and of the "marvels" they had done. They took the message to the people in hiding. After a week they came back with three chiefs and fifteen men but had not found the other Indians, who had fled the slave hunters.

Díaz then preached to the Indians a sermon of sorts. These travelers, he said, were men who "came on the side of God, Who is in Heaven." They had walked across the land many years, telling all the people "that they might believe in God and serve Him, because He was Lord of everything there was on earth." God rewarded good people, and punished evil ones with eternal fire. "When good persons died, He took them to Heaven, where nobody ever died, had hunger or thirst or were cold, or had any other need, but had greater glory than could be imagined." Those who did not believe or obey, "He put under the earth in company with the demons in a great fire, which must never end, but torment them forever."

He ended with a promise and a threat, both of which reflected ideas in the *Requerimiento* (Requirement), a Spanish legal document enacted in about 1512 as an effort to justify the conquest of America. Most often read to Indians as an opening to warfare, it was meant this time for peace. "If they wanted to be Christians," Díaz declared, "and serve God in the way that we commanded them, then the Christians would have them as brothers and treat them very well." He would order them not to be harmed or taken away from their lands, "but to be their great friends." Otherwise, "the Christians would treat them very badly, and take them as slaves to other lands." The Indians answered that "they would be very good Christians, and serve God." Asked about their beliefs, they answered that they worshipped Aguar, who was in heaven and who had created the world and everything in it. "We told them that the One they spoke of, we called God," Cabeza de Vaca noted, "and they were also to call Him that, and serve and worship Him as we commanded, and they would fare very well for it." The Indians understood, they said, and would do as they had been told. Aguar later turned up in Casas's *Apologética historia sumaria*.[12]

The task now was to find everyone who had scattered and gone into hiding. The Indians became messengers to their people, calling them back to their land and to make peace with the Spaniards. For a third time the Indians agreed to do as told. A clerk then notarized the event, and Cabeza de Vaca was careful to record it when he wrote his book.[13] A more successful or peaceful example of a Spanish "conquest" would be hard to find in all of the Americas.[14] Meanwhile, Díaz and the four men went to the town of San

Miguel,[15] which served as their headquarters from April 1 to May 15, 1536. Their prestige helped to bring the hidden Indians to the town. The returning Indians were soon building churches, and the children of the chiefs were baptized. The symbol of peace and safety was to be Christianity.

This remarkable success had to be told to Charles I. Even Alcaraz and the Spanish slave hunters were amazed at the change in the Indians who sought the promise of safety. Cabeza de Vaca ended his account by appealing to the king. "God our Lord, by His infinite mercy, is willing in the days of your majesty and under your power and dominion, that these peoples come to be truly and with entire goodwill subjects of the true Lord Who created them and redeemed them." Success would not be difficult to win, he added, for in two thousand leagues of travel by land and sea, he had not seen idolatry or sacrifices.[16] Casas found it useful to quote this plea in his *Apologética historia sumaria.*[17]

Cabeza de Vaca had taken many months to learn how to be responsible for the Indians. His next lesson would be how to give his vision to others. For the present, while he went on to Mexico City, Díaz would keep the Indians safe. Despite Cabeza de Vaca's desire to bring the Indians to a settled life as Christians under Spanish rule, slavers had made it impossible. He could not make the Spaniards treat the Indians as free people. Díaz had answered that lack of power. As a Spanish official, he was the best person to take charge of the frightened Indians. Cabeza de Vaca now wanted to get that kind of legal power for himself, which meant a trip to Spain to see the king.

Not to Go under Another's Banner

The great adventures of Cabeza de Vaca did not end upon reaching New Spain. After mid-May he and his companions went from San Miguel to Compostela and then on to Mexico City.[1] From the coast of Texas they walked a distance of about 2,800 miles between September or October 1534 and late July 1536 (with eight months rest among the Avavares Indians).[2] They entered Mexico City to a splendid welcome. Antonio de Mendoza, the first viceroy of New Spain, and Hernán Cortés, the celebrated conquistador, met them with "great pleasure" and treated them well.[3]

Mendoza was very interested in their journey. He ordered them to make a map for him and wanted to send them back to explore the north. His goal was "to advance the service of God and the king by means of such prodigious men; he proposed that they return with some men wherein they had come, to bring the barbarous Indians into submission." Cabeza de Vaca, having arranged his voyage to Spain, was unwilling to return. Apparently Mendoza was not offended, for he honored a request to look after thirty Indians who had come with Cabeza de Vaca's party to Mexico City. The viceroy agreed to take care of them and arrange for religious training and baptism, a promise that was kept.[4] Also, he wrote to Spain about Cabeza de Vaca's plan to visit the monarch and urged a grant of royal favor.[5]

In October 1536 Cabeza de Vaca was ready to sail for Spain. However, a storm wrecked the ship, and he could not leave until April 1537. Early in July, as his vessel neared the Azores, only the timely arrival of Portuguese warships held off a French privateer. He gave thanks, he recalled, for having escaped from the hardships of the land and the hazards of the sea. At the Azores, he would have heard about the recent death aboard ship of Pedro de Mendoza, founder of the Spanish settlement in the province of Río de la Plata in South America and, as it was to turn out, Cabeza de Vaca's predecessor as its governor.

In August 1537, after ten years in America, Cabeza de Vaca returned to Europe.[6] One might guess that some time was spent at his home town of Jerez de la Frontera. In November he told the officials of the Casa de Contratación (House of Trade) in Seville what he had learned of the province of Florida, and from there he planned to go to the royal court and retell the tale to the king.[7] This risky crossing of the Atlantic had one purpose: to get a license from the king for another conquest of Florida. In Mexico, Viceroy Mendoza had tried to send Cabeza de Vaca back to the land he had explored, but he would not work under a viceroy's power. His goal was to succeed Narváez as governor of Florida, so he had to see Charles I to spark royal interest in his adventures and promote his ideas for the Indians.

Already, unknown to him, he had missed his goal. Even as he crossed the ocean, Hernando de Soto, a prominent captain under Francisco Pizarro and a veteran of the Spanish conquest of the Inca empire in America (1532–33), had gotten the desired capitulations (dated April 20, 1537) from King Charles I to conquer and settle Florida in place of the unlucky Narváez.[8] If that first ship had not been wrecked the previous autumn, Cabeza de Vaca might have been in Spain in time to compete with Soto. Even so, his interest was strong enough for him to discuss exploring with Soto, although their talks came to nothing.

The story of their meeting comes from a Portuguese known as the "Gentleman of Elvas." Apparently this author did not himself meet Cabeza de

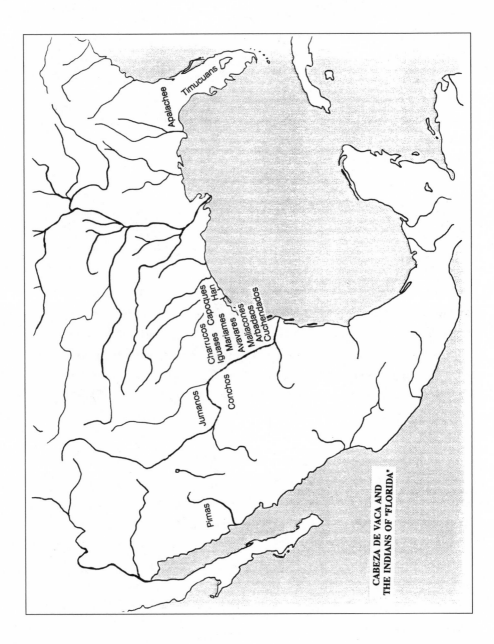

Apalachee

Timucuans

Charrucos
Capoques
Han
Iguases
Mariames
Avavares
Mallacones
Arbadados
Cuchendados

Jumanos

Conchos

Pimas

**CABEZA DE VACA AND
THE INDIANS OF "FLORIDA"**

Vaca but heard him discussed when he later met Soto to go with him to America. Also, he referred to a written "relation" that Cabeza de Vaca took to Spain about what he had seen in Florida, suggesting that his knowledge was secondhand. The Gentleman of Elvas wrote that Soto wanted Cabeza de Vaca to go to America with him and offered a proposal. The two men agreed but then parted "because Soto would not give [Cabeza de Vaca] the money which he asked of him to buy a ship." This reason may have been important, but a better one was that if Cabeza de Vaca "had given up going with Soto, it was because he expected to ask for another government and did not wish to go under another's banner."[9] The same agreement could have been made with Mendoza. Cabeza de Vaca had come to Spain for a different goal, to have his own title and power. Soto's offer was little better than the rank he had held under Narváez, and he did not need to go back to America under someone else's command.

These were sound reasons for turning down Soto's offer. There was, however, another one. Cabeza de Vaca was well aware of how Spaniards were treating American Indians, so he knew what to expect from Soto and his followers. Soto's role in the conquest of America was already disturbing. He had recently carried to Spain great wealth in treasure from the Inca empire, looted under Francisco Pizarro, and had earlier worked with the notorious Pedrarias Dávila (Pedro Arias de Avila), governor of Panama, in a destructive conquest of Nicaragua.[10] Cabeza de Vaca's ideas about a peaceful conquest and how to treat Indians were very clear. So he had to be careful about who held authority. In North America, as it happened, Soto acted as he had earlier. His conquest was quite brutal, but this time there was no treasure, and he was among those who died. Cabeza de Vaca himself was to have much trouble when he went to the Río de la Plata province in South America, but at least he was spared the disaster that befell Soto.

Oviedo's *Historia general* used pointed words against Soto. That conquistador "was given very much to hunting to kill Indians" in Central America. He was also in Peru, "where he enriched himself" when Atahualpa, the Inca emperor, was captured. Although not the same friend to the Indians that Cabeza de Vaca was, Oviedo also spoke forcefully. He wrote his history partly for its moral lessons, and Soto was very useful to him. "O misguided people! O devilish lust! O evil consciences! O wretched soldiers! How you misjudged to what degree of danger you were coming! How you disturbed your lives! How uneasy your souls!" Then, calling on his reader to listen, he made his point: "Do not weep less for the conquered Indians than for their Christian conquerors—or murderers—and be attentive to the outcome of this badly-governed governor: instructed in the school of Pedrarias de Avila in the wasting and devastation of the Indians of Castillo de Oro, graduated in the killing of the inhabitants of Nicaragua, and consecrated in Peru according to the order of the Pizarros." Yet Soto wanted more. He "could not rest without returning to the Indies to shed human blood, unsatisfied with that already shed, and to yield his life, . . . giving occasion for so many sinners, deceived by his vain words, to die after him."[11]

Oviedo was not alone in denouncing Soto. Casas also decried Soto's tyranny and described in vivid terms his eternal end: "Thus the most unhappy captain died as if ill-fated, without confession, and we do not doubt but that he was buried in hell, unless maybe God did not sentence him secretly—according to His divine mercy and not his demerits—for such wickedness."[12] Even the Gentleman of Elvas held a poor opinion of Soto. He agreed with Cabeza de Vaca that Florida was a good land, but that sort of quality was not of interest to Soto, for his purpose "was to seek another treasure like that of Atabalipa [Atahualpa], the lord of Peru." Soto "had no wish to content himself with good land."[13] Whether or not these sharp attacks were entirely fair, Cabeza de Vaca was wise and fortunate not to take up Soto's offer. Soto and his men in Florida were not likely to have welcomed his efforts to treat the Indians in a humane manner. As it was, Cabeza de Vaca's attempt to do so in the Río de la Plata province did not work out well either.

The Gentleman of Elvas raised another question. In Spain, Cabeza de Vaca described the land as being full of hardships, yet the Gentleman still believed that gold and other wealth existed there. He said that Cabeza de Vaca would not answer questions even from his relatives about whether he had seen any rich land in Florida. Andrés Dorantes and he had agreed not to reveal all that they had seen, lest someone take Narváez's place before they could ask for it. Nevertheless, Cabeza de Vaca "gave them to understand that it was the richest land in the world."[14] The question is whether the listeners were misled. No matter what he really said, Soto's men would have heard only of riches. He wrote in his book soon thereafter about rich lands, "very fertile and beautiful, full of water and streams." There also were "great signs of gold" and "other metals." Yet in that land, the Indians "take no notice of gold and silver."[15] He did not say that wealth was there just to be seized. Clearly, it would have to come by working and mining the land, not simply by looting Indians.

Two other remarks from the Gentleman of Elvas suggest that Cabeza de Vaca knew of wealth in America. When two of his kin asked if they should go with Soto, he advised them to do so, for they would act wisely. In addition, after Cabeza de Vaca's talk with Charles I, a nobleman who learned what the explorer had said sent relatives to join Soto's expedition.[16] Neither story tells what lured these people on or what Cabeza de Vaca had stated about America. His own ideas are most clearly found in his book.

Even in America Cabeza de Vaca influenced Soto's men. His name came up again when the Gentleman of Elvas wrote about the hardships that they met in the wilderness. After Soto's death in May 1542, some of his group were ready to give up the conquest. Others, however, wanted to go on in spite of what they had seen. "They hoped to find a rich land before reaching the land of the Christians, because of what Cabeza de Vaca had told the emperor. This was that, while he had found cotton cloth, he had seen gold and silver and precious gems of much value."[17] These men clearly believed that Cabeza de Vaca had revealed something important to Charles I. What they themselves had seen could have given them no such hope. His words to the king are unknown; his book, published later, says only that the mountainous regions had signs of gold and other minerals and that he saw turquoise and what he thought to be emeralds.[18]

Cabeza de Vaca understood wealth to have a wider meaning. Mineral wealth was very important, and he would spend some of his time in South

America searching for it. Fertile lands with good water were also wealth of great value. Even more, he had learned of the wealth to be found in the Indians of America. Wealth was not the gold and silver stolen from dead bodies. It was land and people—Indians and Spaniards joined by Christianity and Spanish civilization. Such wealth had not been Soto's goal, but Cabeza de Vaca hoped to find it in America. If it was not to be found in Florida, perhaps it existed in the Río de la Plata province.

To Conquer and Pacify and Populate the Lands

Seeking a busy ruler's favor could demand great patience. After Hernando de Soto left for America in April 1538, nearly two years passed without much happening to encourage Cabeza de Vaca. Yet a man of his background could be useful to a king. French and Spanish colonial rivalry led to the next step; the king of France, Francis I (1515–47), also had an eye on the New World. During the 1530s explorer Jacques Cartier twice crossed the Atlantic to the St. Lawrence River Valley in the interests of France, and in 1541 he was to do so again.

The Spanish crown became quite anxious about its claims to America. To block the French, it was ready to send a man like Cabeza de Vaca to northeastern North America. An agent wrote to the king of Portugal about "a captain named Joam Cabeza de Vaca who was commissioned . . . to go to explore the Cod Fish River, which is called of the king of France, and he has license from the Council of the Indies, and he told me that he would not go, it being a very doubtful business, and he left here about eight days ago for River Plate."[1] Thus, Cabeza de Vaca's quest at last could begin. After rejecting one offer, he agreed to take over a colony in southeastern South America, the Río de la Plata province. The year was 1540.

European interest in the Río de la Plata estuary had begun early in the sixteenth century. Several explorers sent by the government of Spain sailed along the Atlantic coast of South America looking for a way to the East Indies. Juan Díaz de Solís entered the area in 1516 and lost his life to hostile Indians. Ferdinand Magellan, on his way to the Pacific Ocean, spent a few months there in 1519 and 1520. Sebastian Cabot went upriver to explore in 1526, while he was supposed to be on a voyage to the Moluccas.

Traces or tales of silver, coming from the far west, gave the region its name. Río de la Plata (River of Silver) soon became the title of a whole province. Mineral wealth did not originate there, but by the later fifteenth century local Guaraní Indian bands were crossing a desolate section (now the Chaco) to the fringe of the Inca Empire and returning with looted metal. By the time of the Spanish arrival the amount of silver brought back was enough to get attention when there was little else to attract notice. In their imaginations, the Spaniards had found the entry to a land of gold and silver.[2] The Guaranís were interested in such metal for ornaments or prestige.[3]

A Spanish settlement was founded in 1535. Pedro de Mendoza, a nobleman, landed eleven ships at a site that was named Buenos Aires, bringing livestock, supplies, and a large number of men and women. After a brief period of friendship, the local Indians, nomadic hunters and fishermen who included the Querandí, Charrúa, and Timbú, got tired of supplying food and began to attack. Ulrich Schmidt (or Schmidel), a German soldier who was then in Buenos Aires, saw the friendly relations turn into hostile strife.[4] Inexperience, disease, lack of food, and fierce warfare broke the colonists, and soon more than a thousand had died. Early in 1537 Mendoza gave up, boarded the ship *Magdalena,* and sailed toward Spain.[5] As lieutenant governor he named Captain Juan de Ayolas,[6] who a few months earlier had gone upriver in search of wealth—for "metal or mines," according to an interim successor as governor, Captain Domingo Martínez de Irala.[7]

Mendoza died at sea on board the *Magdalena* in June 1537, when Cabeza de Vaca was sailing from Mexico to Spain. As his ship waited at the Azores for a Portuguese convoy to form, by chance the *Magdalena* landed there. Thus, he would have heard about the Río de la Plata province and its misfortunes but could hardly have imagined that in three years he would replace Mendoza as its governor. At the Azores he met Gonzalo de Acosta from the *Magdalena,* a Portuguese veteran of two trips to the Río de la Plata who was on his way back to Spain. When Cabeza de Vaca went to South America as governor, Acosta was his pilot major and chief guide; when he was sent to Spain in chains four years later, Acosta, now his foe, was again pilot.[8]

Cabeza de Vaca first had to receive the governorship from the crown. According to Antonio de Herrera y Tordesillas, a seventeenth-century Spanish historian, Cabeza de Vaca was at court (*andaba en la corte*), implying frequent or regular presence there.[9] The Gentleman of Elvas said that Cabeza de Vaca spoke to Charles I about his sufferings and what he had seen and learned, a report "made orally to the emperor by Cabeza de Vaca."[10] He also bargained with the late Mendoza's attorney, Martín de Orduña. According to historian Enrique de Gandía, Orduña and his partner were the capitalists of Mendoza's expedition, the men who brought it about and managed it from Spain. Now Orduña was trying to hold on to this venture through the estate of Pedro de Mendoza and the legacy of his lieutenant, Juan de Ayolas, although whether Ayolas was dead or alive was then unknown. For a time Orduña and Cabeza de Vaca worked together for the Río de la Plata province, Orduña looking after his interests and those of the settlers, Cabeza de Vaca thinking about Mendoza's office for himself.[11]

The vacancy in the Río de la Plata was a serious matter. Spain had to have a governor there, and the colonists needed supplies. Also, treatment of the American Indians was again becoming an important issue. The government decided to appoint Cabeza de Vaca, who, besides his other merits, was willing to spend eight thousand ducados to provision the Spaniards and carry on the conquest of the Río de la Plata province.[12] Orduña now saw his stake in the colony threatened and began a lawsuit, but Cabeza de Vaca was not to be overthrown so soon.

The time had come for the Spanish crown to bring conquistadores under control. The adelantados who organized most of the conquests were military or colonizing governors. They risked their money and lives with little support from the government, and those who succeeded were mistrusted and usually replaced with men thought to be more suited for statecraft.[13] As a royal official seasoned in Florida, Cabeza de Vaca would have fit the second category. He was to get his chance at a humane conquest after all.

A capitulation of March 18, 1540, gave him the authority he needed. He took over as governor and captain general of Mendoza's colony, from the Río de la Plata south to the Straits of Magellan. His other titles, *alguacil mayor* and *adelantado,* covered only areas that he himself explored. Besides Mendoza's grant, the document dealt with his duties to the king and matters of finance. His annual salary was two thousand ducados, plus other sources of income, paid only from the revenues of the province. The eight thousand ducados that he invested were to buy horses, supplies, clothing, arms, munitions and other things for the colony. Also, he was exhorted to be zealous in the royal interest.

In the background, nevertheless, remained Ayolas. Mendoza had left him in command, so he was the governor if still alive. Therefore, the capitulation had full effect only if he were dead. Otherwise, Cabeza de Vaca was only the lieutenant governor and captain general, and he and his companions would be subject to Ayolas. In that case, to repay part of his costs, he was to have for twelve years Santa Catalina Island, lying off the coast of Brazil.[14] On April 15, 1540, he received his "license" to "conquer and pacify and populate the lands."[15] Also on April 15, a royal cedula ordered Ayolas, if alive, to appoint Cabeza de Vaca as his lieutenant governor.[16]

The capitulation contained an earlier royal cedula, dated November 17, 1526, that was intended to halt the injury that the Spaniards were causing the Indians and the harm that went with efforts to bring them to Christianity. Twenty or so other conquistadores, including Narváez (1526) and Soto (1537), had it added to their capitulations, so Cabeza de Vaca already knew what it said.[17] For him, however, no special directions were given apart from this ordinance of 1526. Had he been backed by more powerful support, he might have wielded a stronger hand in America. He agreed with the ideas in this cedula more than other conquistadores did and tried to apply them in America. It is odd, then, that when the Spanish government found a governor who was eager to follow its stated policies about Indians, it did not adapt its orders about their treatment specifically to the Río de la Plata province.

By 1540 there was great interest in Spain about converting the Indians peacefully. Much thought was being given to the nature and legality of the Spanish conquest of America. As noted earlier, during the 1530s Bartolomé de las Casas wrote *Del único modo,* advocating persuasion and condemning force in converting the Indians. Another influential Dominican, Francisco de Vitoria, lectured in 1539 at the University of Salamanca against the enslavement of the Indians and about Spain's title over the New World. In 1537 Pope Paul III's bulls, *Veritas ipsa* and *Sublimis Deus,* also dealt with the Indians' slavery and with their humanity and rationality. There were, of course, many opposing arguments as well in this great debate.[18] It would seem unlikely that Cabeza de Vaca could overlook such arguments. Yet his statements and policies show little awareness about the theories and advice that issued from academic, religious, and court circles. Perhaps becoming a soldier at an early age had kept him from the company of scholars and experts. His ideas were directed to general practices: good treatment, justice, payment for work, Christian teaching, and such.

Cabeza de Vaca did ask for one ruling, but it was not about Indians. He wanted an order that no lawyers or attorneys were to be in the Río de la Plata province to avoid the "many lawsuits and controversies, much expense and trouble" that came when they joined the conquerors and settlers. This plea was based on the experience of other newly populated lands. Like Thomas More, he would not have lawyers in his utopia. A cedula of July 1, 1540, gave royal approval: "Inasmuch as we are informed, and by experience it has appeared, that having lawyers and attorneys in newly conquered lands brings in them many lawsuits and arguments which would cease except for having these lawyers and attorneys," they were banned from the Río de la Plata province for ten years. The governor and his officials were to carry out this order in person.[19]

This attack on the practice of law in Spanish America was not the first one. After the conquest of New Spain, according to Bernal Díaz del Castillo, the Spanish conquistadores wrote to the king and begged him not to send lawyers, because in entering the land they would "put it in revolt with their books," and there would be lawsuits and strife.[20] Later, in 1537, the king told Soto not to allow attorneys to "exercise their callings" in his conquest of Florida.[21] A time would come, however, when a lawyer might have helped Cabeza de Vaca.

Fired by the success of his plans, he began getting ready to leave for the New World. Until September 1540 he worked busily, spending fourteen thousand ducados, including salaries, which he borrowed in part on his credit and that of relatives and friends. On July 1 a royal cedula ordered officials in Seville at the Casa de Contratación—the House of Trade, which oversaw trade with the Americas—to arrange with shipowners to give him a fair price for the ships that he needed. Supplies to be carried included flour, wine, clothing, and ecclesiastical items. For the Indians he had such trade goods as shirts, bonnets, blankets, knives, scissors, and axes. In spite of a royal grant allowing him alone to supply provisions to the Río de la Plata province, he ended up giving away much of what he took to America to the people, without any profit for himself.[22] For the Indians, iron had the greatest economic impact. They had long-standing trading ties with each other based on their own agricultural or hunting products, and the coming of Europeans to the Río de la Plata with iron goods added a third vital cultural element to that Neolithic economy.[23]

Not all of the money spent was Cabeza de Vaca's. Pedro Dorantes (not Andrés Dorantes, Cabeza de Vaca's companion in North America), who was appointed royal factor on this venture, also met some of the costs. He wrote in 1548 that to go to America well equipped and "according to the quality of his person," he had sold and spent much of his own property to feed many of those who went on his ship, and he furnished them with arms and other items. A kind of feudal, señorial, or clientage tie clearly existed on expeditions such as this one.[24]

The company numbered about four hundred. Its makeup shows Cabeza de Vaca's desire for peaceful conquest and a readiness to use force. Nine priests, a relatively large number for a province like the Río de la Plata, were to give the sacraments and teach the Indians. Although the military emphasis was much larger, the four hundred soldiers that he enlisted, armed, and trained were not many for the huge area that he had to govern. Well aware of the great value of horses when facing Indians, he had his ships carry forty-eight of the animals.[25] Years in America and the news from Buenos Aires, warned that hostile Indians could be extremely dangerous, and however humane his goals, a Spaniard of the Reconquista was not likely to see that military means might obstruct his religious and political mission.

Juan Friede has suggested that two theories were available for bringing the Indians into a European society. One would enable the Spaniards in America to control the Indians and to force them into an Iberian pattern of civilization. The other would give the task to the missionaries, and the process of civilization would take place gradually and free of domination or force, allowing the Indians to keep their rights as subjects of the crown.[26] Cabeza de Vaca's policies favored the latter method, but he did resort to the former when faced with defiance. Either way, the Indians were expected to take on the culture of the Spaniards.

Two primary sources give Cabeza de Vaca's version of his years in South America. The first is "Relación general," a report to the Council of the Indies, composed in Spain and dated December 7, 1545.[27] The second is the *Comentarios de Alvar Núñez Cabeza de Vaca,* written by and with his secretary and defender, Pero Hernández, the clerk and notary of the province.[28] This book was published in 1555, together with a second edition of Cabeza de Vaca's *La Relación* (retitled *Naufragios*), his account of his adventures in North America. The "Relación general" was part of a legal case prepared by Cabeza de Vaca in which he defended himself for the first time against men who challenged his authority in the Río de la Plata province, rebelled, arrested him, and sent him to Spain in chains. Naturally, he pointed out their faults in it. Such an account clearly was aimed at winning over the Spanish officials and the judges who would handle the legal charges brought by the rebels against his government in America.

The *Comentarios* came a decade later, in 1555, after he had lost that legal case. Because he could not return to the Río de la Plata, he and Hernández may have intended the work as a defense of his actions and policies in South America or as another treatise in the debate about Indian policy in the Spanish empire. Both sources accent his kindness and humanity toward the Indians, whose friendship and esteem became the heart of his story. Both are harsh toward Domingo Martínez de Irala, who held power in the colony after the death of Pedro de Mendoza and again after the overthrow of Cabeza de Vaca.

Readers will find exaggeration, blindness, self-interest, and outbursts of emotion. Nonetheless, these sources—balanced by other, independent ones—give much evidence that Cabeza de Vaca usually made an honest effort to persuade or compel the Spaniards to follow his ideas on the treatment of the Indians of the Río de la Plata province. They are useful statements of his Indian policies.[29]

To Look for a Way
through the Continent

Sailing to America was often a long and dangerous ordeal in the sixteenth century. In late September 1540 Cabeza de Vaca's three ships were ready to leave Cádiz, but the wind held them in port until December 2. When at last they got to sea, they faced more of the trials and adventures that he must have come to expect from life. At the Canary Islands, where he added a caravel to his fleet, the wind stalled him again. The next stop was at the Cape Verde Islands, this time for work on a ship. Finally came the long Atlantic crossing; indeed, the ships nearly went too far. Only the morning crowing of a long-silent rooster woke the crew in time to avoid striking rocks on the coast of Brazil. Everyone called it a miracle. After reaching land, they sailed south, eventually coming to the large island of Santa Catalina (which later became part of Brazil as Santa Catarina Island). This place held much interest for Cabeza de Vaca, for the king had granted it to him whether or not Juan de Ayolas was still alive. On March 29, 1541, travelers and livestock went ashore to recover from the hardships of the voyage.[1]

The Indians of the island spoke a Guaraní dialect. Related Guaranís, whose name for themselves was Mbiazás, also occupied part of the mainland (now the modern Brazilian states of Rio Grande do Sul, Santa Catarina, and

Paraná). An estimated sixty-five thousand Guaranís lived in this region in 1500, and Santa Catalina Island itself had a population of some four thousand.[2] Other Guaranís occupied a wide area westward beyond the Paraguay River, and anthropologist Branislava Susnik has classified, primarily by geographical factors, fourteen subgroups.[3] Although these peoples were known to the Europeans at first as the Carijó or Cario, by the seventeenth century the name *Guaraní* had become general, although local groups had their own names and Indians of different languages or cultures lived in villages dispersed among those of the Guaraní.[4]

While he rested, the new governor had much to think about and do. From the local Indians he needed friendship and much help. "As soon as I arrived at Santa Catalina Island," he wrote, "I gave good treatment to the natives there and to all the others who live on the coast of Brazil, vassals of his majesty, and I gave them many gifts to keep them satisfied."[5] Gifts were the first step in his diplomacy. Just as he had won friends among the Indians of Florida, so he would do in South America. Also, the Santa Catalina Indians were especially important, for even if Ayolas were found, they remained under Cabeza de Vaca. When he claimed the island, he told them that he had come by command of the king to bring help. They seemed to be pleased with his words, and he learned much from them that was of interest, even though other Spaniards had not always acted in so friendly a manner.[6]

Cabeza de Vaca's policies worked as well for his pilot major and chief guide. Gonzalo de Acosta also had good treatment and gifts for the Indians, and he paid them for their work. He arranged for them to build many dwellings, where the people from the ships lodged. When the conquistadores moved to the mainland, Indians again put up the housing. In addition to Acosta's ability to buy or get food and supplies from the Indians, his skills as interpreter, guide, and explorer were welcome. Much traveling and time went into those vital tasks, and he carried out the same roles after the newcomers left the coast to cross half the continent.[7]

One surprise was finding two Franciscan friars in the area. Bernardo de Armenta of Córdoba and Alonso Lebrón of Grand Canary Island had come to America with several other Franciscans in 1538, and they had been teaching the Indians since their arrival.[8] These two friars appeared before Cabeza

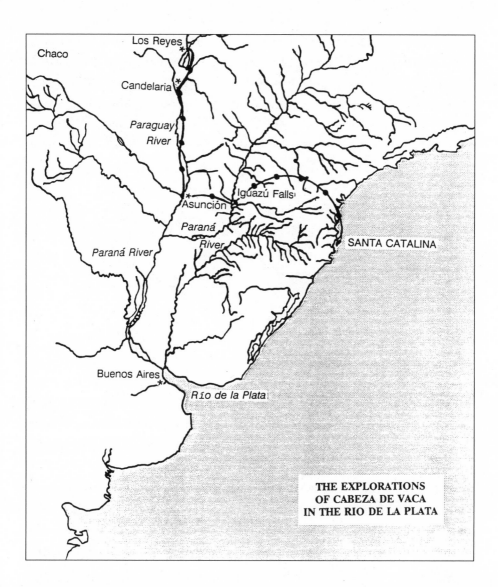

Chaco

Los Reyes

Candelaria

Paraguay
River

Iguazú Falls

Asunción

Paraná
River

Paraná River

SANTA CATALINA

Buenos Aires

Río de la Plata

**THE EXPLORATIONS
OF CABEZA DE VACA
IN THE RIO DE LA PLATA**

de Vaca shocked and terrified, for some Indians had tried to kill them after the natives' dwellings were burned. Two Spaniards had already died in the strife. The governor quickly brought calm, and in making peace with these angry Indians used the skills he had learned in North America. The friars he kept safe, hoping to make use of them despite this crisis.[9]

After the friars' arrival another surprise followed. In May eight or nine Spaniards from Buenos Aires landed on Santa Catalina Island, saying that they were escaping the harsh treatment of their captains. They also brought news about warfare between the Indians and the settlers at that port. Of much interest to the governor was their report that in the interior other Indians, the Payaguáes, had killed Ayolas and his men. Although he would have grieved over the loss of their lives, Cabeza de Vaca would also have felt relief that his own command was now clear. At Buenos Aires, he was told, all but seventy of the colonists were gone, and most of the survivors had settled in Asunción, a town recently founded on the Paraguay River. Further, the settlers and the Indians both were suffering much harm from the royal officials.[10] Actually, Buenos Aires at that moment was being entirely abandoned. While the governor was now assured that the province no longer belonged to Ayolas, he had heard ominous hints of the struggles to come if he tried to install a new order of government.

By September it was time to leave the island. On the nearby mainland, Cabeza de Vaca set up a port named Vera (his family name), and on September 7 he put Hernando de Alvarado in charge of it. Some of the people were to remain there and work at converting the Indians, and for this task the friars would be most useful. However, when the governor later suggested that they stay to teach the Indian converts, they refused, choosing to go with his company to Asunción.[11] Another person with a role in this event was the factor, Pedro Dorantes. In a report to the king he wrote that Armenta actually had wanted to remain there, but Dorantes had argued that no one ought to be left behind. They had not been sent to live in that area but to help the people who were already in the province. If fewer people went to Asunción, their help would have less effect. He also urged that Armenta act as the guide because the Indians of the country liked him very much.[12] Dorantes got his way. The port of Vera was abandoned, and the friars went along, a decision they would soon regret.

Santa Catalina Island had given everyone a needed rest after the voyage. While recovering and awaiting good sailing weather, Cabeza de Vaca thought about the next part of the journey. As he pondered the news from Buenos Aires, he had a startling idea: to get help most quickly to Asunción, why not have some of the people go there overland, while the others went by ship to resettle Buenos Aires?[13] Armenta later declared that the idea had been his. He told the governor what he knew about the land and the people and advised him not to move the ships and people by the river, "because I was sure that there was no Christian on it." Apparently he knew or had guessed about the exodus from Buenos Aires. To get to Asunción, he suggested that the horses and most of the people cross the mainland directly from Santa Catalina Island. Indeed, he was willing to go along. "For the safety of their lives, as for being well-provided in the necessary things of supplies, my presence was very necessary." That decision was hard to make, he added, because he did not want to leave the Indians he had been teaching and baptizing.[14]

Such a journey would not be the first in the region. During the mid-1520s Aleixo Garcia, a Portuguese survivor of the Juan Díaz de Solís voyage of 1516, traveled from Santa Catalina Island all the way to the fringes of the Inca empire, looking for wealth. He and five or six other Europeans accompanied two thousand Guaraní Indians who were taking part in one of a series of migrations westward. After gathering some wealth, Garcia was killed by Indians near the upper Paraguay River on his way back to the coast.[15] At issue was not whether a route toward Asunción existed, but as Dorantes noted, the quality of the route by which Garcia went. To Cabeza de Vaca, Dorantes said, "I want to employ my hand to go to discover that route."

Dorantes had a varied background. After military service during a communal uprising in Toledo (an event like the one that Cabeza de Vaca had faced), Dorantes lived in New Spain from 1529 to 1536. Also like the governor, he clearly was an able explorer. With fourteen Spaniards, his black slave, and a few Indian guides and carriers, he set out "to discover the land and look for a way through the continent" to Asunción. Three and a half months later he was back with a good report. The country turned out to be very rough, but there was a way to cross it. After a long trek over empty land, he had met some Indians who received him well, both for the gifts he gave them and because the Indians with him said that he was the son of Armenta, and they held the two friars in high esteem. Also, there was ample maize there.

He had learned of a river, the Itabucu (Itapocu), which entered the sea eighteen or twenty leagues north of Santa Catalina Island. The Indians declared that it was the nearest and safest way to go inland. With Dorantes still tired from his journey, the governor sent Acosta to scout that river as a route into the interior.[16]

These surveys were important. The Portuguese had been active in the region, and Cabeza de Vaca wanted full control for himself and Spain. Also, he regarded exploring as worthwhile and enjoyable for its own sake. Another interest was likely present as well. Earlier travelers had fought with hostile Indians, and several Portuguese had been killed. His goal was to explore and hold onto the land while avoiding such strife. For Cabeza de Vaca, the report was good news. He decided to make an entrada to explore and to bring relief more quickly to the Spaniards who remained in the province. There were good reasons to go overland. The Indians near Buenos Aires were dangerous, so a landing there might be costly. Even if that hazard were overcome, the journey to Asunción by river was hard for men and impossible for horses, or so the refugees from Buenos Aires assured him. The horses were a major concern, for at least twenty had died during the voyage across the ocean.

Meanwhile, from March until November 1541 (fall and winter in the Southern Hemisphere) the people rested. The arrival of spring would make it easier for those who were sailing to Asunción unless the water level of the rivers was low. In May, Felipe de Cáceres, the newly appointed royal accountant, tried to take a caravel to Buenos Aires, but winds made it impossible to enter the Río de la Plata estuary. His ship returned to the island.[17] A caravel was also sent by the governor from Santa Catalina to get supplies. Some Indians attacked the caravel, and only a vigorous defense by the crew kept it in Spanish hands.[18]

Throughout these months the Indians remained friendly with the visitors. When it was time to go, Cabeza de Vaca gave them "many caps and shirts and other things to leave them satisfied." Some of them, "of their own will," went along with him, "both to show me the way and to carry the supplies for sustaining the people." After they had finished their work as guides and carriers, they went back to their homes, "very content and happy" both with his good treatment and with the presents he had given them.[19]

The Good Treatment That Was Done to Them

With the coming of spring, it was time to go to Asunción. On October 18, 1541, all who were taking the overland route sailed up the coast. After landing at the river that Acosta had surveyed, Cabeza de Vaca took formal possession in the name of the king. From there, on November 2, some 250 soldiers, a few wives, the two friars, many Indian carriers, and twenty-five horses began the long march inland.[1] The first days were a great challenge, as the travelers, with Acosta as the guide, had to cut their way through uninhabited forests. After nineteen days of strenuous effort they came at last to some villages. The Indians were Guaraní, known to be "lovers of war" who ate human flesh, and they already had killed many Portuguese. Despite the danger, Cabeza de Vaca needed their help because his supplies were low. Fortunately, the Indians proved to be friendly and responded to his kindness and persuasion. He paid them for food and gave shirts, caps, and other gifts to their chiefs. Then, in the name of the king, he stated a claim over the land—the province of Vera.

The natives got along quite well with the Spaniards. When word spread that the travelers paid for what they wanted, Indians from all over came to sell goods—more, even, than were needed. Besides paying them, Cabeza de

Vaca gave them many things to keep the land in peace (Acosta took much credit for their good behavior in his own version of the trek).[2] Cabeza de Vaca had learned in North America the importance of gifts. He assumed that in South America he would find things the same. Indeed, gifts also had meaning for the Guaraní Indians, for example in family or personal relations and supplying services. Also, giving gifts had a rule of exchange, for to give was to receive, to do a favor meant to receive a favor.[3]

Nevertheless, friendship rested very much on how Cabeza de Vaca managed his own people. Bartolomé de las Casas, who had much zeal on the Indians' behalf, discovered from similar trials how hard it was when Spaniards were nearby. Between 1516 and 1540 he had faced a series of such problems on the islands of Hispaniola and Puerto Rico, in Central America, and in northern South America.[4] Cabeza de Vaca used strict means to avoid trouble. His people were newcomers who did not know the customs of the Indians, and to avoid strife he tried to keep the groups apart. Even so, disputes caused more trouble than did the hardships of travel, felling trees, or bridging rivers. A century later in Paraguay, Jesuit missionaries also thought it best to keep a good distance between Spaniards and Indians.

Cabeza de Vaca ordered the Spaniards not to go to the Indian villages or trade with the people. Instead, men who knew the Indians' language and methods of trade purchased needed supplies, which the governor sold to the colonists at no profit. Further, he camped far enough away from villages to avoid harming or upsetting anyone. His rules caused grumbling and bitterness among his own company, the first hint of the unrest that in two years resulted in his overthrow. To keep the Spaniards away from the Indians was not only nearly impossible but also was likely to antagonize people beyond endurance.

On this journey Cabeza de Vaca's methods worked very well. He managed his people firmly and the Indians kindly, giving them gifts or paying for what he needed. Pero Hernández, who was living in Asunción at the time,

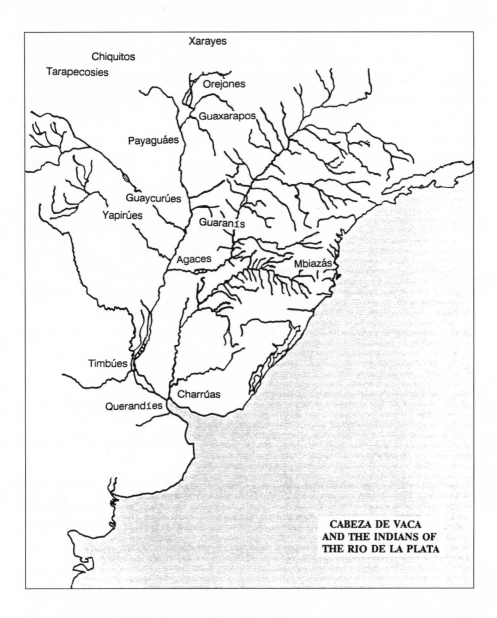

Map labels: Xarayes, Chiquitos, Tarapecosies, Orejones, Guaxarapos, Payaguáes, Guaycurúes, Yapirúes, Guaranís, Agaces, Mbiazás, Timbúes, Charrúas, Querandíes

**CABEZA DE VACA
AND THE INDIANS OF
THE RIO DE LA PLATA**

later heard about the excitement and drama. With this system, he said, and "seeing that the governor punished whoever offended them in something, all the Indians, so confident, came with their wives and children, which was a thing to see." As the news spread, the effect was more and more stirring. Indians came from far away, loaded with supplies, to look at the Spaniards and their horses—awesome creatures that had never been seen in their land. Curiosity disarmed fear. The Indians became "very happy and contented," going from place to place to tell of the "good treatment that was done to them" and to show off what they were given. On the way to Asunción the Spaniards came to another Guaraní-speaking area, where the villagers also sold them food. The usual presents of scissors, knives, and such objects made the Indians "so happy and content that for pleasure they danced and sang."[5]

Guaraní lived near Asunción as well, so friendship with them was vital. The Spanish settlement depended on their help for its survival, and their trust could be won. The best method was to have Indians spread the news of Cabeza de Vaca's peaceful mission. In North America the stories that preceded him excited curiosity and drew people from each village to him. In the Río de la Plata province, he found, the same approach worked. Those earlier years of adventure and hardship served as useful training. One difference, nonetheless, was striking. Healing (or magic), the main reason for his first triumph, was not used in South America; there, the Indians looked to him for other things.

The journey also had its problems. Although food was ample in populated areas and the Indians were paid and were happy, some villages were many days apart. The travelers had to cut through dense forests and climb mountains. Some rivers had to be crossed repeatedly, a difficult task in marshlands. In vacant areas they had to live off the land, and sometimes they had no food at all. For a time they ate white worms, found in the hollows of reeds. They were the size of a finger, and "very good" fried. Other places had game, which was a welcome addition to their diet.

Cabeza de Vaca often praised the land, calling it pleasant, with large fields, woodlands, and abundant water, "very fit for cultivating." The Indians seemed to be prospering. Their culture at that time was Neolithic, but not late Neolithic, and they used slash-and-burn methods of farming. "All the province of Bera is the best land," he rejoiced, "with more good water, rivers, streams, springs, fields and woodlands than I have seen, very suitable to populate and breed livestock of all kinds, and very healthy." Later in the journey he called it "the most fertile land in the world." Much of Cabeza de Vaca's vision of Spanish settlement centered on land and people. Indeed, he had come back to America to help Indians as well as Spaniards. These Guaraní, he wrote, "are farmers and keepers of ducks and hens, like those of Spain, domestic people, friends of the Christians, ready, with some work, to be brought to the knowledge of our Holy Catholic faith." This sentence was written after his defeat and failure in South America. He had earlier pointed out land that was good for farming in North America.[6] It is notable that Casas, following Aristotle, later argued for the capacity of the American Indians in part on the basis of their skill as farmers.[7]

The passage to Asunción brought other troubles. When the Spaniards came to a village they usually found more food than needed, but if there was too little, anger and strife followed. Bernardo de Armenta and Alonso Lebrón, the two friars, had gone ahead of the others with a number of Indians that Cabeza de Vaca called useless—clearly women. Relations between the friars and Indian women later became a problem. When this first group came to a village and ate the food there, sometimes little was left when the rest arrived. Hungry latecomers began to demand that the friars give up their Indians.

The governor had to act with care for both political and religious reasons. He told the friars not to go ahead of the company and that too many people were with them for it was "better to give bread to the Christians than to dogs." His use of this verse from the Bible (Matt. 15:26) for a policy statement is both revealing and at odds with his desire to treat the Indians well. As later actions would show clearly, the welfare of Spaniards under his authority was his first duty, for the Indians were better able to care for themselves. Also, like other Europeans of his day, his sense of ethnic or cultural superiority was strong.

This clash led to another. The friars refused to obey him and tried to take their followers by another route. He made them come back—a good thing, he believed, for "they would have found themselves in very great trouble." Then he had a notary record the "disorders" that they had caused on the journey and ordered that they not take charge of so many women. The friars became furious, speaking evil of him and conveying a different version of events to the king.[8] The future brought more disagreement about these friars, the supplies they used, and especially their collection of Indian women. Another account came from Pedro Dorantes, the royal factor, who reported that when Cabeza de Vaca ran out of gifts, he was ready to take supplies from the Indians by force. However, Armenta and Dorantes changed the governor's mind, and their Indian guide to Asunción, Miguel, was able to get necessities from villages on the way. This idea remained in Dorantes's memory for a long time. Twenty-five years later he repeated the story in a list of his services to the crown.[9] A future crisis would confirm Cabeza de Vaca's willingness to seize food from Indians who refused to sell it to starving Spaniards.

On the last day of January 1542 the travelers came to the Iguazú River. This tributary of the Paraná River entered a land where Indians were said to be waiting to attack and kill the Spaniards. For safety, one group went down the river in canoes, while the other led the horses along its banks. The strong current and rocky falls made passage difficult. After bypassing the great Iguazú falls, they reached the confluence of the Iguazú and Paraná Rivers. Suddenly, they came upon the dreaded Indians, who were Guaraní, all painted for war. The Indians were so unnerved that Cabeza de Vaca was able to assure them that he meant no harm. His presents and words spoken through an interpreter again led to friendship.[10]

By now a number of the travelers were ill, and when Cabeza de Vaca was ready to go on, they had to be left behind despite protests. Earlier, he had sent orders to Asunción for two bergantinas (Samuel Eliot Morison's term for these boats) to meet him at that point in the rivers, but Asunción was farther away than he knew, and the boats had not arrived. Leaving a guard with those who had to stay, the rest went on their way. Later, Cabeza de Vaca wrote about the success of this great march overland. During five months he and his people walked more than four hundred leagues "without causing disturbance or disagreement" with the Indians. "I always traveled on foot and barefoot to encourage the people that they might not be dismayed, because, besides the difficulty of the journey in cutting trees and making roads and bridges to cross the rivers, which were many, we suffered great and excessive hardship." His sense of satisfaction long remained, and turned up even in the final defense of his career as governor.[11]

As Was Customary in the Kingdom of Spain

When Pedro de Mendoza gave up on his colony at Buenos Aires in 1537, the whole venture might well have ended. For the Spaniards, survival came to depend on a new location for their settlement and a new form of statecraft. For five years they managed to avoid collapse while a new governing system was created. With Cabeza de Vaca's arrival as governor and adelantado of the province, the existing officials faced the loss of hard-gained power. Their resulting hostility led months later to his overthrow and a revival of the practices that had existed between the eras of Mendoza and Cabeza de Vaca.

Cabeza de Vaca had set sail from Spain bound for Buenos Aires.[1] On Santa Catalina Island, however, he learned that many settlers had moved upriver to Asunción, a new town located on the Paraguay River. Between Buenos Aires and Asunción the river zone was inhabited by nomadic Indian hunters and fishermen whose manner of life made them unsuited for Spanish control. The Spaniards needed farmers to get the economic help they wanted, and where they first met such farmers, they founded Asunción. They saw those Guaraní Indians as a vital base for the search to the west for gold and silver. Indeed, the Guaraní themselves had long been going on great journeys for these metals and could offer direct knowledge, guides, porters, and fighters.[2]

Asunción was in quite a good place. Three Spanish captains, all part of Mendoza's expedition, had a role in its foundation. In 1537 Juan de Salazar de Espinosa, Gonzalo de Mendoza, and Domingo Martínez de Irala were searching the Paraná and Paraguay Rivers for Ayolas. On August 15, the feast day of the assumption of the Virgin, Salazar founded a town, Nuestra Señora de la Asunción, at the bay of Caracara on the eastern bank of the Paraguay.[3] At first there was only a stronghouse, but it is not clear who raised it. Ulrich Schmidel (Schmidt), a German soldier who came to America with Pedro de Mendoza, wrote that the local Guaraní Indians were made to build a house of stone, earth, and wood.[4] On the other hand, Francisco de Villalta, who also came with Mendoza, said that the Indians were unwilling to do anything for the Spaniards, who had to build it themselves.[5]

The leading figure in the Río de la Plata conquest was Irala. Of Basque origin, he had come to America as a secretary to Pedro de Mendoza. While not one to act very quickly or openly, his strength, ability, and force of will put him above others who had as good a claim to rule.[6] When Pedro de Mendoza left Buenos Aires, the lives of those who stayed depended on getting help from Spain. Alonso Cabrera, another Spanish captain, went there for aid. When he returned to the Río de la Plata he carried a royal cedula (dated September 12, 1537), signed by the queen. He also had for himself the title of overseer of the struggling colony.[7]

The cedula dealt with the position of governor. It stated that if Mendoza had not left a lieutenant or if he was dead and had not named someone else, "and in that case and in no other," the people might elect as governor and captain general of the province "the person who, under God and their consciences, seemed to be most suitable." If the person who was elected also died, only one further election might be held.[8] This cedula was unique, for nowhere else in Spain's American empire existed such a grant of popular elections.[9] In January 1539 at Buenos Aires, Cabrera enacted the cedula and declared Ayolas to be Mendoza's successor.[10]

Because Ayolas was still out exploring, someone had to rule for him. One choice was Captain Francisco Ruiz Galán, left as lieutenant over Buenos Aires when Mendoza sailed for Spain in 1537.[11] In June 1539 Ruiz Galán was at Asunción seeking power over the whole province, but he was known as a cruel man, and some people opposed him. Cabrera was especially angry and unpleasant toward him, reportedly because Ruiz Galán would not do what Cabrera wanted.[12] In 1543 a number of witnesses at a legal hearing recalled the antagonism between the two men.[13]

Irala also had a claim to rule. When Ayolas went to explore in early 1537, he landed at a port on the Paraguay River that he named Candelaria (not the later Jesuit mission capital by the same name). Before Ayolas went inland to look for wealth, he ordered Irala to stay at Candelaria as his lieutenant with the bergantinas and thirty men, who were told to obey Irala's commands "like those of myself" while he was gone. In 1539 Irala was able to use this grant of power—with support from Cabrera, among others—to take over the province in the name of the absent Ayolas. A civil war between Ruiz Galán and Irala nearly broke out, but other leaders among the Spaniards averted it.[14] However, angry factions and bitterness, typical of Spanish conquests in America, existed long after Cabeza de Vaca had left the Río de la Plata.

Irala soon had control of the colony. At Asunción in July 1539, under the royal cedula that allowed the election of an acting governor, he became lieutenant to Ayolas until the latter returned from his journey. Salazar then turned the fort at Asunción over to Irala.[15] For Ruiz Galán the struggle was lost. Later, when Ayolas was known to be dead, Irala strengthened his grasp on power. Then, early in 1541, he received news at Buenos Aires that other Spaniards had landed on the coast. He said later that he waited for them until June, but when Cabrera demanded that he withdraw all the people from Buenos Aires, he abandoned it and moved the settlers to Asunción.[16]

Whether or not Buenos Aires had to be deserted in 1541 was later disputed. Irala explained that he was doing what Cabrera required of him to protect the safety of the people and end the harm caused by the Indians there.[17] Others disagreed. Pero Hernández said in 1545 that the port was surrendered against the will of all the Spaniards, it being "the key and entry of their relief and remedy." He wrote elsewhere that the leaders shared in the spoils produced by the move.[18] Bartolomé de Cuéllar, who had come to America with Mendoza, saw a different reason: Irala deserted because of a report from the Indians that Cabeza de Vaca was on the coast of Brazil with many Spaniards.[19] Cuéllar's words suggest that Irala moved deep into the interior to hold onto his own power, expecting the newcomers to resettle Buenos Aires. Ironically, most of them bypassed that port and went directly to Asunción. Another explanation involved Ruiz Galán and his challenge for power. Cabrera was known as Ruiz Galán's foremost enemy, and Irala was his victorious rival. In August 1543 Cabeza de Vaca charged at a legal hearing in Asunción that Cabrera, for his own interests, wanted to leave Buenos Aires in order to strip Ruiz Galán of his power as lieutenant governor of the port. Three years later he repeated that charge to the Royal Council of the Indies.[20]

Historians have ideas of their own. Enrique de Gandía believed the move may have occurred to get the colonists closer to the rumored wealth of the Incas of Peru, a view also expressed by Cabeza de Vaca.[21] Hipólito Sánchez Quell pointed out that the Guaraní Indians were hospitable while the pampas peoples were terrible enemies and that Paraguay was a fertile land already worked by farmers. Irala's biographer, Ricardo de Lafuente Machain, denied any sinister purpose in making the move but instead explained it as obedience to long-standing orders from Pedro de Mendoza to Ayolas, even though Buenos Aires was in a relatively good situation by 1541.[22]

Mendoza's remaining colonists landed at Asunción early in September 1541. Their winter journey up the river was a great ordeal, as Isabel de Guevara recalled in 1556. Her letter to the Spanish government describing her services and those of her husband, Pedro de Esquivel, and requesting royal favors, gives a unique account of the role of the Spanish women in the conquest.[23] Asunción was probably the best site in the region and made it possible for the settlers to survive. The key was the Guaraní, who served the Spaniards in many ways. There was a cost, nevertheless, since the loss of

Buenos Aires meant that reaching the new inland port was a much longer and harder voyage from Spain. Along the riverside the people built themselves huts of wood or adobe, roofed with straw. Only 350 or 400 Spaniards remained in the entire province, except for the newcomers, who were resting on the Island of Santa Catalina.[24]

Later in September a government was fashioned in Asunción. Irala and the other officials drafted the legal documents to form a *cabildo,* or town council, an action that was illegal according to historian Adalberto López. Whether legal or not, public welfare seemed to require officials to keep order, check weights and measures, oversee meat and fish shops, and carry out similar duties. A sense of isolation shows clearly in these documents: "Until now there have appeared no persons provided by his majesty as officials of the towns founded and built in this province." The officials in Asunción had created a government, until the king decided otherwise, "as was customary in the kingdom of Spain," to make needed laws.[25] An example of its laws, reflecting the lack of currency, came on October 3, giving monetary value to such items as fishhooks and knives.[26] The creation of a cabildo changed Asunción from a stronghouse under military discipline into a city of free men with equal rights. Only six months later Cabeza de Vaca supplanted the cabildo, another element in the political crisis that led to his eventual overthrow.[27]

How effectively Irala's officials brought about order and security is another matter. Pero Hernández, a bitter foe, spoke sharply against them. His "Relación" of 1545 cataloged their misdeeds and self-interest and portrayed life in the colony as involving abuse and terror for many of the Spaniards and Indians.[28] Other victims told similar stories. However, a new government was on its way: Cabeza de Vaca had already left Santa Catalina Island and the coast of Brazil.

At nine o'clock on the morning of March 11, 1542, the new governor walked into Asunción. The journey across half the continent had lasted four months. Although he and his people brought the supplies that had been promised, the three hundred or so Europeans there suddenly had 250 additional mouths to feed. The welcome expressed unbelievable rejoicing and pleasure. Afraid that Indians would kill everyone, the settlers had lost hope of ever getting help. Cabeza de Vaca had come by the king's command, he declared, to help them. After some discussion about the death of Ayolas, Cabeza de Vaca showed his royal writs and authority to Irala, the lieutenant governor, and the other officials. Then came the formal change in command, when the officials, clergy, soldiers, and people heard the reading of the royal documents. They accepted his authority, submitted to him as governor and captain general, and gave him the staffs of justice. With the legal steps over, he was ready to meet the tasks of government.[29]

Some members of Cabeza de Vaca's party did not enter the town with him. One group, because of illness, had been left where the Iguazú and Paraná rivers joined, and a month passed before they appeared. While drifting down the Paraná on rafts, they spent fourteen days fighting a long, tough battle against Guaraní Indians. Everyone faced extreme danger and many were injured, but the only death at this time was the victim of a jaguar.[30] It is notable that during the passage to Asunción, Indians attacked only when Cabeza de Vaca was not present to turn aside trouble.

The loss of life on the whole journey was amazingly small. According to Armenta, no Spaniards died. Dorantes stated that no more than two men died, one killed by the jaguar, another who became sick and, helped along by an arrow, died. Cabeza de Vaca spoke of a drowning and the jaguar's attack. Yet Schmidt, who was not on the trip, had quite a different story. The governor, he said, "brought not more than three hundred out of the four hundred men with him, the remainder having died of hunger and disease."[31] His dislike for Cabeza de Vaca was so great that he would not admit his success.

Cabeza de Vaca's other company had a much worse experience. In late December 1541 the ship sailed from Santa Catalina Island for Buenos Aires, with his cousin, Pedro Estopiñán Cabeza de Vaca, in charge as lieutenant. This group was to stay at Buenos Aires until orders came. Of 140 passengers, eighty were men. A striking local tie had all who were from Jerez, the governor's birthplace in Spain, going with Estopiñán. According to Pedro de

Fuentes, who wrote about this voyage to relatives in March 1545, after the pilot died they had to trust themselves to a boatswain who knew a little about fixing latitude. Many times they nearly turned back to Santa Catalina Island because the sailors were unsure whether they had passed the entrance to the Río de la Plata. Eventually they found themselves in the estuary, "without knowing where we were."[32] Francisco González Paniagua also told about the hardships of the journey. Although they had two pilots, one died and the other deserted, hiding among the Indians. The result was much work and weariness because of storms and contrary winds, as an eight- or ten-day passage took forty.[33]

Buenos Aires shocked the voyagers. They were expecting a town of a hundred people but found it destroyed instead. When a note was discovered explaining that the original occupants had fled up the river to Asunción a few months earlier, the group decided to follow despite their orders to stay there. Fortunately, the route was marked with signposts, and a storehouse along the river had some maize that saved them from dying of hunger.[34] In Asunción, when Cabeza de Vaca heard that Buenos Aires was deserted, the danger to the ship travelers became clear. To help them, and because he thought it important to hold onto Buenos Aires, late in April 1542 he ordered Captain Juan Romero to take supplies on two bergantinas to resettle that port with Estopiñán's group.

Romero met them coming up the river, and both parties returned to Buenos Aires.[35] Two other bergantinas, under Gonzalo de Mendoza, followed with more aid.[36] In addition to concern for his own people, the governor wanted to heal relations with the Indians. He ordered both captains to see that those who lived along the Paraná River "be given good treatment, and be brought by peace to obedience to his majesty." Nevertheless, the second attempt to occupy Buenos Aires also failed. Not only did the Indians renew their attacks, but a ship capsized and an earthquake struck. Once more the settlers decided to flee upriver, and in December 1542 they docked at Asunción. It was a year after they had left Santa Catalina Island and nine months after Cabeza de Vaca had arrived. They had suffered many hardships and some loss of life from storms, floods, Indians, and the earthquake.[37]

The Paradise of Muhammad

One of the basic goals of Cabeza de Vaca's mission was to apply his ideas about teaching the Indians. Since his plan was new in the province, it was vital to win support from the clerics and religious who lived there. Thus, he called them to a meeting with the royal officials, captains, and settlers, where he encouraged them to have care in teaching the Indians as "vassals" of the king. Part of a letter from Charles I was read, telling them to use special care to see that the Indians were not treated badly. Cabeza de Vaca directed the clergy to obey the royal order and to tell him about anything that was to the contrary. To be as clear as possible, he gave them copies of this policy.[1] In 1546, at a legal hearing in Spain, he added other points that he had made at this meeting. All of the Spaniards were to treat the Indians well, to pay them for their labor, and not to harm them or take their possessions. Likewise, to help the Indians understand, he had the royal provisions and the ordinance for their good treatment explained to their chiefs. Warnings about these rules went to every Spaniard in the province. Cabeza de Vaca had stated his ideas frankly at the start and explained them to everyone.

He also expected their help with his plans. Bernardo de Armenta and Alonso de Lebrón, the two friars, might have been valuable because of their favor among the Indians. After they had arrived from the coast, both went off to live among Indians. To make use of them, Cabeza de Vaca called them back to Asunción and provided a building site and the means to erect a church and house. There, like the other religious and clergy, they might begin to teach the Indians.[2] However, they were unwilling to work with him. Perhaps they were upset about the troubles on the route to Asunción, and they obviously wished to live among the Indians without close official control. Armenta, for his part, later blamed Cabeza de Vaca and said publicly that the governor was not interested in the Indians. Armenta quoted Cabeza de Vaca as saying that "where there was no gold or silver, there was no need of baptism."[3] Even so, too many Spaniards stated on oath that the governor's handling of the Indians was very good and that he threatened to punish those who harmed them for Armenta's words to be accepted. He was too angry to be convincing.

Very soon, if not from the start, Cabeza de Vaca's orders were ignored. It was not easy for a new governor to grasp the complex ties already fashioned among the peoples in the Río de la Plata province. His ideas about Indians were born of a long and close (though unintended) study of North American peoples. The Guaraní of Paraguay were different and lived in far different surroundings. When the Spaniards first settled at Buenos Aires, they had to battle fierce and able fighters who defended their land and drove out the colonists. When they resettled far up the river at Asunción, they found that the Guaraní who lived in that region were much easier to manage. The causes of such harmony help to make sense of the problems that Cabeza de Vaca faced and that in time led to his downfall.

These Guaraní saw many reasons to welcome the Spaniards as allies. Perhaps most important, they needed help in struggles against other enemies. The newcomers also had amazing weapons of an unknown metal and great skill in warfare. For the Guaraní it was entirely reasonable to understand those novel powers in terms of magic, which was very important to their culture. Another bond was that some of the Guaraní shared the Spanish interest in journeys to the west. Not only had they a tradition of going there for gold and silver, but their legends spoke of Candiré, the lord of all good things, who was to be found to the west (and was linked to the Inca empire).[4] Also, the Spaniards at first had to act with care because they were so few in number, and their search for wealth showed that they did not come to America primarily for settlement.[5]

The key to this alliance was that the Guaraní chiefs gave women to the Spaniards. In 1541 Domingo de Irala said that the Guaraní served the Spaniards both personally and with their women, so that seven hundred women lived in Spanish houses and fields.[6] The Guaraní used women to cement such unions.[7] In a society where women supplied food and labor as well as sexual activity, they supported the Spanish leaders in the same way as they did their own chiefs. It was part of the nature of the alliance.[8] The result was a blending of Spanish and Indian religious, economic, and political systems. Yoked to the goal of Christianization was the need for workers. The Spaniards accepted the Guaraní custom of sealing political loyalty by creating kinship through "marriages" with Indian women, and the Christian sacraments of baptism and marriage evidently "civilized" them enough for marital purposes.[9] Although this pattern may be seen as a kind of seraglio of female laborers, their use as a work force did not mean that they all were sexual partners.[10]

Ulrich Schmidel (Schmidt) also observed the custom: "Among these Indians the father sells his daughter, the husband his wife if she does not please him, and the brother sells or exchanges his sister." After a defeat in battle, he noted, women were used to make peace. Thus, Ayolas was given six women, and the Spanish soldiers each got two women to act as servants.[11] What to the Spaniards looked like the sale of daughters, wives, and sisters was to the Indians quite different. The emerging system of service by kindred or blood ties was based on Indian kinship labor customs and duties, fitted into the Spanish demand for workers.[12]

How terms were used could also confuse the Spaniards. In Guaraní social order, cousins were called siblings, aunts and uncles were called mothers and fathers, and nieces and nephews were called daughters and sons. To distort matters further, Cabeza de Vaca's idea that the Indians were to be paid for their labor was at odds with the Guaraní custom, which tied work to kinship. Indeed, even if the Indians and Spaniards had been agreeable, there was too little money to make Cabeza de Vaca's system operate.[13] His hope that gold and silver would become available in Paraguay for currency was not realized during the colonial era.[14]

The governor saw European marriage customs overcome by local ones. Spaniards were having sexual relations with women who were related—mothers and daughters, sisters, aunts, and nieces. To have sexual relationships with women who were related to each other within the degrees of affinity prohibited by canon law was a worse offense than to do so with unrelated women. Incest clearly was a problem, and even if some of the Indian "sisters" or "daughters" actually were cousins or nieces, the canon law ban of affinity still applied.[15]

Some Spaniards had dozens of women, particularly, he later charged, Irala. Cabeza de Vaca wanted the Indians to learn Christian and Spanish ways and to replace their own practices. Other actions upset him as well. He accused some men, especially among the captains and royal officials, of being cruel to the Indians and causing them harm. Natives were beaten, forced to work hard without pay, and deprived of their property. Some were even killed. Furthermore, "Christian Indian women" were sold or exchanged like slaves. If Cabeza de Vaca's Indian policy were to succeed, these abuses had to end. Because of such "serious sin and offense against God," he had a cleric examine the problem. Then he took many women away from the Spaniards, an action that aroused great hatred against him.[16] Memories of New Spain, where Spanish slave hunters killed helpless people and ruined large areas, still affected Cabeza de Vaca's outlook. Nevertheless, to view Paraguay in those terms was to misjudge how the Europeans and the Guaraní Indians had linked their interests.

This behavior shocked others besides the governor. Their reports gave birth to a legend that came to be called the "paradise of Muhammad." Alonso Agudo, a former official of the Holy Office of the Inquisition of Granada, wrote at length about this furor on February 25, 1545, nearly a year after Cabeza de Vaca had been arrested and his reforms ended. The letter went to a powerful church leader, Cardinal Don Juan Pardo de Tavira, inquisitor general and, as archbishop of Toledo, primate of Spain—an office second only to the papacy in income value. Agudo attacked the "dissolution and evil living" that he had seen, especially among the leaders. The Spaniards did not live as Christians, "but worse than Sodom." They had managed to take the Indian women, "calling them wives" and their kinfolk "in-laws." This practice went on "with much shamelessness and little fear of God."

He made a comparison with Islam that was quite pointed for post-Reconquest Spain. "We do not content ourselves with imitating the sect of Muhammad and his *Koran,* which commanded that they might have seven women," for some of the settlers had as many as sixty. Except for the prayers being said in Spain for the settlers, Agudo believed, the land would have swallowed them up like Sodom. When Cabeza de Vaca decreed that related females could not live with a Spaniard, the men began to hate the governor for his meddling. They grumbled that he was taking servants from them, despite "having no reason to complain [because] some cases [were] so obscene and so alarming."[17]

Another priest, Francisco González Paniagua, wrote to Cardinal Tavira on March 3, 1545. His ideas were so much like Agudo's that the two surely had talked together. Both agreed that Muhammad, in the *Koran,* allowed men to have "not more than seven women" and that the Spaniards did not call their women servants but wives, and their kinfolk were in-laws. So great was the moral breakdown, added González Paniagua, that Spaniards who held only four Indian women did so because they could not get eight, and those who had eight did so because they could not get sixteen. Anyone with only five or six women was just too poor to take the dozens that the captains and interpreters had. The "wickedness" that they did in their dwellings was plain to see in the streets and plazas, where mestizo children ran.[18]

Clerics were not the only ones decrying the settlers' behavior: other Spaniards said the same thing. Gerónimo Ochoa de Eizaguirre, who witnessed but did not take part in the rebellion against the governor in 1544, wrote to the Council of the Indies in March 1545. His stories about the Spaniards and their women are like those of the priests, even speaking of the *Koran.* Indian fathers or kinsmen gave women to the Spaniards as servants, who then sold or traded them like slaves—at a price that was too high. The worst effect came when teaching Indians to be Christians. If they were told that they might not have more than one wife and that they could not have sexual relations with related women, they asked, "How do you order us not to have more than one wife when you have ten or twenty, and among them sisters and relatives, having sexual relations with all of them?" Finally, the Spaniards had become so ensnared in "sexual vices" that some of them thought about little else. They had even lost interest in going back to Spain.[19] The conquistadores who had come to America seeking wealth in the form of gold or silver stayed for the Indian women.

Thus, the Spaniards were soon outnumbered at Asunción by their mestizo offspring. Cabeza de Vaca's nephew, Alonso Riquelme de Guzmán (who later fathered a family by one of Irala's mestiza daughters), wrote to an uncle in Spain about these children in 1545. The Guaraní "serve us as slaves and give us their daughters, that they might serve us at home and in the field." The result was more than four hundred mestizos, "because, your honor may see, indeed we are good populators, not conquistadores."[20] In July 1545 Pedro Dorantes, the factor, made a similar point. Rather than undertake another entrada, he warned Irala, the Spaniards "want to populate, and not to conquer."[21] The Indian women had become more attractive than silver or gold.

This racial union struck others as well. Francisco de Andrada, a priest who came with Pedro de Mendoza, noted in a letter of March 1545 that in Asunción there were at least five hundred mestizo children.[22] Armenta's October 1544 tally was even larger—six hundred children.[23] As will be seen, his rebuke was not honest; he himself was scolded about the Indian girls that he collected. By midcentury, according to Irala, Asunción had three thousand mestizo children.[24] In 1556 a writer said of the Indian women and mestizas, "Praise God, they are plentiful."[25] The replacement of the Indian population by a mestizo one was underway. Besides the attractiveness of the Indian women and the scarcity of European women, it should be noted that the "paradise of Muhammad" image was based in the political, economic, and social or status reasons that encouraged Spaniards to acquire so many Indian females.[26]

Cabeza de Vaca's efforts to help the Indians went beyond separating related women and Spaniards. He also decided that edicts were needed to keep the Indians from being molested or disturbed. The first of these decrees came on April 5, 1542, about a year after his arrival, when he was also in the midst of a crisis over authority with the royal officials (see chapter 13). The governor ordered that the Indians, especially women, not be sold or traded without a license. Within six days, any related women had to be removed from Spanish dwellings. Edicts touched on military security as well. No one was to trade machetes, daggers, iron arrowheads, or other weapons with the Indians. Even useless or damaged swords and crossbows, for example, were to be turned over to Cabeza de Vaca. In addition, the Spaniards now had a curfew at night and rules for carrying their firearms. Another item banned from trade was wax, which was needed to pitch the bergantinas. The Indians' property and privacy were also covered. Spaniards were not to go to Indian dwellings without the governor's approval, and sales of Indian land or homes would be reviewed to avoid deception or an unjust price. A later edict stated that no one could force Indians to trade against their will. One decree may have been for Cabeza de Vaca's personal benefit: any trade in parrots or monkeys had to have his license. Apart, perhaps, from the last one, his measures were aimed at correcting problems that existed. Interpreters, who had at times caused disorder while trading at Indian villages, were also regulated. They were to make visits only on the governor's business or with his approval and only for tasks that he assigned. When their work was done, they were to return at once and report to him. When some Spaniards used the edicts to prevent the mothers of their women from visiting because related females were not allowed together in Spanish households, Cabeza de Vaca revised the rules so that visits might again take place.

By custom, the edicts were read to the people of Asunción and posted publicly. Offenses could bring either a fine (to be split among the royal exchequer, the local public works fund, the judges, and any informers), a sentence to jail or the stocks, or service in the bergantinas.[27] The penalties were harsh enough to show that Cabeza de Vaca was serious. They counteract arguments that his "humane" Indian policy was aimed only at persuading the Spanish government of his innocence when he was accused of crimes.

Any effort to manage trade with Indians was bound to anger the Spaniards, and these edicts sharpened dissatisfaction with the governor. Felipe de Cáceres, the royal accountant, tried in 1545 to justify rebellion by charging that Cabeza de Vaca's edicts against trade with the Indians were made only to control it for himself.[28] Pedro Dorantes wrote to the king at the same time about Cabeza de Vaca and the Indians. He claimed to have told the governor in public that restraints on trade were against the service of God and of the king, as well as contrary to the welfare and advantage of both the Indians and Spaniards. Even Indians had spoken against it and were dissatisfied for these as well as for other reasons.[29] As Dorantes made clear, not all of Cabeza de Vaca's ideas for a humane conquest were agreeable to the Indians, who had their own ideas about the Spaniards.

The government of Spain also issued a series of reforms in 1542. These "New Laws," largely the work of Bartolomé de Las Casas, met rejection and rebellion in the Americas.[30] Cabeza de Vaca likely did not know about these laws, but they shared with his edicts the goal of protecting Indians. Two years later, in 1544, his enemies arrested him largely because of that goal, and in the same year a civil war began in Peru against the New Laws, a war that shook the whole campaign to protect the American Indians.

Were his edicts enforced? One night in May 1543 a Spaniard named Bernardo (or Hernando) de Castañeda entered an Indian's dwelling and forced a woman to have sex with him in front of her husband. The husband went to Cabeza de Vaca, who sentenced Castañeda to one hundred lashes.[31] Yet, Francisco González Paniagua recalled that this punishment was unique, the only whipping he remembered being imposed by the governor.[32] Cabeza de Vaca was probably much more lenient than severe. Alonso Riquelme de Guzmán, his nephew, later said that no one had ever been hanged, and Pedro Estopiñán Cabeza de Vaca, his cousin, added that when Indians complained of being mistreated, he warned and punished the guilty Spaniards "with complete moderation and mildness" and quieted the Indians with gifts.[33]

The Spaniards held onto their Indian women long after Cabeza de Vaca had lost the power to protect them. Martín González, a cleric, wrote in 1556 that there were Spaniards who had between eighty and one hundred Indian women, groups that surely included relatives. He thought that it was a bad example for the Indian men, yet this practice appears to have been borrowed, at least in part, from the way that the Indian men treated their own women.[34]

Christians and Vassals
of His Majesty

In his own way, Cabeza de Vaca did come back to the New World as a missionary. By the latter part of his great adventure in North America he was trying to teach the Indians about Christianity, and this task remained very important to him in South America. At Santa Catalina Island he wanted the two Franciscans to stay and teach the Indians Christian doctrine, and after his arrival at Asunción he told the clergy to do the same for the local people. He called together all the Indian vassals of the crown, the chiefs especially, and in the presence of the clergy and officials spoke to them "useful words" so that they might be "good Christians." Yet, while lending his prestige to this teaching, his primary role with the Indians was to protect them. Religious training generally was left to the clergy. Otherwise he avoided challenging Indian customs, unless they seemed to be monstrous, to undermine Spanish morals, or to imperil the safety of the province.

One exception to his relative tolerance was cannibalism. Shortly after he came to Asunción he warned the Indians there to stop eating human flesh or allowing it to be eaten in their towns—"for the serious sin and offense that they were committing by it against God our Lord." It was to him a common, serious problem, and on April 29, 1542, he ordered the Guaraní

Indians to cease eating human flesh.[1] The issue was not a new one, for years earlier, when he was on the coast of Texas, five Spanish castaways reached such an extreme that they ate one another until only one was left. When the Indians there learned of the incident, they were so horrified that if they had known about it, Cabeza de Vaca believed, the Spaniards would have been killed.[2]

In South America it happened again. Gregorio de Acosta (who had come to America with Mendoza and may have been a son of the pilot Gonzalo de Acosta), said that when Pedro de Mendoza was at Buenos Aires, many men ate each other because of a great famine. Ulrich Schmidt gave two such examples in his book.[3] There were enough cases that in 1539 Charles I granted a pardon by royal cedula to the Spaniards of the Río de la Plata province who had eaten human flesh.[4]

Cabeza de Vaca was not inventing stories about cannibalism among the Indians of Paraguay. The people who were ordered to give up the custom were loyal and helpful allies, and no excuse was needed to enslave them because they were already under Spanish control. His target was the friendly Guaraní Indians, who had been eating the bodies of their enemies, the Agaz Indians, "cooked and roasted," in full view of the Spaniards.[5] Pero Hernández, a man who knew both the region and its people well, wrote at length about how the women diverted and fattened such captives until they were killed and their flesh eaten with much festivity and rejoicing.[6]

Was the campaign against cannibalism a success? Some of the clergy thought that it did not work very well. On September 28, 1542, the two Franciscans, Armenta and Lebrón, and a priest, Francisco de Andrada, urged the governor to require more enforcement because the Guaraní Indian allies had not fully broken with the custom. While helping the Spaniards to make war on hostile Indians, they legally took slaves and then sold them to people living in the interior of the land. These slaves were being eaten, they charged, although both the church and the king opposed the practice. The priests wanted the Guaraní to stop trading slaves.

The next day Cabeza de Vaca and the three men met with his officials and the captains. He told them that he had given the Indians orders not to eat human flesh or allow it to be eaten anywhere. Until now, he had not known that they were doing so, but if they were, he would punish them by making war, as the king had commanded. Then the chiefs of the Indians of the region, who had also been called, joined the meeting. He told them again not to eat human flesh or to give slaves for others to eat. If they did so, they would be enemies. Turning to the clergy, he directed them to teach and preach to those Indians to do what was best to serve God and the king. Finally, Armenta preached a sermon to the Indians to obey the governor's commands and not to eat human flesh.[7]

On the other hand, there may have been no problem at all. Luis de Miranda, a priest and friend of the governor, said on oath that after the Indians were warned to avoid human flesh, they "guarded against eating it and held it as an evil thing." He himself never saw them doing so again.[8] Other Spaniards agreed. In August 1543, at a hearing on the topic, a dozen witnesses stated that the Indians had ceased eating human flesh after the governor ordered them to stop.[9] Pero Hernández described carefully the elements of Guaraní cannibalism, and if all of the time-consuming ritualistic steps set forth were closely followed, it would not have been difficult for the Spaniards to discover and discourage the practice among friendly Indians.[10]

Cabeza de Vaca's policy did not last long. After his foes arrested him, they told the Indians that they did so because he was an evil person who did not allow them to kill and eat their enemies. Thereafter, the new government again let friendly Indians eat the flesh of slaves and foes to win the Guaraní's support. Even newly converted Christian Indians took part, which Hernández called "a thing so against the service of God and his majesty, and so abhorrent to all who heard it." He and the governor claimed that three hundred were killed, there was a "public meat market," and the dead were roasted.[11] The victims were the Agaz Indians, part of the Guaycurú cultural-linguistic group, who dominated the Paraguay River and fisheries with their canoes north and south of Asunción. The name Payaguá (from which the word Paraguay comes) was given to them by the Guaraní and taken over by the Spaniards; they called themselves the Evueví—people of the river.[12]

Cannibalism did not make Irala squeamish. Captain Hernando de Ribera, writing to the king in 1545, told how Irala had handled the practice in 1539, after becoming acting lieutenant governor for the first time at Asunción. When he and the Guaraní allies defeated the Agaz Indians at war, the Guaraní roasted their foes in the presence of Irala and the royal officials. Irala did not mention cannibalism in his report of the fight.[13] Captain Francisco de Ribera told a similar story. An unpublished letter, cited by Julio César Chaves, tells about some Payaguá Indians who were punished for the death of Ayolas by being cut into pieces and eaten by Guaraní. Present were Irala, Felipe de Cáceres, and Alonso Cabrera.[14] On one point, however, Ribera may have been mistaken. Ayolas apparently died in June or July 1538, but when the Spaniards learned about it in March 1540, Cáceres was back in Spain and could not have been present if such revenge took place before Cabeza de Vaca became governor.[15] In a letter of January 1545 to the king, Hernández virtually confirmed the story: he said that the Payaguá Indians were divided among the Carios (Guaraní) Indians and were killed and cut into pieces in the presence of Irala, Cabrera, and Garci Venegas.[16] Perhaps Ribera got the name wrong.

Besides cannibalism, another challenge for Cabeza de Vaca was the violent opposition of a few neighbors. The Agaz Indians had been a problem ever since the founding of Asunción.[17] Ulrich Schmidt saw them as warlike from first contact (probably in 1537). When the Spaniards approached the Agaz, they "wished to make war against us by not allowing us to pass through." He judged them to be the "best warriors that can be found on water," but after the Spaniards fought and killed many of them, they made peace for a time.[18] Irala wrote in 1541 about the struggle against the Agaz: "With God's help, and the service of Guaraní Indians, we have destroyed many offspring of other Indians who have not been friends, especially the Agaces."[19] Cabeza de Vaca later recalled them as "a warlike people, indomitable, with evil practices, the enemies of all the river peoples, owing to their making war on everyone and never keeping friendship or peace with anyone."[20] According to Hernández, they were the most feared of all the tribes. Time after time they promised peace, only to plan treachery and war against Spaniards or other Indians.[21]

These Indians soon gave the governor's peacemaking skill its extreme test. Just before he first entered Asunción they had been troublesome again, but when their chiefs came to meet with him, they declared that they desired friendship. He answered that he was pleased to have them as vassals of the crown and friends of the Spaniards but warned of war if they broke the peace. His terms were that they stop preying on the Guaraní, release their hostages, allow Christian Agaces to practice their religion, and grant safe passage to the Spaniards. If they did not keep their word, they would be punished.[22] Soon, as it turned out, they were back at war, for the Agaz agreed to peace only to carry on trade and prepare for more warfare. In their long struggle against the Spaniards, a time of peace was only a chance for rest.[23]

Meanwhile there came a more urgent threat from the Guaycurú Indians. The Mbayá-Guaycurúes called themselves the Eyiguayegis. Indeed, *Guaycurú* was not an ethnic name; rather, it described a late Paleolithic culture (in contrast to the Neolithic Guaraní Indians) of aggressive hunters. Their population in the year 1500 was some fifteen thousand, and these brave fighters were greatly feared by the other Indians in the region.[24] Hernández respected them as a warlike and valiant people who lived solely by hunting and fishing. He reported that women were treated well and had "much preeminence among them." Perhaps passing on Guaraní stories, he added that female captives of war were set free and not harmed, a statement that the Spaniards themselves could not make. A few pages later he added, "It is certain that the women have more liberty than what our lady Queen Isabel gave to the women of Spain."[25] According to Branislava Susnik, such good treatment of women—their own or captives—was an important psychological and social factor when hunter-gatherers got ready to fight each other.[26]

The Guaycurúes were among the chief enemies of the Guaraní. They lived across the Paraguay River from Asunción and fought some Guaranís for hunting, fishing, and farming areas. The Guaranís called for help, and the governor asked the clergy for their advice. They answered that a war against the Guaycurú Indians would be just and lawful. Nevertheless, Cabeza de Vaca first tried for peace. Two interpreters, a cleric, and an escort of fifty soldiers were sent to order the Guaycurúes to obey the king and stop the raids on the Guaraní. If they did so, Cabeza de Vaca would be their friend and help them; if not, he would make war on them.[27] The basis of this warning was the *Requerimiento,* which the government of Spain had issued in 1513. In *Relación,* Cabeza de Vaca had shown that he was aware of its main points.[28] Now he was using its ideas again. Indians were to be won by peaceful means, he hoped, but if force had to be used, it was to be done legally, as set forth by the laws of Spain.

This time peace did not come easily. The Guaycurúes, in spite of his warnings, answered that they meant to keep up the war: "They did not wish to give obedience, or be friends with the Spaniards and the Guaraní." They forced the messengers to leave by shooting arrows and wounding them. For the sake of the Spanish-Guaraní alliance, the governor had to go to war. On July 12, 1542, a dozen horsemen and two hundred soldiers, joined by ten thousand Guaraní, marched out of Asunción, to go after the Guaycurúes, who had "four thousand men of war."[29] Hernández found the order of march impressive: "the adornments of war, the many arrows with parrot feathers, their bows painted many ways, their instruments of war, their drums, trumpets, cornets, and other such things." The chiefs, recognizing the governor as war chief in this action, each handed him a splendidly painted bow and arrow, according to custom, and all the Indians brought him painted arrows trimmed with parrot feathers.[30]

While on the march, the army just barely escaped disaster. When a jaguar suddenly panicked the Guaraní Indians, the Spanish soldiers mistook the confusion for treachery and began to strike at them. Only by a great effort did the governor hold the Indians on his side. Yet his ability to handle them even in an extreme crisis saved the alliance, which was truly the basis of the Spanish settlement in the province.[31] Such fear of the jaguar was general in the Guaraní areas, even among great warriors. The "jaguar-man" was believed to be an Indian possessed by the wild animal, stealing the prey of another's snares and being blamed for the evils that the community suffered. One so identified, according to historian Rafael Eladio Velásquez, was immediately killed by his companions.[32] Another fear was that shamans were thought to change themselves into jaguars, to attack people and eat them.[33]

Later, while in prison, Cabeza de Vaca found out that this misadventure had not run its course entirely by chance. After the royal officials and Domingo de Irala arrested him, they bragged about shooting at him with harquebuses that night. Indeed, two bullets had barely missed.[34]

In time the scouts found their quarry, and the next part of the plan began. The Spaniards aimed not to destroy the Guaycurúes but to stop their raids on the Guaraní. A solid victory might be enough, so the governor had his men leave an opening for flight into the woods so as not to kill too many. He told the Guaraní that this attack was entirely for their benefit, for their safety and defense, because the Guaycurúes had never seen or known the Spaniards or caused them any trouble. At dawn the clash began. Hernández saw the Guaycurúes fighting with "impetuosity and valor," while the Guaraní "died from fear of them, and nothing could make them attack their enemies." They would have fled if they had dared, so the Spaniards carried the battle. Yet, perhaps there was good reason to flee. Although the Guaraní had marked their bodies with white crosses, in the darkness the Europeans could not tell one Indian from the rest. They killed and wounded both friend and foe.

From the back of his horse, Cabeza de Vaca led his men into battle with the ancient cry of "Santiago!" The horses caused much fear among the Guaycurúes, who had never before seen such a beast, and they set fire to their dwellings to escape in the smoke and chaos. Victory came quickly, with only two Spaniards dead and a few wounded. Despite defeat, the Guaycurúes held onto their fame as warriors. Twenty of them trailed the Guaraní to Asunción and killed a thousand stragglers.[35]

Now was the time to try another way. The Guaycurúes had been shocked by European skill and power in battle, so perhaps they were ready for peace. Four hundred prisoners of war became the bait. The governor announced to the soldiers and Guaraní chiefs that the king had ordered that none of those Guaycurúes were to be enslaved. The legal steps called for had not been carried out, he explained, and the king was better served by giving them liberty. He picked out one man, handed him gifts, and sent him to tell the Guaycurúes to come and make peace.[36] If the Spaniards were astounded by the governor's ban against enslavement, the Guaraní as well would have seen it as meddling with their usual handling of captives.[37]

A few days later the emissary was back with his people. Twenty chiefs spoke with the governor. They and their ancestors had gone to war against everyone, they boasted, and had "always defeated and destroyed them. Never had they been conquered by any people, nor did they imagine that it might happen. Since they had met others more valiant than themselves, they were coming to put themselves under their power and be their slaves, to serve the Spaniards." [38]

Cabeza de Vaca used his victory to present the Christian religion to the Guaycurúes. He said that he had come there by royal command, "so that all the inhabitants might grow in knowledge of God our Lord and be Christians and vassals of his majesty, to place them in peace and tranquility, to favor them and treat them well." If they stopped their wars against the Guaraní Indians, he would protect and defend them and have them as friends. Then, he gave the chiefs all the prisoners taken in battle. They agreed to his terms and promised to help supply Asunción, which they did, according to Hernández. They came when the governor called, and they obeyed his orders. Every week they brought fish, game, and other trophies from their hunting. Their ties with the Spaniards, and even with the Guaraní, were happy, their visits festive. Hernández may well have been stretching the case to make a point. Even so, for the moment it was a striking triumph, a success of great importance. The Guaycurúes were the most feared in all that land, Cabeza de Vaca noted, and might never have come under Spanish authority if he had not made war.[39] Yet victory by itself did not justify his conquest; he still had to defend his use of force in achieving it.

His confidence, however, was not well founded. The Guaycurú Indians did not suspend their hostility toward the Guaraní for long, and after Cabeza de Vaca's era had ended they renewed violence against the Spaniards. Susnik saw peace as a tactic to allow them a look at such novelties as iron and horses, and to barter or recover captives.[40] In the sixteenth and seventeenth centuries some Guaycurúes rejected Spanish material culture when ancient ways of life could still be upheld. Only in the eighteenth century did they begin adopting Spanish elements that allowed an easing of the rigors of their traditional way of life.[41]

The governor's victory led to others. Various Indian peoples "came of their own will to ask for peace."[42] Relations with the Guaycurúes showed that a modest amount of force, used to frighten but not destroy, might win peace and friendship. Soon the Yapirú Indians, known as excellent hunters, arrived at Asunción to see the governor. They were also one of the Guaycurú groups, although foes of the recently defeated Guaycurúes, and they lived inland to the west of Asunción.[43] The Yapirúes wanted to have good relations with those who had overcome their enemies. To show their good faith, the chiefs gave to the governor several of their daughters, suggesting that they also used females to encourage good relations and common bonds.[44]

The governor again seized the chance to speak about Christianity. He stated that he had come to tell the Indians to be Christians. They were to submit to the king and live in peace and friendship with his vassals, the Guaraní. If they agreed to do so, they would become his vassals as well, and he, as governor, would protect them and keep them in harmony with all the people of the land. The other Indian allies would treat them as friends, and they could trade with the Spaniards and Indians at Asunción, as the Guaycurúes had done since making peace.

The gift from the Yapirúes was used as a model for the Spaniards in handling Indian women. According to Luis de Herrezuelo, a friar, the governor never touched Indian women, but he welcomed the women and girls to avoid upsetting the chiefs. Instead of keeping them for himself, he turned them over to the clergy to be taught Christian doctrine and customs. The Yapirúes were happy and content, said Hernández, but he did not say what the settlers thought about this way of treating Indian women.

The Yapirú Indians kept their promises of friendship, at least for a time. Their way of life, however, impeded even more than usual the duty of Christianization. They were nomadic, and the clergy did not trust them enough to live and travel with them, but to force them to change to a settled life would likely mean that they would starve. The only way to expose them to the Christian faith, it seemed, was to teach it to the women that they had given to the governor and send them back later to inform their own people.[45] The desire for peace likely came from rivalry with neighbors over Spanish friendship and trade. In time they reversed that policy and resumed their attacks on the Guaraní.[46]

Questions were later raised about the seriousness and effectiveness of Cabeza de Vaca's peace efforts. At a legal hearing on these methods held during August 1543, a number of people testified on oath about his success. The witnesses' statements give a useful summary of Cabeza de Vaca's Indian policies. After his arrival, they agreed, he had informed himself about the conversion of the Indians. Then, "by good treatment and coaxing, he has convinced the chief Indians of this province, their wives, children, relatives, and everybody in general, of the knowledge of our Christian religion, and service and obedience to the royal crown." He also protected and defended the Indians so that the Spaniards were not causing them harm and punished any who did so. Finally, he "attracted and pacified many warlike and untamed Indians" for friendship and trade, helping the Indians and the Spaniards, and "making a great service to God our Lord."[47] This source is particularly valuable because it dates from before Cabeza de Vaca's arrest, and he was not yet attempting to defend himself against his enemies' charges. More than a dozen witnesses stated under oath that the governor's gifts and good treatment satisfied the Indians and made them happy. Even rival Indians made peace under his administration. The situation benefited both Indians and Spaniards. His policies served as a legal code for managing Indians, for the public notices and decrees were meant to avoid future wrongdoing. Nevertheless, how deeply he had affected these Indian peoples could not be measured by testimony from Spanish witnesses. Only time would reveal his long-term success, and he did not have time.

They Would Go from the Land and Leave Them Free

Peace and friendship grew between Cabeza de Vaca and most of the Indians, but he met failure too. Well-known for treachery, the Agaz Indians soon tested his willpower and skill. Despite having signed a treaty, they attacked the garrison at Asunción as soon as he went off to fight the Guaycurú Indians. Each night they came to loot and carry away Guaraní women. After returning to Asunción, Cabeza de Vaca asked the officials and clergy for advice. Their signed opinion was to make war against the Agaces "by fire and blood" because of the evil and havoc that they were causing. Four earlier legal cases had shown the Indians to be liars, so the latest raids only confirmed previous knowledge. Even so, the struggle had been as costly to them as it was to the Spaniards and Guaraní Indians, for a thousand or more Agaces died in the warfare.[1]

The Agaz Indians knew what they were doing. As one of their chiefs said regarding Asunción, "These walls are washed with our blood, for everyone knows that in their buildings the Christians are killing those who come to them to see about peace and bring them their things."[2] Their boldness led to a tougher policy. The governor ordered that a dozen Agaz captives be hanged.[3] At that time the factor, Pedro Dorantes, learned a solemn example of Agaz philosophy. When one of them, facing death, was about to weep, another told him, "As you are sad about dying, die like a man. Those who are binding us must also die like us, and it is all a small advantage, since in the end we all have to die."[4]

To Cabeza de Vaca, the hangings seemed necessary. As much as he desired goodwill from the Indians and as hard as he worked to win it, he would not allow any who agreed to come under Spanish authority to carry on their old quarrels. The Guaycurú Indians, despite a hard-fought battle, were pardoned because they had not yet made peace. The Agaces, on the other hand, had vowed to be friends and knew what it meant to break their word, so he treated them harshly. Yet hanging Agaz prisoners did not end the turmoil. While this strife grew, he was too busy getting ready for his entrada to give it much thought. Before the next chance came to face these Indians, the royal officials had seized power from him and the Agaz problem fell into their hands.[5]

By October 1542 Cabeza de Vaca was again taking the first steps toward exploring. Long talks with Indians and Spaniards who knew the area fired his interest, and he was eager to carry on with his travels and discovery into the unknown parts of the country. When he asked the Guaraní chiefs for guides, many were willing to go. First among them was Aracaré, a Guaraní from upriver who said that he was an important chief. The choice of Aracaré, however, led to a struggle against Spanish power itself. (In fact, he was a chief of the Guarambarense, a Guaraní subgroup.) His goal actually was to stop the settlers and drive them away. That ambition outraged the governor, for among his titles was that of adelantado, under which he was charged with opening the land for settlement.

Their contest began on October 20. Captain Domingo de Irala and ninety Spaniards left Asunción to go up the Paraguay River, taking three bergantinas and many Indians. He planned to go north of his earlier landings, to avoid the people who had killed Juan de Ayolas, and then look for a place to enter the region to the west of the river. On the way, three Spaniards and eight hundred Indians landed to explore the interior (in the area of what now is Fuerte Olimpo), guided by Aracaré. About twenty days later the three Spaniards came back to Asunción. Aracaré, they charged, had betrayed them and caused extreme danger, nearly destroying the mission. As they ventured into the interior, he set fires to alert nearby Indians to kill them. Then he bid the friendly Guaraní to desert them and urged the other guides not to show them the way. "The Christians were evil," Aracaré insisted, for he could see where their search would likely lead. He warned the Indians not to show the Spaniards the way to their villages "because they would be their slaves." Without guides, the Spaniards "would go from the land and leave [the Indians] free." The guides were swayed and did as he said, despite the pleas of the Spaniards. Forsaken, lost, and in much danger, nonetheless the Spaniards "miraculously" escaped the hostile Indians and made it back to the settlement.[6]

In mid-December four Spaniards and 1,500 Indians repeated the journey. When they turned inland, Aracaré again tried to block them. However, this time there was no mutiny, and the Spaniards finished their task. After a month of exploring an empty countryside, facing hunger, thirst, and death, they returned. Aracaré was waiting and caused more harm by attacking both the Spaniards and their allies. This defiance, the first by a Guaraní leader, could not be ignored. Cabeza de Vaca, the officials, and the clergy held an inquiry, which declared Aracaré a "principal enemy." The next step was to notify the accused of the judgment; Aracaré tried to kill the Spaniards sent to inform him. Then came the sentence of death, and, for the Indian allies, its "just causes." Aracaré's crime was that he "impeded the discovery of the land," further proof of the great value that the governor placed on exploring. With everything done "according to law," Irala, still exploring, was ordered to carry out the penalty. With his usual ability, he had Aracaré arrested and hanged.[7]

Aracaré's sense that the European alliance held dangers was unique. At first the Spanish use of the Guaraní on the entradas corresponded to the Indians' own interests and desires. They took part in the expeditions against the Agaces and the Guaycurúes because of ancient hostilities between the two cultures of hunters and farmers on the opposite banks of the Paraguay River.[8] Guaraní youth also joined Spanish explorations to capture women, settle other areas, or free themselves from customary Guaraní ways of life.[9]

Yet for Aracaré, there was nothing new in his struggle with the settlers. In 1540 he had agreed to help Irala and the other Spaniards search for Ayolas but tried to take them where hostile Indians would kill them or where they would get lost. Then he secretly won over the Spaniards' allies, who deserted them. Thus, his tactics had been tried several years earlier. When he met the governor he again had acted friendly, so he was treated well and given presents as a show of goodwill toward him and his people. Aracaré then had gotten another chance to guide for the Spaniards—another chance to try to ruin them. Cabeza de Vaca did not say what he knew about the earlier clashes. Perhaps he believed too much in his ability to win the friendship of all Indians.

The death sentence for Aracaré was used later to attack Cabeza de Vaca. When his rivals took over the government, they needed to charge him with crimes to justify their rebellion. One useful example was this execution, because by saying that it was unjust and had caused the Indians to go to war, they could raise doubts about how he had treated the natives. Only after returning to Spain was Cabeza de Vaca able to defend himself. In 1546 he asked witnesses who knew about the Río de la Plata to explain that Aracaré, "an Indian, native to the Paraguay River, pretended friendship with the Christians, saying that he was a chief (it not being so) and offered to help the Christians and discover the land. Therefore they treated him well." The witnesses also swore that Aracaré had betrayed the Spaniards, and one of them added that the Indian had made war even on his own kinfolk and forced them to flee to safety, so much did he hate their affection for the Spaniards.[10]

For Cabeza de Vaca the issue was rebellion by an Indian who had agreed to submit to Spanish rule. He could not see it as a war for freedom against Spanish power. Thus, the threats uttered in the *Requerimiento* ("Requirement") against Indians who defied Spanish authority gave a legal basis for Aracaré to be hanged. Whether it was wise or just to do so may be debated, and one person who could see the grounds for Indian self-defense was

Bartolomé de Las Casas.[11] In his own lifetime Aracaré inspired a great debate, and his defiance of Spanish imperialism has won him the respect of historians such as Fulgencio R. Moreno and Julián M. Rubio.[12] Cabeza de Vaca's denial that Aracaré was a chief may reflect the provision in his capitulation with the king that any wealth taken from enemy chiefs who were captured, killed, or executed in war be shared with the crown.[13]

Meanwhile, Irala was carrying out his original orders. About 250 leagues up the river he found some villagers who were willing to help explore the interior. With them were some Guaraní captives, who spoke to him freely. He had a list of questions for anyone he met about the local geography and Indians, supplies, and travel on the river. Also, if the local people knew about gold or silver, he was to find out how they got it, how much they had, and who owned the sources. One question dealt with other Europeans in the region. Of much interest was Aleixo Garcia, the Portuguese who had traveled there in search of gold during the 1520s. In fact, Irala met many Indians who had been Garcia's slaves before the local Guaraní killed him. In addition, Irala was to ask about myths and legends. For example, was there a great chief in the land of gold and silver? Was there a white king? Finally, would the Indians guide the Spaniards to the places they described?

By February 15, 1543, Irala was back in Asunción with good news. The Indians had shown him a way from the river into the interior, and he had followed it for three days through a very agreeable land. They had some gold and silver and ample supplies for the conquest, and they were willing to serve as guides. He had named the site Puerto de los Reyes (Port of the Kings [Magi]), because he arrived there around January 6, the day of Epiphany. It seemed to him that there was no better spot for exploration to begin.[14]

Shortly before Irala's return, a disaster struck Asunción. Prior to daybreak on February 4, a Sunday morning, fire broke out and raged for four days through the crude straw and wooden dwellings that made up the town. Two hundred houses had burned when it was over, leaving only fifty standing.

Losses of clothing, food, livestock, and munitions were also serious. The Spaniards were so ruined, devastated, and naked, Pero Hernández wrote, "that nothing remained for them to cover their bodies with." Although some colonists suspected that the Indians were trying to burn them out of the land, the fire actually started by chance when an Indian woman living with a Spaniard shook a spark onto a straw wall.

Cabeza de Vaca met the settlers' staggering needs. At "great cost" to himself he bought supplies to support the people, "without charging them anything." The fire was a dangerous blow, and he called it an obstacle and great hindrance to the entrada and discovery of the land. Nevertheless, Asunción was soon rebuilt, this time with materials, such as adobe, that were less likely to burn. He helped the townsfolk himself and even urged them to get their houses finished, but it is likely that the Indians did much of the labor. A new church also rose from the ashes. Cabeza de Vaca spent many days trying to get the royal officials to help build it, but they did not work until he did so himself.[15]

The great fire was not the governor's only problem in early 1543. Troubles with angry Indians survived the death of Aracaré, for his brother, Tabaré, and members of his family struck back at the Spaniards and their allies. Cries for help soon reached Cabeza de Vaca, and, following royal instructions, he again called on the officials and clergy for advice. Because the Indians had attacked, the officials and clergy advised sending soldiers to restore royal authority: "If they were not willing to agree, warn them once, twice, three or more times as they were able, declaring that all the deaths, injury and damage done in the land was their fault." War might then be made on them as enemies, in order to protect the friendly Indians in that country.[16]

To crush Tabaré, Irala was summoned once again. Cabeza de Vaca told him to attack the Indians, as the clergy and officials had urged, but first he was to warn them and try to restore peace. If his men had to fight, they were to cause "the least injury that they were able, avoiding death and robbery and other evils."[17] At first Tabaré and the Guaraní chiefs were defiant. Their numbers were strong and their defenses securely fenced with wooden walls protected by wide pits. Indeed, sixteen Spaniards died in the attack, and many others were wounded. The Indian allies also had many losses. However, more than three thousand of the enemy were slain, many of their women captured, and they had to surrender.[18] According to Branislava Susnik, Tabaré made peace because he feared that the loss of the captured women would mean a population collapse, a major crisis for his people.[19]

When the Indians came to make peace, the governor pardoned them. They claimed that "they had been deceived and wanted nevermore to be evil, but to be great friends of the Christians." He gave back their women and added some gifts, but he also warned that if they went to war again, he would punish them. Thereafter Tabaré remained on good terms with Cabeza de Vaca and later agreed to help him when he went to explore the interior of the province.[20]

Tabaré's uprising, like Aracaré's, stirred debate among the settlers. Some blamed the Indian revolt on the governor. For example, Ulrich Schmidt often treated Cabeza de Vaca with scorn, for their ideas and values were not at all the same. He looked with great disfavor at the governor's "nice virtue," frowned at his "arrogant and vain inspiration," and twice faulted him for having "no great respect among us." In brief, "he was not the right sort of man," a statement that perhaps says as much about Schmidt as about the governor. Samuel Eliot Morison saw Schmidt as unpleasant and relied on Cabeza de Vaca when the two men's statements disagreed. According to Schmidt, war followed Aracaré's execution because Tabaré wished to avenge his brother's death. Irala and others among the governor's foes spread this tale as well.[21]

Other accounts refute these charges. A notable historian of this conquest, Enrique de Gandía, contended that the rebellion was not started by Aracaré's death but by the mistreatment caused by members of Irala's expedition to Puerto de los Reyes. Documents written by rivals of Cabeza de Vaca reveal the Indians' complaints of robbery, abuse of daughters and wives, and other wrongs. The mistreatment that Gandía cited happened during Irala's journey of exploration, when Aracaré was hanged.[22]

Tabaré's uprising gave rise to a second charge against the governor. His enemies said later that when he sent Irala to punish Tabaré, Cabeza de Vaca took the royal standard from the mast of his ship, "saying words of anger against it," and in its place set a standard with his own coat of arms.[23] How much truth is in this story or in the other accusations leveled after Cabeza de Vaca's arrest is not easy to say. Whether his enemies were lying or twisting the truth, any hint of such ambition or pride was well suited to encourage royal distrust of him.

Cabeza de Vaca still sought a humane and just conquest. In spite of Aracaré's clear scorn for Spanish sovereignty, the governor did not understand that some Indians would reject any attempt at peace and friendship that meant submitting to Spanish authority. Thus, a later Guaraní uprising called for a return to the old ways, which for them meant liberty.[24] Cabeza de Vaca could see only that the civilization of Christian Spain was superior to Indian cultures. Unlike another defender of the Indians, Casas, he could not imagine that a Spanish conquest might mean greater harm to the Indians than would leaving them to be free within their own culture, or that they had a right to fight for freedom. Thus, Cabeza de Vaca did not hesitate to stop Aracaré, Tabaré, or any others who inflamed or attacked the Indians who accepted the Spaniards.

That They Might Be the Governors and Not He

The Indians did not overcome Cabeza de Vaca. Most often he handled them quite well, and they proved to be far less dangerous to him than were the Spaniards—the royal officials in particular. Indeed, the first major problem he faced after coming to Asunción was with the royal officials who held power: the treasurer, Garci Venegas; the accountant, Felipe de Cáceres; the factor, Pedro Dorantes; and the overseer, Alonso Cabrera (called "the white-tailed fox" because of the way that he worked).[1]

Another important official was the notary of the province, Martín de Orúe, whom the governor removed within a year at the request of traders and the overseer of the goods of the deceased. After an inquiry was made to find the "most able and loyal" person for the post, Cabeza de Vaca chose Pero Hernández, a former secretary to Pedro de Mendoza.[2] Hernández proved to be a loyal friend, Orúe a perilous foe. Orúe and Cáceres had first come to the Río de la Plata with Mendoza. After his death they returned to Spain to obtain royal approval of their titles, and they returned to the Río de la Plata with Dorantes and Cabeza de Vaca in 1540. These officials soon joined with the other officials as his enemies, Cáceres the first and most bitter.[3]

At issue was the officials' use of rank for their own gain. The *quinto,* or royal fifth, was a tax levied by the Spanish crown on precious metals or gems. Although little gold or silver had turned up in the Río de la Plata province, scarcity did not hinder these men. They simply taxed whatever people had, even items as essential to life as fish, meat, hens, fat, honey, maize, hides, and other goods received from the Indians. While others pointed to Cabrera, Hernández blamed both Cabrera and Venegas for inventing the system of fees. These taxes, he charged, were contrary to justice and the practices of Spain and the Indies. The royal officials arrested those who could not pay, seized their goods, and put the "naked and starving" debtors in jail. Whatever the officials got was sold at auction—to their friends, said the victims—to raise the funds to pay governmental salaries. Also, Cabrera and Venegas had been taking advantage of various taxes since Mendoza's flight, "spending it all on their houses."[4]

Late in 1542 this abuse of power by the royal officials was stopped. Cabeza de Vaca ordered the quinto payments ended, and the issue was to go to Spain for a ruling. If the tax was upheld in its existing form, he promised to repay from his own salary whatever might be owed. The officials, whose duties in the province included finances, were enraged and now had a reason to unite against him. During the early part of 1543 they tried to get the quinto back, but Cabeza de Vaca would not give in. It was against "just charity and the royal service," he scolded Cáceres, done solely for personal gain. The quinto was not the only source of trouble. Many of the people in Asunción were quite poor, and to help them the governor canceled other taxes as well. He had Orúe tell the mayor, officials, and constables not to demand their fees of office until gold and silver were circulating. Also, those who were put in prison for debt no longer had to surrender their weapons or clothing. Thereafter the officials hated him, and their hostility grew.[5]

Once the officials began quarreling about the quinto, they quickly found other faults with the governor. They wanted a larger share of power and on April 2, 1543, sent a note asking him to discuss government matters and to revoke his earlier edicts. A week later he wrote a long and severe answer defending his actions and blaming the officials for any lack of discussion.

This reply again denied them the quinto taxes, which clearly were at the heart of their displeasure. With his policies and goals in such conflict with their interests, both the old and new officials joined in plotting against him.[6]

Cabeza de Vaca commented before he came, "the officials took them all, leaving them naked and disarmed."[7] The use of the word "naked" may be relative, more symbolic than literal, yet it is found in several sources. In August and September 1543, at a legal hearing, more than a dozen witnesses stated on oath that the quinto had brought great hardship to many settlers. Some spoke of their own distress; others had seen the jail full of arrested people, or those who were "poor and naked" or dead of hunger.[8] In 1545 Francisco González Paniagua, a priest, wrote of how the settlers had suffered from those payments. After failing to persuade Cabeza de Vaca to reinstate the quinto, the officials accused him of enriching himself at their expense. Eventually they gathered enough support to remove him. Antonio de Escalera, a priest who had come to America with the governor, made the same point about the settlers' suffering to the king in 1556.[9]

Memories of the quinto lasted into the next generation. Ruy Díaz de Guzmán wrote long after the event and from a unique position (he was related to both Cabeza de Vaca and Irala). He explained the struggle with the royal officials as coming from their desire to have a hand in the government and from their insistence that he could not do anything without their advice. The governor's answer had been that he had no need to consult with them in ordinary matters of little weight. Otherwise his office would be destroyed, "that they might be the governors and not he." They then became "very hostile, with great disgust" for him, which "he tolerated with much patience." As historian Marco Antonio Laconich has pointed out, they wanted a return to conditions under Irala.[10]

Revealing in another way is a letter to the king by one of the royal officials. Cáceres wrote in March 1545 to denounce Cabeza de Vaca for mismanagement. Cáceres was defending rebellion because he had helped to overthrow the governor. Although he mentioned the quinto, he did not admit that it had injured the public or how its payment had been enforced. Instead, he complained that the governor had encroached into tax matters and meddled with long-standing practices. Also, Cáceres accused Cabeza de

Vaca of having insulted the royal officials and ignoring their demands that he heed their advice.[11]

The quinto issue and the abuse of power by Cáceres came up again two decades later. Pedro Fernández de la Torre, the first bishop in the province of the Río de la Plata, held an inquiry in 1564 about Cáceres, part of a long conflict between the two men. Among other crimes, the bishop accused the official of opposing Cabeza de Vaca from the start and plotting rebellion even before reaching Asunción. Witnesses for the bishop recalled the quinto tax strife. Gaspar de Ortigosa, who had collected these payments, said on oath that as soon as Cáceres arrived at Asunción, he acted to claim the quinto that was levied on goods that the soldiers traded. The hardships caused by jailing people and making them pay quinto debts led the governor to tell the officials not to collect the tax until the king could be informed of the matter. Pedro de Esquivel, who came to America with Cabeza de Vaca, then testified that henceforth he "always saw the officials acting in an evil way toward the governor."[12]

Halting the quinto payments was aimed at ending extortion. Yet, within a subsistence economy based on the farms and labor of Indians, Cabeza de Vaca still faced the problem of paying for the costs of government. If he had held power for a longer time, he might have found it necessary to use Indian labor to support his government, for few other resources existed, but he had not made that discovery before he was overthrown. Before his arrival, Irala, as lieutenant governor, had met this crisis in part by seizing the property of the dead adelantado, Pedro de Mendoza, and of traders and other persons.[13] Later, in 1544, Cabeza de Vaca's property was also taken. The governor apparently placed his hope for future economic growth and provincial finances on the success of the entrada to a land of gold and silver. Meanwhile, by agreement with the king, he bore the costs of the colony himself.

The first half of 1543 was busy. Besides rebuilding Asunción, Cabeza de Vaca was getting ready to make his entrada. While he planned and arranged for exploration, his rivals were also hard at work, seeking to stop him from acting against their interests. Two groups already hated him. The royal officials were in a fury about losing the quinto revenues, and the friars, Bernardo de Armenta and Alonso Lebrón, were also angry. Although he asked them for advice along with the other clergy, they had been unable to get along with him from the start. Whatever good they did by teaching and baptizing the Indians was undermined, in his eyes, by their disciplinary shortcomings and unwillingness to work according to his terms.

The quarrel began on Santa Catalina Island. Cabeza de Vaca wanted the friars to stay there, to train the Indians in religion, but they had refused. Then they were unruly on the long overland journey. Finally, he urged them at Asunción to be good models of Christian morality for the Indians and Europeans, especially in their behavior toward the Indian women. Indians and Spaniards alike had trouble with the two men. Owing to jealousy they whipped an Indian chief and were going to "cut off his member," but he escaped. For the same reason they threatened Spaniards and had some beaten and shackled. In his legal defense the governor later said that Armenta and Lebrón "privately wished me much harm" and sought to injure him because he had rebuked them for having in their house and monastery more than thirty Indian women and girls. He ordered them to release the women, but the friars instead moved a few leagues away.

By June 1543 Armenta and Lebrón were ready to strike. With the royal officials and other allies, they formed a league to obstruct Cabeza de Vaca's entrada and discovery of the country. To keep the conspiracy secret, they took an oath over the "Holy Gospels" (or, in other accounts, a crucifix or a missal). The officials wrote letters and reports accusing the governor of causing great harm to the country. The friars were to carry the dispatches to the coast of Brazil and on to Spain. They wanted Irala to head the government again and Armenta to become bishop of the province. The Franciscans' prestige was expected to add support to their charges.[14]

Dorantes's letter of June 8, 1543, to Charles I shows what the officials were writing. He defended the quinto as having its basis in local custom and law and pointed out that the region lacked gold and silver. Also, he stressed the need to encourage Spanish settlement by granting "liberties" and royal favors and advised sending a "solicitor for the Indians, and for our souls." That person should be charged "to reform our vices." Although this letter failed to recount the vices that needed reform, he later wrote another one that did.[15]

On June 10, just as Cabeza de Vaca was ready to begin his entrada, Armenta and Lebrón fled with their household of Indian women and girls. The girls had been given to the friars to be taught Christian doctrine, and their distraught parents had the chiefs beg the governor for the girls' return. He sent his cousin, Francisco de Estopiñán Cabeza de Vaca, and some soldiers after the friars, and two leagues away they were caught. The Indian girls were soon returned to their families.[16]

This plot might have cost the governor his life, as Pedro de Esquivel testified in 1564. When the friars were caught, one of their company asked if the governor was alive. He was supposed to be killed after Armenta and Lebrón fled.[17]

Cabeza de Vaca lost patience with the friars. They had caused "a great scandal and disturbance" among the Spaniards and Indians by their bad example and by carrying away the Indian women and girls. He was determined to make them and the officials pay for "the crime which they had committed against his majesty." His anger also reflected the delay that they had caused his entrada.[18] Armenta related this event quite differently. He wrote to the king in October 1544 that he had left Asunción because he "could not make any fruit or profit" there and wished to return to the work he had started at Santa Catalina Island. He had told the royal officials of his plan but had not informed the governor, and he agreed to take secret reports about the Río de la Plata province from the officials to Spain. However, the governor's men came after him, found the dispatches, and arrested him and Lebrón. His letter did not refer to the Indian girls who had hampered the flight.[19]

After a time the governor found support for his view of the event from other Spaniards.[20] One letter notable for its bluntness came in 1545 from González Paniagua, who denied that Lebrón and Armenta had left Asunción to tell the king about the state of the land and its conquest. Their flight, he declared, "was more to fulfill their passions and interests."[21] Juan de Salazar, friar of the Order of Our Lady of Mercy, also saw Armenta and Lebrón in a poor light, although he gave the royal officials even more of the blame.[22]

Asunción was again under control. Pedro Estopiñán Cabeza de Vaca held a legal hearing during June and July so that the governor could prepare for the entrada. To discover what was written to the king, Orúe, who would have recorded the complaints against Cabeza de Vaca, was arrested and nearly tortured. The royal officials then decided to confess, and Dorantes, Cáceres, Venegas, and Cabrera lost their positions as punishment. The first two were soon back in office, for Cabeza de Vaca wanted to keep his eye on both of them while he went to explore the interior. (Venegas and Cabrera stayed in jail for a time.) Enrique de Gandiá pointed to Cabrera as the force behind this revolt, although Cáceres seems to have hated the governor from the beginning. Armenta and Lebrón were put under house arrest. Irala escaped punishment. Cabeza de Vaca said that Irala was the most guilty but did not allow him to be charged or mentioned in the evidence or sentences, hoping to "restore" him to the service of the king. Irala was not one to be won over by such leniency. González Paniagua thought that the governor should have had them all hanged, but that was not his way.[23]

Historian Carlos Zubizarreta blamed the strife on Cabeza de Vaca, whose arrival led to antagonism between the newcomers and the original settlers in Asunción. Also, he ignored the power of the town council and replaced its members with men holding his confidence. Ricardo de Lafuente Machain, in a biography of Irala, concurred. Complaints brought about a growing uneasiness that was promoted by royal officials who believed they had been ill treated by the governor. They were joined by the old conquistadores, whose privileges and rights he had threatened.[24]

Yet, the rift did not arise simply between the old conquistadores and the newcomers. Juan Pavón de Badajoz, Cabeza de Vaca's mayor of Asunción, and Pero Hernández, his notary, were early residents of the colony, whereas

Dorantes, who opposed him, had come to America on one of his ships. Other examples could be listed, and the biographical sketches of settlers who came to the province between 1535 and 1541 show many exceptions to the old-comer–newcomer thesis.[25] Bitter factions had flourished before he took over the government and lasted for years after he was gone.

Before They and Their Souls Are Lost

One of the charges made against Cabeza de Vaca after his overthrow was that he did not take advice. Indeed, his orders were to ask the royal officials and clergy about such matters as exploration, settlement, or trade, and yet he did hear what they had to say, and his frequent summons to the captains and clergy for counsel brings to mind the insistence of Bernal Díaz del Castillo that in the conquest of New Spain Hernán Cortés did not act alone but in agreement with his captains and followers.[1] The problem in Asunción was that Cabeza de Vaca's goals were often at odds with those of his advisers.

Yet there was one topic on which all agreed. The time had come to make a new entrada. On May 24, 1543, shortly before the friars Armenta and Lebrón began their flight, Cabeza de Vaca called for ideas about beginning such a journey into the interior. After pointing out that he had come by royal command to the Río de la Plata to help settle and extend the province, he said that he did not intend to leave until he had found the best way for an "entrada and discovery of this conquest." His hopes had clearly been boosted in February by Irala's account of Puerto de los Reyes. An entrada and discovery might succeed there, even though other scouts had failed and some of the Indians with them had died of hunger or thirst in barren areas.

Irala's route seemed to be the best and most likely, and more delay would be "very dangerous" and a "disservice" to God and the king.

His request for advice on how to proceed allowed the royal officials and clergy a useful outlet for their problems and complaints. Thus, Luis de Herrezuelo, a friar of the Order of San Gerónimo, urged quick action for many reasons. However, the goals of exploring were less important to him than was "the disservice that now we are all doing to God." The people had too much leisure and were not living morally. An entrada would fill their time and enforce greater order, which could help them to serve God and the king. Another problem was death, for "each day we are fewer." Also, the settlers were losing strength and using up their supplies, although the recent harvest had added somewhat to their stores.

Friar Juan de Salazar held similar ideas. Everyone knew, he began, that the king had sent Cabeza de Vaca to discover and conquer that land so that the people might know and worship God and obey the monarch. Nonetheless, there were other reasons for acting. Think about those who had come to this land and were dead, he urged, the many who died from hunger or at the hands of enemies before they were able to reach Asunción. Before the few who were still alive also perished, they should enter and discover the land. His words about Spanish immorality were graphic: "Get out of Babylon, not to call it Sodom, before they and their souls are lost!" Even if nothing was found at all, it would be very good "for the souls of those who enter" to get away from existing problems. Wait for a month, he said. The winter would have ended by then, and the people would have time to prepare.[2]

Luis de Miranda de Villafaña was quite a strange fellow. Historian Enrique de Gandía called him a poet-cleric and expert swordsman, the first heretic of Spanish America, and the most congenial fellow in the Río de la Plata conquest.[3] Miranda advised Cabeza de Vaca to send two groups to Puerto de los Reyes and carry on the bergantinas as much food as possible from the previous harvest. Half of the people should go in the first party, the rest to come with extra food after the September and October harvest. They could bring more goods that way and not have to take as much from the Indians along the river. He opposed using many Indians from Asunción. They added to the risk and gave little help, being a people "without order," who just ate up the food. The campaign required four hundred soldiers, but nearly everyone was very weak, so only the most robust and well armed ought to take part. Asunción also had to be defended, yet barely two hundred soldiers could be left there, a third of them injured or aged. Because Cabeza de Vaca had also asked for advice about who to put in charge of Asunción, Miranda named two captains, Juan de Salazar de Espinosa or Gonzalo de Mendoza. The Indians loved the first and feared the other, he said, but Miranda preferred Mendoza.

Ideas came also from the royal officials. Alonso Cabrera, the overseer, worried about the safety of Asunción. The Indians were becoming troublesome as well as grieved by the deaths they had suffered from the Spaniards. He expected their desire for revenge to cause an attack after the soldiers had left Asunción. Therefore, he opposed leaving too early. It was better to wait until the end of winter (which was just beginning as he gave this advice in May), when the river would be lower. Because the people were already weak and tired, it would be unwise to spend cold nights out in the open. There also might be illness and death. Further, with the river high above its bed, the explorers could not fish or hunt for food. His third point showed a realism based on the hardships at Buenos Aires. The Spaniards had to have enough to eat. "We have seen and felt hunger—it has been the cause of so much death and the loss of people." He wanted the bergantinas to carry from five to six hundred *quintales* (hundredweights) of flour. If they had to retreat, then they need not die from hunger. Although Irala said that Puerto de los Reyes had ample supplies and people, Cabrera insisted that "What is a lot for the Indians, and is enough for them, is for us a small quantity"—a revealing comment by a royal official about Spanish eating habits. He wanted to allow six months to a year to get ready. For a man who was angry and bitter toward Cabeza de Vaca and who later helped to ruin him, he gave sound and reasonable advice.

A second royal official to reply was Felipe de Cáceres, the accountant. Some of his ideas were like Cabrera's, but he differed in his view of how best to act. He agreed that something had to be done, seeing the great needs and the daily decline of the people. Their flour, munitions, clothing, and other basic goods were giving out. Also, they were without hope of help, each day going from bad to worse. God either was punishing "our great sins" or was somehow served by such extreme losses. The remedy was the conquest and discovery, to convert the Indians and keep order for everyone's welfare. Unlike Cabrera, Cáceres found hope in Irala's report. Believing that the land was populated and fertile, rich with gold and silver, he advised that the entrada begin as soon as possible, in mid-August. The company should be three hundred Spaniards, ready and armed, and two hundred Indians, "all courageous and orderly men, not including a rabble of boys and useless folk." Up to four hundred Indian women would carry the burdens of food, munitions, and necessities.[4]

This role for women as carriers, apart from their work as servants, is notable. According to historian Silvio Zavala, using Indian females for hard labor was not a European invention. The Spaniards adopted native Indian customs, even those opposed to Iberian ideals. Gandía quoted the Indian chief Tabaré as complaining that "we are women to the Christians, for we are being burdened like them."[5] Even Cabeza de Vaca did not prevent the women from working this way. During his war against the Guaycurú Indians in 1542, Spanish soldiers took their women along as carriers, and when Alonso Riquel de Guzmán went to Puerto de los Reyes late in 1543, he noted that there was not a soldier without an Indian woman carrying his load of fifty pounds of flour.[6]

Cáceres was confident about finding food. "God will be pleased to supply fishing so that there is not any need." The food, supplies, and munitions carried by the bergantinas should last for the two months it took to reach Puerto de los Reyes. Unlike most of the others, he did not like the idea of sending two separate groups of people. That plan allowed the Indians to see what the settlers were doing and revealed Spanish weaknesses. It was better to arrive quickly, everybody at once. As he pointed out, whenever the Spaniards met Indians, "we eat to excess, and they try to kill us or flee from us." Finally, he added that it was three years since they sailed from Castile, and the king had not been told of events. The officials clearly had something that they wished to say to the king, and they may already have been writing the secret reports that Armenta and Lebrón would take along on their flight.

Pedro Dorantes, the factor, had explored part of Brazil across from Santa

Catalina Island months earlier. His experience and awareness of how hard it was to live off the land made him wary. Only a few Spaniards, three hundred or so, were necessary, he argued, with as many female Indian servants and some Indian males. Four boats could bring the supplies. Because the lack of food had been a problem in the past, the settlers should bring enough to cover any loss or damage. The time to start was the middle of July, the period of high water at Puerto de los Reyes. They would not be able to fish, and they should not expect to get supplies there, for Irala had found none.

Dorantes did not trust the Indians' stories. On one occasion it had taken him twenty-eight days to cover a distance that they said needed five, and his Indian guides knew the route. Another example was Captain Andrés de Arcamendia, who had searched for what some Indians reported to be a good country where he and his men could find a land with food in a short time. After thirty-six days of travel, ten with no water, they came back without having seen any dwellings or people. Many of their own Indians had died of hunger and thirst. Dorantes warned that Indians told lies for their own reasons. One Indian, for example, stated that a journey through unpopulated areas would take only a few days, although other Indians disagreed. Apparently this man simply wanted to be taken to his native land. "Believe the worst," Dorantes advised, "to defend against it." He wanted to send about two hundred Spaniards to Puerto de los Reyes at first. They and their Indian servants could make a settlement and sow a crop for food. In December or January, when the governor and the others arrived with their own supplies, the local harvest would also be ripe. He disagreed with those who did not like having many Indians along. These allies already had been very helpful, he argued, both in battle and as servants, so they were needed. Indeed, for the safety of Asunción, any Indians who had said or done anything wrong should necessarily be taken to Puerto de los Reyes.

Garci Venegas, the treasurer, also agreed about sending one group of people ahead to prepare Puerto de los Reyes. They would build a fortress with dwellings and clear and plant the land. He stressed having enough supplies and gave much the same advice as the other officials.[7]

Martín de Armencia, a cleric, gave another reason for using two parties. To put all the people together was a great risk. At least four hundred Spaniards were needed, plus many Indians, both male and female. All of them had to be fed during a long and hard navigation, and they would use more supplies than they could carry at one time. Also, Puerto de los Reyes was not in an area able to supply much food, yet there had to be enough to feed both the garrison at the port and those who went exploring, in addition to a reserve in case of retreat. The best way, in his opinion, was to send half the company with horses and supplies. They would take over Puerto de los Reyes, get whatever was possible from the Indians, and then clear the land and sow it. The Indians would help, he thought, if they were treated well. When the planted fields, supplies, and housing were ready, the captain at the port could send the bergantinas back for Cabeza de Vaca and the others.

Armencia saw several clear advantages to his plan. The Spaniards would be rested, and the Indians would have had enough time to get used to the settlers and become friendly. Exploring should then begin easily, without risk or danger. Knowing the governor's eagerness to go, he warned that delay was less dangerous than rashness: "You are wise and prudent; govern and overcome the dangers in order to carry on to a good end."[8]

Another priest who urged patience was the prebendary, Juan Gabriel de Lezcano. He advised waiting for the winter to pass, because people without clothing ought to be in houses away from the harsh weather, not navigating on the river. The settlers needed to be clothed with cotton from the harvest, and those who were tired or injured had to recover. Many had been hurt or had lost their belongings in the great fire or through other misfortunes and were still in need. For the Spaniards and Indians, many provisions would have to be gathered, and time was needed to build another large *bergantín,* because the smaller ones could not bring everything. A large company was vital for such a serious undertaking. Altogether, he suggested using three hundred Spaniards, as many Indian women servants, two hundred Indian men, and two thousand quintales of supplies. While the groundwork was being done at Asunción, some of these people could survey the region, sow the land, and build housing for whoever came later.

Francisco de Andrada, a cleric, wrote briefly but to the point. Enter quickly, he said, for three very clear reasons. First, the old ships were ruined, and the new ones soon would be worn out. To build more, the settlers needed wood, which was difficult to obtain. Second, the Spaniards were losing their strength by the day. The healthy were falling ill, the sick were dying. Third, they were using up their flour. He added a fourth reason that reflected his spiritual office. The Spaniards were dying in peril of losing not only their lives but also their eternal souls. He urged the governor to send some men to the area of Puerto de los Reyes, and to bring the rest when a camp was ready.

Five of the captains gave a joint opinion. Juan de Salazar, Gonzalo de Mendoza, Irala, Agustín de Campos, and Gonzalo de Acosta had listened to the ideas of the other men and agreed to answer Cabeza de Vaca's summons for advice together. Because of the heat, they thought it best to leave in winter. According to the pilots and mariners, Puerto de los Reyes was at sixteen degrees from the equator, so the summer was likely to be hard, adding to the risk of failure. Like many others, they favored occupying the city in stages. The local Indians could plant crops, so that after the harvest the rest of the company might arrive and go out exploring right away, thereby easing the drain on supplies. To avoid troubling the local Indians, a small garrison ought to keep some food on hand in a fortress for when the explorers came back.[9]

Cabeza de Vaca had quite an array of viewpoints by the end of the survey. On June 8 he called a "junta of many people" to look at his plans. With so many often opposing ideas to pick from, he was free to take whatever suited him. The opinions agreed, he told the junta, that the entrada begin at Puerto de los Reyes. The widest variety of advice had been on timing. He chose to leave as quickly as possible. Delay, he argued, was dangerous and was in disservice to God and the king. The people were sick and dying, and their war stores and other vital goods were becoming exhausted. He liked the idea of traveling in two companies but was not willing to go with the second one, as some advisers had suggested. It was his duty to lead the Spaniards to Puerto de los Reyes.[10]

Despite his eagerness to begin, much had yet to be done. A venture on such a scale depended on the help of the Guaraní and other Indians who lived along the way. Because the recent fire had ruined most of what Asunción held, the first task was to gather supplies. To replace the lost food, he sent Gonzalo de Mendoza upriver with three bergantinas to buy what he could from the "vassals of his majesty," paying them and treating them well.

The advice of the royal officials was very interesting. Some of them already opposed the governor, Cabeza de Vaca later stated, because he had curbed their abuses of the settlers and Indians.[11] They would soon usurp his power and take it for themselves. Nevertheless, their ideas were realistic and useful. He listened to them, as his orders demanded, but his plans reflected his own views. So strong was his desire to explore that he set out as soon as the company was able to leave. While his planning was adequate, he might have lessened the chance of failure by taking the more cautious advice of the people who knew the land well.

To See If I Could Find
the Gold and Silver

As an adelantado, Cabeza de Vaca had been sent to discover new lands and peoples.[1] During his first months in Asunción he naturally had spent most of his time setting up a government, but for many reasons he was eager to explore. Perhaps the root of this interest was the time he had spent in North America. Those years had affected him deeply, changing his goals and values and even his character. Despite being captive for nearly a decade in one wilderness, he had come willingly to live in another. This time, perhaps, he might bring it under control. Even the location was not important. When Hernando de Soto got Florida, Cabeza de Vaca agreed to take part of South America that was almost equally untamed. He loved to explore and reach unknown peoples, to attract them to Spanish rule—which was, after all, one of his duties. His captains might have done this work for him, but he wanted to take part himself, and this urge spurred him to act.

Astounding myths and marvelous tales of wonders and riches lured the explorers of the New World. South America abounded in amazing legends, such as El Dorado, the Amazons, and fabulous cities. The very name of the province, the River of Silver, was a legacy of their dreams, for at first the Europeans thought that abundant silver would be found there. Silver and gold had some importance for Cabeza de Vaca as well, because they were vital to the success of his government. However, unlike many conquistadores, he was not obsessed by precious metals. During his major journey of exploration, for example, the Indians at one place told him that in the past their ancestors had taken the "white metal" from there. Yet, he did not stop to look for it, passing on toward the port that was his destination.[2]

Cabeza de Vaca said little about the economic basis of his government. He stocked trade goods from Spain but used them more for diplomacy with Indians and relief for Spaniards than to make a profit. Without access to the mineral wealth of the Inca empire, the economic potential of Paraguay was quite limited. Nevertheless, he had come to the New World in debt. Some way had to be found to pay for his costs if he hoped to keep his post. The Río de la Plata province did not promise to earn very much for him or for most of the others, so he could not wait much longer to look for some income. Opening a road to the area of Francisco Pizarro's conquest, the Inca empire, for example, might tap some of that wealth. There were, thus, many reasons for exploring the interior.[3]

Ironically, nonexistent gold and silver helped to bring about Cabeza de Vaca's overthrow in 1544. After that event, as a prisoner in Asunción, he learned from Domingo de Irala and his enemies that they expected him to find gold and silver if he succeeded in entering the wilderness, for they had seen those metals there. Accordingly, they were afraid that he would win favor with the king and retain power, and they would never again control the land. To stop him, they plotted to turn the other Spaniards against him.[4] Naturally, he wanted to believe that rich metals were to be found. If the Spanish crown ever sent him back to govern the Río de la Plata province, that wealth was necessary to carry out his policies. Many other Spaniards wanted to believe the same thing, although for different reasons. Irala himself may have been sure that he knew where gold and silver were to be found, but when he made his own entrada in 1547, he also did not find any.

By September 1543 Cabeza de Vaca was working out the final details. He assigned Captain Juan de Salazar to stay in Asunción as his lieutenant with two hundred soldiers. Salazar's orders dealt in part with the nearby Indians, who were to be handled with peace and justice and treated with care, for until recently some of them had been enemies. As a people newly converted, they were to be taught Christianity by the clergy. In addition to good relations with the Indians, the governor wanted Salazar to uphold peace among all the local people. Because trade between Indian tribes had already led to trouble, such steps as taking hostages might be needed to ensure safety. Because of the recent fire in Asunción, Salazar was to pull down any buildings that might block escape in case of fire or hamper a call to arms. There was also work to do on a caravel being built to carry a report to the king about the governor's work in America. Finally, Salazar was to keep an eye on the friars, Armenta and Lebrón, owing to their recent attempt at flight.[5]

The governor's other enemies had to be kept away from each other. He decided to put Felipe de Cáceres and Pedro Dorantes back in their offices and to bring them with him to Puerto de los Reyes. Eight days before he left, they went ahead with about a dozen horses, but Dorantes asked to withdraw because his horse died and his health was poor. A son, also named Pedro, became acting factor or perhaps a hostage to his father's good behavior. Irala, useful as a guide, went along also. However, Garci Venegas and Alonso Cabrera stayed in Asunción, under arrest.[6]

Cabeza de Vaca's great entrada began on September 8, 1543. After mass was celebrated in the church that he had helped to build, he and the members of his party set out for Puerto de los Reyes. There were ten bergantinas, built by Gonzalo de Acosta, to carry supplies and people—four hundred Spaniards. In 120 canoes were 1,200 allies. The Indians dazzled Pero Hernández, appearing "very strangely beautiful" riding in canoes with their bows and arrows. They had colorful ornaments of feathers and plumes, with bright metal forehead plates that glittered in the sun. They wore these plates, they said, because the brightness hindered their enemies' vision. All of these "friendly Indians," claimed the governor, came of their own choice. Although those who went along may have been eager to do so, not all among the Guaraní were pleased. Eventually, as Branislava Susnik has noted, the Indian traditionalists rebelled, although without success, against the continual supplying of provisions for such journeys as well as the loss of their young people. Spanish demands for food weakened the Guaraní's interest in farming and cut their economic strength, and many of the young chose to settle where the Spaniards had gone to explore.

Cabeza de Vaca took great care with the Indians who lived along the river. He greeted them as friends and gave them presents. After explaining his plans to explore, he asked them to keep peace with Asunción.[7] Other Indians were met in the same way, and nearly all of the people on the way to Puerto de los Reyes showed him friendship. Taking his gifts, they agreed to stay at peace with Asunción and sold Cabeza de Vaca what he needed.

A special visitor was Tabaré, who came with the other Guaraní chiefs who had recently been at war when they heard that the governor was near. Cabeza de Vaca was pleased to greet them "because they were keeping the peace terms that they had made." Tabaré offered to join the company, a welcome proof of friendship. His goodwill ensured peace and security throughout his land, as he was greatly feared. Asunción and the river region would therefore be less cause of worry during the entrada. Friendship and peace with these chiefs also helped the Indian allies feel confident.[8] The governor's skill in handling them, backed by Irala's military triumphs, had gained peace with all except the Agaz Indians. At last, a year and a half after entering Asunción, Cabeza de Vaca was again exploring.

On October 12 the Spaniards came to the port of Candelaria. A few years earlier, around 1538, Juan de Ayolas and his men had come back to this point from the west with gold and silver. Irala had orders to be waiting there with the ships, but he had gone elsewhere. After four months the Payaguá Indians had attacked, killing Ayolas, eighty other Spaniards, and some porters. Knowledge of that massacre made Cabeza de Vaca uneasy as he neared the port, but the wealth that Ayolas had carried drew him on "to see if I could find the gold and silver that they took from him."

One of those Payaguá Indians came to talk to the Spaniards. Through a Guaraní interpreter he stated that his chief wanted to know what people they were. The Payaguáes desired peace, and the chief offered to give up the gold and silver taken from Ayolas if he were pardoned for the Spaniard's death. The governor promised a pardon and asked how much had been taken from Ayolas. Sixty-six Indians had carried it all, was the reply. In the beginning Ayolas and the Payaguáes were friendly, or so the man said, but then Irala had abused them and treated them so badly that they slaughtered Ayolas and his men when they returned.[9] Irala's version of that disaster was reported later, in March 1545. Early in 1540, he said, he had learned from an Indian about the death of Ayolas and also that the carriers had some twenty loads of metal. His excuse for not meeting Ayolas with the ships was that river flooding had left him short of supplies, so he had gone to get more.[10]

Other sources tell a different tale. For example, the nine Spaniards who fled Buenos Aires in 1541 and met Cabeza de Vaca on Santa Catalina Island blamed Irala for the deaths of Ayolas and his companions. In 1545 Pero Hernández, who long opposed Irala, charged that Irala deserted the port where Ayolas had left him. Irala had traveled eighty leagues to a port where he had a chief's daughter and remained there fifteen or twenty days. Also, Ayolas had placed in Irala's care the daughter of a chief, and the Indians grew angry because Irala "had sexual relations with her, and was with her all day in the cabin of the bergantín." Greatly upset, they killed some Spaniards and took her away. A second cause for Irala's absence was that the Payaguá Indians had stopped supplying food for him.[11] As a hunting-gathering people, they would have much less surplus to give than the agricultural Guaraní. Ten years later Hernández gave a more sinister reason for Irala's absence. It was done "with an evil purpose": the Indians would kill Ayolas and Irala could take over power, which he did "against God and against his king." "He has destroyed and devastated all that land, and has held it tyrannically for twelve years."[12]

Irala's defenders have denied that he was guilty. Historian Harris Gaylord Warren wrote that there was no basis for the charge of deserting his post. That absence came in the summer of 1538 during a struggle for power with Francisco Ruiz Galán in Asunción, and Irala returned too late to save Ayolas. Indeed, an "anonymous account" of March 9, 1545, related that Ruiz Galán caused Irala to arrive late.[13] Irala, however, was silent about Ruiz Galán's role.[14]

Hernández and the nine refugees were not the only ones who reported that story. Captain Francisco de Ribera said that Irala was very fond of the Guaraní women, "for which cause he was distant from the town of Candelaria."[15] Gregorio de Acosta also recalled that Ayolas did not find Irala or the bergantinas when he got back, and that "by such a cause did the Payaguá Indians kill Juan de Ayolas and those who came with him."[16] Even the meeting with the Payaguá Indians suggests that this summary is true. They wanted to know if Cabeza de Vaca and his men were the same ones who had come in the past. The Spaniards had been warned to say that they were not. In fact, Irala was there, but he was carefully hidden.

The Payaguáes were not fooled. Their own spokesman was outwitting the Spaniards when he said that the chief would visit the next morning and show them the gold and silver of Ayolas. Five days passed before the governor decided that the Indians really were not coming. The interpreter was sure that the Payaguáes were gone, having used a trick to allow time to flee. As they were likely to head up the river, he advised chasing them right away, for their belongings would slow them. From what he knew of the area, he guessed that they would not stop before reaching a lagoon they had taken over from other Indians some time ago.

The hunt began, and soon the Spaniards caught the stragglers. After a week they reached the lagoon, but the Payaguáes were not there; they had gone deeper into the interior. The governor and some others kept after them, trying for peace, but finally decided to give up and go on to Puerto de los Reyes.[17] Cabeza de Vaca was sure that the gold and silver of Ayolas still existed, but its lure did not distract him from his goal of discovery. Whether or not the Payaguáes still had the loot taken from Ayolas is not known. That treasure was never found.[18] It may be that after Ayolas was killed his wealth was soon scattered among the people of the region.

The journey up the Paraguay River was long and hard. Much time had to be spent hunting and gathering fruit from trees along its banks. When the

Spaniards neared Puerto de los Reyes, Cabeza de Vaca decided to enter in stages, lest too many men and boats coming at once alarm the Indians and cause them to flee. He led one group, and Gonzalo de Mendoza took the rest. Mendoza was a hidalgo and a man of much experience in the Río de la Plata. He came to America with Pedro de Mendoza in early 1536 and took part in the founding of Asunción in 1537. The governor already had given him several important tasks, and now he had charge of part of the expedition to Puerto de los Reyes. Mendoza's orders were to govern both Spaniards and Indians gently and kindly. He was not to allow his men to be unjust to the local Indians but to pay for all supplies and see that trading between them and the Spaniards or Guaraní allies "conserve the peace, which is fitting for his majesty's service and the good of the land."[19]

The journey to Puerto de los Reyes was another success. Except for the Payaguá Indians, the governor had made or kept peace with everyone. His skill with the Indians and his control over his own party had given this entrada a promising beginning.

A Land That Was
Newly Discovered

For two months Cabeza de Vaca made his way up the Paraguay River. On November 8 he came to Domingo de Irala's Puerto de los Reyes (whose location is uncertain but may be near modern Corumbá, Lake Gaíba, or Lake Cáceres, all north of present-day Paraguay and in the border region of Brazil and eastern Bolivia). His successes were about to come to an end. After the bergantinas had been hauled across some shallows, the explorers went ashore to a friendly greeting from the local people. Officials, clergy, Spaniards, and Indians then witnessed him state a claim in the king's name "as a land that was newly discovered." Puerto de los Reyes was a farming community of some eight hundred dwellings. Nearby were populations of the Sacocis, Socorinos (Surucusis), Xaquetes or Xaqueses, and Chanés Indians. The Spaniards called these Indians *Orejones* (Big Ears) because of the large gourds or discs put into holes made in their ears, perhaps meant to prevent evil spirits from entering. The Orejones' relations with the Guaraní were soon marked by varying degrees of hostility.

A great crowd of people had watched the landing. Turning to them, the governor explained why he had come and what he hoped to do. The king of Spain had sent him there to teach them "to accept Christian teaching and believe in God, the Creator of Heaven and earth, and to be vassals of his majesty." If they did so, Cabeza de Vaca would protect them and treat them well. He spoke also about erecting a church for celebrating mass and other services, an example for the Indians and a comfort for the Christians. Then, fixing a large wooden cross in the ground near the river, he gathered the people for the formal action of taking possession in the king's name. Also, he gave the usual gifts to these new subjects of the crown. At the end of the ceremony he warned the Spaniards and Guaraní not to injure or use force against the local people, who were friends and vassals of the king and were not to be harmed. Nobody was to go to the Indian villages, and everything accepted in trade was to be paid for.[1]

Cabeza de Vaca spoke further to the Indians about religion. They were the first tribes using idols that the Spaniards had seen in that part of America. These objects were made of wood, but it was said that gold and silver were used farther inland. He told the chiefs "with kind words" to give up their idols, to burn them and halt their use. Instead of worshiping the devil, who misled them, they should "believe in the true God, who created Heaven and earth, mankind, the fish and the sea, and everything else."

The chiefs agreed to burn some of the idols, but they did so with great fear that the devil would be very angry and would kill them. Hernández, however, believed that as soon as the church had been built and mass said, "the devil fled from there," and the Indians went about "feeling secure and without fear."[2] This use of "kind words" to attack idolatry is another parallel with the ideas of Casas, who called the destruction of idols on the Yucatán by Hernán Cortés as one of many "errors and blunders." He advised instead using indoctrination and the good example of "virtuous and Christian works."[3]

Irala received a new office at this time. On November 10 he became *maese (maestre) de campo* (comparable to a military rank of colonel) and chief magistrate. The governor praised Irala's "capacity, ability and fidelity" but soon found his loyalty lacking.[4]

By the time that he reached Puerto de los Reyes, Cabeza de Vaca's policy was clearly set. He wanted to keep the Spaniards and Guaraní away from the native people and punish anyone who abused them. With kind treatment, payment for labor and goods, careful teaching of Christian doctrine, and an end to all idolatry, he expected his exploring to prosper and the Indians to gain the blessings of Spanish religion and culture. Yet these goals were not to be won so easily. The Indians at Puerto de los Reyes did not get along with the newcomers as he hoped. Some were unhappy about having their homes entered and things taken. Others were robbed along the trails. Again he ordered the Spaniards and Guaranís to stay away from native villages and dwellings. He declared that the explorers did not need to take anything because he was giving his company food and clothing.

The Spaniards were not the only cause of trouble. Fighting between Guaraní and local Indians led to a major uprising. Eventually Cabeza de Vaca managed to restore peace. Again, he ordered the Guaraní not to rob the Orejones' houses or touch any of their property. Later, he called back those villagers who had fled during the fighting to reassure them.[5] These fights took away time that he needed to organize the entrada. His refusal to turn this problem over to another official shows his desire to set up a just rule, but the time might have been better spent getting ready.

He did learn about the region, however. As the camp was put into order and the Indians were exposed to Spanish ways, he talked to people who could tell him about the land he was to enter. Some of them had known Aleixo Garcia when he passed near there twenty years earlier, and they remembered him with favor. A chief who had come to the region when Garcia's party arrived from the far west wanted to go along with the Spaniards in order to return to his own country. Other news came from scouts sent out to look over the nearby area. One party had traded for gold and silver with some Xaray Indians (who lived by Lake Mandioré and came to be well regarded by Spaniards). The governor called a meeting of the clergy and officials, who agreed that he send Antonio Correa and Hector de Acuña, with two Guaraní and ten other Indians, to survey the villages along the route to where the Xarayes lived. The party would look for any Guaraní-speakers who might provide an account of the region. As always, he told them to make friends with those they met and supplied presents to ease their way. He also gave them several questions to ask: Who lived there? What was their manner of life? How did they make war? How far away were their villages?

After a week the scouts were back with a guide from the Xaray chief. Their journey had been quite hard, noted Hernández. While the people caused them no trouble—indeed they were helpful—the land itself had al-most stopped them. Swamps and lagoons were all but impassable, and the extreme heat turned discomfort into torture. Sometimes food and drinking water could not be found, apart from what the Indians gave them. One night they slept on the ground, "with great misery, thirst, hunger and fatigue." The next day, happily, they found good water. After two more days of agony they reached the village of the Xarayes. They were so worn out that when the chief offered them some girls to sleep with, "they did not want them," and answered that they were exhausted.

The Xaray chief, whose name was Camiré, already knew about the Span-iards. He had long wanted to see them, he declared, "because he had known that [Cabeza de Vaca] was a good man and a great friend of the Indians," giving them gifts and "not stingy." Among the Xaray Indians the chiefs were obligated to give their people feasts, so Cabeza de Vaca's gift-giving would have been understood and welcomed.[6] Even in a part of the province so remote, his generosity had won him favor and renown.

The scouts were guided back by a Guaraní. Earlier journeys by the Guaraní from the Paraguay River to the Andes had left many stragglers, who settled in the northern Chaco zone. They were often willing to guide Spaniards across it and to help fight other Indians met on the way. This man had lived with the Xarayes for many years; he had arrived there with some Guaraní raiders who were then overwhelmed. When asked what route his war party had used, he could not recall much of it because at the time he was just a boy. The Guaranís had come to get silver and gold and had taken a large amount, but it was lost when they were defeated. He thought some of the plunder might yet be found, and he said that he was willing to guide the explorers to the Xaray village where he lived. Spaniards clearly were not the only looters who had come to this land after those metals. He said that villages were located within five days' travel and offered to go with the Spanish party to show the way. Cabeza de Vaca agreed to let the Guaraní guide them into the interior, but the tale of gold and silver left him skeptical—"I did not allow much confidence." Still, historian Enrique de Gandía saw Cabeza de Vaca's purpose in leaving Puerto de los Reyes solely as the pursuit of silver and gold.[7]

The scouts' report was both cheering and sobering. The Spaniards could expect a friendly welcome from the Xaray chief, but the route that had been opened was not fit for a large number of explorers. Although Cabeza de Vaca would not admit it to himself, he had been forewarned about how unlikely success would be. If the weather conditions were not right, the land to the west of Puerto de los Reyes did not allow travel very easily.

One other cloud began to darken this venture. The Indians, so recently befriended, were already clashing with the newcomers, and the fighting got worse as the days passed. Although the company had traveled to Puerto de los Reyes in two groups to avoid causing alarm, when Captain Gonzalo de Mendoza brought in the second party a week after the first had arrived, he reported that the Guaxarapo (Guachí) Indians had attacked and killed five or six Spaniards.[8] These Indians were noted for their skills at warfare and with canoes (they lived along the western bank of the Paraguay River, north of the Payaguá Indians and to the south of Lake Mandioré).[9] The governor had treated them well and left them at peace.

Their change of behavior had two causes. Martín de Orúe, the former notary, was partly to blame. He was one of the governor's bitter enemies and was unlikely to help carry out his policies. During the journey he had outraged one of the Guaxarapos by putting him in manacles as punishment for taking an axe. The Indian escaped but was very angry. Mendoza brought on the second problem. He had traded for a piece of cotton cloth with the Indians but did not keep his part of the bargain.[10] Hernández noted that having the Spaniards killed was "a very great loss for our reputation." Soon the Guaxarapos came by canoe to Puerto de los Reyes to boast about how they had slain the invaders and to urge the Indians there also to kill the Spaniards, who "were not brave, and . . . had soft heads" (they were not wearing helmets). Thereafter the Indians of Puerto de los Reyes began to rise up in arms "and bring forth evil plans."[11]

Uninhabited and Uninhabitable

Before three weeks had passed Cabeza de Vaca was ready to begin the entrada into the interior. He planned to go from Puerto de los Reyes around and west of a mass of land that divides the Andes Mountain range, with its silver, from the Río de la Plata province. This large section, soon to be known as the Chaco, served as a refuge for displaced tribes of Paleolithic and Neolithic Indians. A hundred Spaniards and twice as many Guaraní would protect the bergantinas and Puerto de los Reyes, led by Captain Juan Romero, who earlier had carried out similar duties in Buenos Aires.[1]

Several explorers entered this "Green Hell" in the first half of the sixteenth century. As related earlier, Aleixo Garcia led the way in the 1520s, and Juan de Ayolas followed about a decade later. In 1547–48, Domingo de Irala tried to do so as well, but by then the source of the legends and wealth that drew them on, the great Inca empire, had fallen into the hands of Francisco Pizarro in 1532.[2]

There is some question about whether in 1543 Irala had found the best spot to begin the quest. Historian Julio César Chaves noted with some surprise that Garcia picked the place most suitable for beginning the march to the west. The three other leaders—Ayolas, Cabeza de Vaca, and Irala—went later by unsuitable ways.[3] Garcia's passage may have been easier because he had few Europeans (five or six) following a great mass of Indians. In

Branislava Susnik's view, Puerto de los Reyes did make a good starting point. Despite the great troubles that befell Cabeza de Vaca's entrada, it was possible from there to find Indian villages, whereas other routes were likely to pass by hunter-gatherers or vacant areas.[4] Later in the colonial era a trail linking Asunción to the Andes followed the route that Cabeza de Vaca had started.[5] It went into what is now part of eastern Bolivia, mostly north of the Bolivian Chaco. The semitropical climate, with rain from December until February, creates seasonal swamps that dry up during the rest of the year.[6] The rain made Cabeza de Vaca's journey impossible.

On November 26, 1543, the explorers set out from Puerto de los Reyes. There were a great number of Guaraní allies, three hundred Spaniards, and ten horses, and they took enough supplies for twenty days. That they ran short much earlier became a topic of great controversy. After five days of travel the guide became confused. Soon he confessed that he did not know where to lead them. It had been so long since he had last gone that way that he could not find it again. In truth, getting lost must have been easy; cutting a path into the forest and brush proved very difficult.

Then, for a moment, they had help. A few Guaraní Indians, stranded in the area by ancient migrations and wars, came to the aid of the governor. They could not find the guide's lost trail, for their fear of enemies had kept them hidden in the dense, thickly wooded forest, but a kinsman who lived in a village some distance away knew the route better. Two Spaniards, an interpreter, and two Indians went to find him, and the next day the rest of the party followed. After three days an Indian came back with an alarming report. The nearest populated land, according to the man who knew the region, was sixteen days away from his village, over a hard and deserted passage with deep undergrowth and heavy forest. Even the trip to that man's village was not easy, for they had gone most of the way on their hands and knees. Indeed, the scout did not overstate the obstacles. The Spaniards tried to use his path and found it to be so heavily forested that in a whole day they could not cut through as much distance "as a cross-bow shot carried." To make matters worse, the rainy season was upon them. The obstacles that they were trying to cross were truly overwhelming.

A day later the interpreter brought the man supposed to know the way, and he said that to go any further would bring great trouble. He had not taken the trail for a long time, and, judging from the smoke sent up from new villages, other people were moving into the area. He was afraid to return. The land was so wild that crossing it meant a great struggle, and it would take sixteen days, he thought, to cut a road through the forest. When asked to guide the Spaniards there, he agreed to do so in spite of his fear.

Cabeza de Vaca went to the clergy and officials for advice. Clearly upset by the warnings of what lay ahead, they strongly opposed going forward. Almost everyone was out of supplies, they answered, and many had not eaten in three days. Because the soldiers had thought that within five days they would find food and people, they had not been careful. In six days they would have nothing to eat, and it was dangerous to go on without support for themselves, especially as Indians "never say anything certain." Besides, the new guide's guess of sixteen days might also be wrong. All the explorers could die of hunger, "as has happened many times in new discoveries made in these regions." They urged Cabeza de Vaca to go to Puerto de los Reyes for supplies before he explored any further. If the governor failed to follow their advice, "they would require it of him by command of his majesty."[7] Because many of these advisers soon helped to overthrow the governor, this incident suggests that his rivals were already plotting and acting against him. As Alonso Agudo, a priest, later wrote, the return to the bergantinas was urged "maliciously . . . by those already acting wickedly."[8] Cabeza de Vaca and Hernández blamed the failure on the officials and clergy who forced the return, as well as on the men who had not taken care of their supplies.

Sometime later, after Cabeza de Vaca's arrest, his enemies said that the fault was his own. He had taken along too much cargo, small boxes, and other baggage—clothing, furnishings, and a camp bed. These items, borne by Spaniards and Indians, were "superfluous" and displaced necessities. Given Cabeza de Vaca's character, this charge is not easy to believe.[9] When his accusers described the events, they had become desperate and sought to justify their rebellion. It is notable that the garrison at Puerto de los Reyes was also short of food, so the governor had taken with him as much as possible, expecting to supplement it with whatever the explorers could find. However, they managed their food supply badly, and they were located where they could not live off the land.

Cabeza de Vaca had other defenders beside Agudo. Francisco González Paniagua agreed with the governor's handling of both the entrada and the supplies. The soldiers, he noted, went from Puerto de los Reyes with stores enough for twenty days, and some had more. He blamed the shortage on the guide, who said that after a few days of wilderness they would reach a settled area. When the men heard that Indian towns were ahead, they "rejoiced." Trusting the news or greedy because of rationing, "they treated the provisions that they carried with such excess" that soon they had nothing to eat. Even stronger words of defense for the governor came from Friar Juan de Salazar, who claimed that the entrada was so well supplied and directed "that one could not do more in the Indies." Alonso Riquelme de Guzmán, the governor's nephew, told much the same story. The Spaniards began the entrada well supplied, he recalled, for there was not a soldier without a woman carrying for him a fifty-pound load of flour from roots (likely to be manioc). However, the people were new to that land and squandered the supplies they brought, believing that after five days they would find a populated place. Unwillingly, the governor had to abandon the entrada, so as "not to risk the life of one man." Naturally Cabeza de Vaca was furious about this gluttony and reckless waste. He scolded the soldiers, saying they "lacked reason" and were not men but "beasts" who "might die like pigs" for being careless with their food. However, such scorn only angered them and gave Irala another opening to win their support. Irala issued them part of his own food, which originally had come from the governor himself.[10]

Thus, Cabeza de Vaca had no choice. When faced with the united opinion of the officials and clergy, he agreed to go back to Puerto de los Reyes. Perhaps it was well that he did so, for he soon learned that otherwise his life would have been in great danger. Irala and his men later told him that they had agreed to kill him during the next battle with Indians.[11] The retreat was a great blow to him. Although unhappy about not going further, he admitted that the obstacles were overwhelming. He blamed the land, calling it "un-inhabited and uninhabitable, without people, without supplies, and without pathways." Before turning back, to get some advantage from the distance already covered, he sent scouts to look for the settled area that the Indian guide had reported. Captain Francisco de Ribera, who was skilled in such tasks, took the guide, some Indians from the local village, six Spaniards, and several Guaraní. The goal was sixteen days to the west, a hill called Ytapoa Guazú (spelled Tapuaguazú by Pero Hernández), where Indians known as "Lords of the Metal" were to be found. A few weeks later, Ribera brought back marvelous news of a place that was both fruitful and rich, but the report came too late for Cabeza de Vaca to learn whether it was true.[12]

Everyone Was Dying of Hunger

By mid-December the explorers were back at Puerto de los Reyes. Although he had left it only twenty days earlier, the governor found the garrison in turmoil. As soon as Cabeza de Vaca departed, reported Juan Romero, the Indians attacked the fortress and tried to seize the bergantinas. They had roused the neighboring peoples and were plotting with the Guaxarapo Indians, who were now enemies of the Spaniards. Also, the Indians were spying on the settlers and clearly were planning to strike again. The governor called in the chiefs and told them to be calm and keep the peace, that he and the others were their friends and had not caused them trouble or unhappiness. Instead, he had given them gifts and promises of help against their enemies. If they broke the peace, he warned, they would have war, but he then handed out more presents.[1] The chiefs agreed to be peaceful and to drive his enemies away, but they spoke only to gain time, for they could see the weakness among the explorers.

Another problem was the shortage of food. Very little was on hand, and the next harvest would not come until later in the season. To meet the shortage, Cabeza de Vaca traded for flour (maize and manioc were grown in the region) with the Indians for as long as they could supply it. He shared this flour, as well as linen cloth and iron from his own stock, with more than two hundred men who were "somewhat naked and badly sheltered," according to Francisco González Paniagua, who knew all about their misery because his job was to report on what the company needed for shelter. After the rebels had arrested the governor and charged him with tyranny, Gonzáles Paniagua recalled how he had cared for the people: "To clothe them and remedy their needs, these are the tyrannies that I have seen him do in this land."[2]

The breakdown of friendship with the Indians can be seen in an order dealing with slavery. In their ongoing warfare with hostile Indians, both the Guaraní and the local Indian allies were taking slaves. Spaniards then acquired some of those slaves, saying that they had traded for them and calling them servants. Cabeza de Vaca understood the Indians to be unhappy about these dealings and feared that the Guaraní Indians would not want to remain in his company. To avoid that danger, on January 6, 1544, he ordered that no one "take, ask for, or demand from the Guaraní Indians or the natives of this port any male or female slave of any rank." Slaves in Spanish hands were to be given back, "freely and without obstacle." The penalty was a fine of two thousand *castellanos,* to be divided among the royal exchequer, a fund for building bergantinas, and whoever exposed the offender. (Where the castellanos to pay such fines would come from remains unexplained.)

Then, possibly to avoid defiance, came a bribe for the Spaniards. If the entrada did not succeed, Cabeza de Vaca promised, he would "give them liberty in order that they can own and catch slaves." Further, he would reveal a way that slaves could be used that was agreeable "to the service of his majesty" and would also suit the Indians who had come in his company. It was a promise not in keeping with his usual policy. Perhaps he was so sure of success that he expected not to have to pay the bribe. Or he may have lost patience with the local Indians and made up his mind to punish them. In spite of the promise tied to his order and regardless of the strong words against slavery, some of the Spaniards disobeyed him. A few weeks later, on March 1, he again had to command an end to slave trading, this time by the Spanish interpreters.[3]

When they began to run out of food themselves, the nearby Indians stopped selling it. With very little left, Cabeza de Vaca somehow had to locate more. The Spaniards and their allies numbered about three thousand, and at Puerto de los Reyes the bergantinas held food for only ten or twelve days more. Calling the chief Indians of the region to another meeting, he explained that his interpreters had taken many gifts to the villages in the area to trade for food, but they had not been able to get any. Where, he asked them, might his people find something to eat? Their reply was that several leagues away the Arrianicosi Indians lived by some large lagoons; they had much food and could sell him what he wanted.[4] These Indians lived along the Paraguay River near Lake Gaíba, where, with two harvests a year, food was abundant.[5]

Panic was overwhelming Puerto de los Reyes. All the people were begging for food, wrote Pero Hernández, and there was none to give them. They were ready to scatter throughout the land, looking for something to eat. As usual when making a major decision, the governor called his officials and clergy. The hunger and danger were so great, he said, that unless help were soon to be found, he expected all to die. Then he disclosed that the Arrianicosies had supplies of food. The advisers suggested that he send men to those Indian villages to buy supplies for the people. Because "everyone was dying of hunger," if the Indians would not sell food, it could be taken by force; if they resisted, the governor could make war. With that advice, Cabeza de Vaca sent Captain Gonzalo de Mendoza with 120 Spaniards and six hundred Indians to get the food. If the Arrianicosies refused to sell, they would be robbed.

This advice appears to be a reversal in Cabeza de Vaca's Indian policy. Nonetheless, in his mind the crisis justified taking such a drastic step. As governor he was responsible for the safety of his people. They had to have food, even if someone else thereby had less. Although he came to America to Christianize Indians, any who defied the authority of Spain would not be treated as well as Spaniards or Indians who were already Christians. If he had to choose, he thought that his first duty was to his own followers, even if it cost others. In addition, as he later argued in self-defense, the local chiefs had told him that the Arrianicosies Indians and others nearby held plenty of food and supplies.

Mendoza's orders were to treat the people in the villages with care. He was to warn both Spaniards and Indian allies not to lay hands on the natives and to punish violators to avoid trouble. The governor stressed that Mendoza should establish friendship while getting the food and say that the governor wanted to see and know the Arrianicosies, to give them gifts. If they submitted to royal authority, he promised to help them. Finally, Mendoza was to pay enough to make them content.

Only if peaceful efforts failed could Mendoza change his tactics. Should the Indians not be willing to sell food, he was to repeat his terms to them "once, twice, three and more times, as many as you should and are able." Finally, if they refused food to starving and begging men, the Spaniards might seize it. "If they still are unwilling to give it to us, take it by force; if they resist by arms, make war on them." Force, even war itself, could be used "because the hunger in which we are left does not allow anything else." Even after conceding the use of force, he added that whatever took place was to be as restrained "as was fitting to the service of God and his majesty." When, on December 16, Mendoza set out, there were two parties exploring the interior: his own and the one led by Captain Francisco de Ribera.[6]

The Indians at Puerto de los Reyes also knew about other sources of food. The Xaray Indians, who had welcomed scouts early on the entrada, lived on a river that might be navigable, for the waters had risen. They and their neighbors interested the governor, and on December 20 he sent Captain Hernando de Ribera with fifty-two men to find the Xarayes. A man with much experience, Hernando de Ribera had sailed to the Río de la Plata with Sebastian Cabot in 1526. The Xarayes were notable for other reasons besides food; Cabeza de Vaca had heard about them being linked with gold and silver.

Unlike Captain Mendoza, who had power to make war, these explorers were to stay on board their bergantín, "to see and discover with their eyes." Only a single interpreter was to disembark and trade with the Indians. These Spaniards were to come back informed about the land.[7]

Sending three captains and their men into the wilderness thus allowed Cabeza de Vaca to explore more territory. A shortage of supplies, even starvation, did not stop him from trying to open up the interior so that his government could succeed. Only his own men could defeat him.

Only What Was Needed

Although the governor had agreed to end his entrada in December, three captains were still exploring. On January 12, 1544, Francisco de Ribera entered Puerto de los Reyes with exciting news. After having struggled through thick woods for seventy leagues, the party had come to a land of good water, pleasant groves of trees, fruit, abundant honey in the hollows of trees, and good hunting for pigs and deer.

In that fair place dwelt the Tarapecosi people. Using signs, Ribera learned that three days' journey away there were Spaniards. These Indians had plenty of supplies, and he saw gold and silver ornaments. Before he could learn about their origin, however, the Tarapecosies began an attack. By acting as if other soldiers were nearby, he and his men got away, but all were wounded during the escape. By chance, some Tarapecosies were then at Puerto de los Reyes. That attack, they believed, had not been against the Spaniards but against the accompanying Guaraní, who were their enemies. If explorers went back with Tarapecosi interpreters, they would be welcomed with food, gold, and silver. Plenty of supplies were there, and they could trade for the gold and silver.[1]

Ribera's account brought him a reward from Cabeza de Vaca. Nevertheless, this scouting report was as close as the governor ever got to his goals. The dream of settling a colony where he might Christianize Indians and recover the money he had spent was soon to fade. A nearly impassable forest and growing disfavor among the Spaniards joined to crush this trace of hope. Not imagining that disaster was coming, Cabeza de Vaca tried to act on the promising news and began planning another exploration, although Ribera warned him that the journey was hard and the land still flooded. The Indians had said that the water would not go down until the end of February, as it did every year.[2]

To make a new entrada, Cabeza de Vaca recalled Gonzalo de Mendoza and his men. In his message he said that a sickness had struck at Puerto de los Reyes. The reply was quite discouraging, for Mendoza's people were also sick, and he was having trouble getting food from the Arrianicosies Indians. When the interpreter tried to tell them why he had come and to trade beads, knives, fishhooks, iron wedges, or such goods as they might want in exchange for food, they refused to let him display these items or even to explain that the Spaniards meant no harm. Instead, they tried to kill him, and he fled. They said that no Spaniards were to be in their land, and they did not want to give them anything because "they had to kill them all." The Guaxarapo Indians (who earlier had killed several Spaniards) were aiding the Arrianicosies.

Mendoza had ordered the interpreter and some Spaniards to try again. The Indians, feathered and painted for war, shot arrows at the invaders and chased them away. As a result, he led most of his men to the villages, where they were met by more arrows. However, Spanish firearms killed two Indians and the rest fled, for in their view of warfare casualties were to be avoided. They left food and other goods, but they refused to return and accept payment for the food. Instead, angry and hostile, they rallied others to make war on the Spaniards.

The governor sent new orders to Mendoza. He was to try to return the Indians to their dwellings without harm or trouble. Any supplies that he took had to be paid for, and the Spaniards were to leave them in peace and look elsewhere for food. The prisoners were to be set free, with presents, to attract the others. Later, as it turned out, Mendoza had to report that efforts at peace failed, for the Arrianicosies, Guaxarapos, and other allied Indians were set on making war. He did capture a good supply of food, including maize and roots, but left enough for them to live on, he thought.[3] The food crisis, for a time, seemed to be over.

Cabeza de Vaca had not heard the end of those Indians. When his enemies arrested him in Asunción, they needed reasons to excuse and defend rebellion against a royal governor. One was to blame the deaths of thousands of Arrianicosies on him because Mendoza had carried off their food. The dishonesty of this charge is clear when one looks at two accounts of this event by Felipe de Cáceres. First, in a letter of March 8, 1544, to the governor calling for an end to the entrada and a return to Asunción, Cáceres wrote that when Mendoza and his men had gone in search of food, many places had been destroyed and laid waste by those Indians, "according to choice," and that "our friends the Guaraní" took many Arrianicosies as slaves. Also, the maize taken fed the Spaniards for about three months. At this time he had nothing to say about any great loss of life.[4]

A year later, on March 7, 1545, Cáceres wrote to Charles I. Cabeza de Vaca was then in prison, and this letter, to justify his arrest, stated that he "caused to be killed so many Indians, and with such cruelty," that eleven towns were ruined and burnt, "wherein died more than three thousand souls without cause or just reason."[5] However, Cáceres had no choice but to write in this way. Cabeza de Vaca's good name with the Indians had to be offset by accusing him of cruelty against them. Any esteem or support that he enjoyed in Spain had to be countered with defamation, or he might get help from those with influence who shared his views about how to treat the native Americans.

Eventually came the chance to deny these charges. In 1546 sworn witnesses in Spain verified the governor's story, a long and careful account of how Mendoza and he had struggled for peace with the Arrianicosies. Cabeza de Vaca cited the Indians' defiance and warfare, their scorn for peace and friendship, and Mendoza's threats to punish their attacks. Yet they and their allies never were willing to come to peace. Naturally, some of them were hurt. The Spaniards "killed one or two Indians—and no more," he said. They did not kill any others, and except for the food, Spaniards did not take any loot from those people, who had no gold or silver or other goods but lived "solely by fishing and farming." Even the food that was lost would not cause them to starve. "Only what was needed" was removed—"no more."

He also refuted the charge that villages were destroyed. In those villages there were small straw dwellings, and altogether perhaps eighty were burned. Further, the Spaniards did not set the fires, which did them no good. The Indians did it themselves, for in America this behavior was widespread. It was their custom in war, and new huts were easy to make. Among witnesses called to his defense in 1546 were conquistadores of varied backgrounds, such as Alonso de Montalbán and Pedro de Heredia, who were active in northern South America, and Andrés de Cobasrubias and Andrés de Tapia, from New Spain. Also, men who were present or had heard about the event took his side. For example, Alonso de Medina, a friar of the Order of San Gerónimo, said that he had not seen more than one or two dead Indians and affirmed Mendoza's report that he had ordered that none be killed.[6]

This testimony does not end the controversy. In the Río de la Plata province other Spaniards heard charges against Mendoza in his battle with the Arrianicosies. Friar Bernardo de Armenta had no trouble believing the worst. He was in Asunción at the time but "was informed by many people" who were with Cabeza de Vaca "that there were made many wars, deaths and arrests unjustly against many Indian nations, without having cause or reason for it," or so he told the king in October 1544, when the governor was under arrest.[7]

Francisco González Paniagua spoke about the same event in early 1545. He did not go on that search for food, but he knew the story of the slaughtered Indians. "Some say that Captain Gonzalo de Mendoza defeated them with moderation, and others say without it, and the one and the other can be believed as one wishes." He blamed both Indians and Spaniards. "The best offspring of this land," he wrote, "are so villainous that if it were not on account of fear, they would have no goodness." Yet, the Spaniards were even worse. "So great was the greed and so little the fear of God, that we might debase ourselves to any cruelty or meanness." His own belief was that Mendoza "defeated those towns and their people in such a way that he destroyed them and killed or captured a very large part of the people."[8] Because González Paniagua usually supported the governor, for him to grant his rivals some truth in their case against Cabeza de Vaca encourages trust in his account of events in the Río de la Plata province.

Mendoza's return to Puerto de los Reyes, on about January 22, brought another problem. The Guaraní Indians who were with him had taken about four hundred captives. Because Cabeza de Vaca was worried how they might affect the Guaraní and Spaniards on the entrada that he hoped to resume, he asked the officials if it would be better, for ease of travel and greater mobility in battle, not to be burdened by these "useless" (female?) persons. Unwilling or not, they agreed to leave such captives behind.[9]

The third party of explorers reached Puerto de los Reyes on January 30, 1544. Its captain, Hernando de Ribera, was unable to report directly to the governor, who was very ill.[10] Indeed, Cabeza de Vaca never did hear this account, for before he could recover his enemies overthrew him. On March 3, 1545, Ribera made a secret report to be sent to the king. He swore an oath that all he stated was true, and several of the governor's friends signed the document as witnesses.

In this account Ribera admitted that he had ignored his orders to stay aboard the bergantín. After reaching the Xaray Indians he went on into the interior, where he found a fruitful country. Even more enchanting, he heard amazing legends from the people about silver and gold, large villages of female warriors ruled by a woman, and black people with beards—wonders that were sure to lure sixteenth-century Spaniards back to search after them. The Indians had a rich heritage of myth and legend, as did the Spaniards, who were eager to bring life to Old World fantasies in the New World. When the Indians spoke of Amazons, they may have been simply answering leading questions.

Ribera tried to hide some of the Indian tales from the clerk who was recording his discovery. He wished to keep to himself "the truth of the riches and towns and variety of people" until he could report to the governor.[11] Nonetheless, Pedro de Fuentes at that time also wrote a letter that included some of Ribera's stories, and others, such as Ulrich Schmidt, repeated them as well, so secrets were not very well kept.[12] Cabeza de Vaca became angry because Ribera had disobeyed orders and reprimanded the captain for not continuing the discovery of the Ygatú River. Because of the governor's illness, however, he was not able to get a formal report of this discovery.[13]

Like Ribera, Schmidt told of the wonders that interested him. As always, he could not forget the Indian women, who "are absolutely naked and are beautiful after their manner, and also commit transgressions in the dark." He recalled how angry the governor was when Ribera's group reached Puerto de los Reyes and that Cabeza de Vaca made everyone stay on the boat. Then he ordered Ribera "to be cast into prison" and took what the soldiers had brought from the country. Finally, the governor "would have hanged our commander" as the penalty for disobeying orders and trading with the Indians. Instantly there was mutiny. The men in the bergantín and their friends on shore demanded that Ribera be set free and that their trade items be returned. The governor met their demands, "giving us fair words that we might be pacified." The outcome was that "he desired our commander . . . and us to give him a report on the country we had been to."[14]

Schmidt's story has some problems. While historian Enrique de Gandía accepted his account as truthful, he noted that no other writer about the conquest mentioned this conflict. Pero Hernández recalled that Ribera gave no report of his discovery because the governor was so ill.[15] Also, an order by Cabeza de Vaca to have Ribera hanged is not easy to believe, because he was unwilling to kill any other Spaniards as punishment for their crimes. Finally, Ribera, in the year to come, took the governor's side against the men who acted to remove him from power.[16] Surely one would expect to find Ribera among Cabeza de Vaca's enemies if he had been treated as badly as Schmidt stated.

Many other problems hindered the governor while he tried to devise plans to explore again. The supply of food got lower, and the land remained flooded. Time after time he sent men out to see if the water could be passed.

"I wanted to go at once, with all the people," he wrote, quite ready to make another entrada. Yet the high water trapped him just as effectively as the dense forest had done weeks earlier. Finally the worst blow hit, as serious illness began to spread among the explorers.[17] The decision to advance or retreat was soon taken out of his hands.

That He Might Not Discover Gold and Silver

Cabeza de Vaca's entrada was coming to its end. During his last year in the Río de la Plata province he faced danger and failure, but not while exploring new areas. The first blow came from sickness. While they were awaiting the food from Captain Mendoza, fever struck down so many men that the camp could not be guarded. Almost everyone became sick, and some of the Guaraní Indians died. The sole Spanish loss to illness was an "elderly" cleric, Martín de Armencia. Mendoza's men were also ill, even before they could come back to Puerto de los Reyes with their captured food. Francisco González Paniagua reported that of almost four hundred men, there were not four who were well. Many got better, only to become sick again.[1]

The local Indians knew how serious matters now were. These people, the Sacocis (Socorinos) and Xaqueses, lived along the Paraguay River, north of the Guaxarapo and south of the Arrianicosi Indians. At first these tribes had been helpful, trading goods and warning about other Indians who planned trouble. Now even they became hostile, owing to Spanish weakness and demands for food. Hernández wrote that the Indians claimed that the land was theirs and the Spaniards were not to fish there. Cabeza de Vaca quoted the Indians as calling "the Spaniards . . . cowards, and [the Indians] were brave, and that they had to kill and drive them from the land."[2]

Indian attacks began against small parties of Spanish and Guaraní fishermen. The captives were killed and cut into pieces to eat. Another tactic was to get the Guaraní drunk and slaughter them when they were helpless. According to González Paniagua, the Orejones intended to destroy the Spaniards' allies so that "none might be left," and "little by little, the Christians would die." Clearly these Indians could see that the cornerstone of the Spanish settlement was the alliance with the Guaraní. Puerto de los Reyes itself soon was attacked, and a number of Spaniards who were too weak to defend themselves were killed. One battle left at least fifty-eight dead. Cabeza de Vaca tried to end the trouble. He sent messengers to demand that the attackers free their captives and offered friendship, warning that he would punish the Indians if they did not stop. However, the fighting went on as the Spaniards grew weaker. In February 1544 Cabeza de Vaca brought charges against the Indians before the officials and clergy, who agreed that it was lawful to go to war. Then, after they had legally been judged to be enemies, he "declared them as slaves, and made war on them."[3]

Cabeza de Vaca had previously opposed enslaving Indians. What had changed his mind? He argued that they had called on their neighbors to make war on land and water and had attacked the Spaniards and spurned his calls for peace. Because they had rebelled without cause "against the peace and friendship" that had been made with them and because "each day they made war on the Christians and Indian allies," they were declared to be rebels who might be taken as slaves. This order actually did follow his past policy, as he pointed out, for he had earlier declared war on the Agaz Indians. Further, Spanish law allowed a sentence of slavery as a penalty for serious crimes, such as cannibalism or resistance to royal authority, so he could apply it in this case. Later, in 1546, he explained that to defend his people from these enemies and to punish them, he had some arrested and made slaves.

What had shaken Cabeza de Vaca's hopes for a peaceful conquest? In Spain he made a comment that implies a loss of faith. All over the Indies, he said, the Indians "always have joined to resist the Spaniards, trying to kill them and throw them out of the land, without having received any evil from them." They did so by making war and by withholding supplies. When they could not overcome the Spaniards, they feigned peace, but when the Spaniards became trusting, they attacked them and looked for chances to kill them. Other factors affected his judgments as well. The Indians hated the Spaniards, he said, "because they forbid their vices and sins, which they have against nature, and of eating human flesh." Hernández also spoke about the role of cannibalism in this conflict. Despite all efforts to pacify them, they killed five Christians and ate them, "for which the governor proceeded against them legally, and with the advice of the clergy, sentenced them as slaves." Steadfast disapproval of eating human flesh, if it did actually occur in this instance, may have led to a change in the governor's ideas about slavery. Nevertheless, despite his belief in the higher value of Spanish civilization and religion, even he was able to grasp one reason for Indian warfare that was very noble: "They wanted to be seen free, and that is why they try to kill [Spaniards] every way they can."[4]

The origins of this struggle later became part of his legal case, so the governor explained it with great care. When his enemies had to find reasons to justify arresting him, they used this war, as they did Gonzalo Mendoza's seizure of food, to stir up doubts about his Indian policy.[5] Ulrich Schmidt described the struggle against the "Surukusis" (Sacocis or Socorinos) Indians, adding that because of their past help to the Spaniards, "God knows that we did them wrong." His story, however, contains a puzzle. The "Surukusis" lived in a land so unhealthy that he could not find "a single Indian there who was forty or fifty years of age," yet he also said that the governor's order was to "destroy all persons from forty to fifty years of age."[6] Cabeza de Vaca denied any blame. There was no loss of towns, he said, unless the Indians themselves burned three or four, "by their choice—which would not be ten small houses of straw each."[7] Even before this event became an issue, González Paniagua wrote that the Sacocis had given help to the Guaxarapos when they seized five Spaniards and that they worked with them to kill friendly Guaraní Indians.

For three months almost everyone at Puerto de los Reyes was sick. Cabeza de Vaca hoped "that God would be pleased to give them health," so that when the waters went down they might be able to explore further. Yet, every day "illness increased, and the waters did the same." González Paniagua remembered the governor "always waiting for God our Lord to send health to the people," so that the entrada could begin. Cabeza de Vaca was unwilling to return Asunción until pushed by the officials and soldiers to do so.[8] The end came as his rivals used one of his own methods against him. Before taking any major step, he discussed it and reached some kind of agreement with his officials and the clergy. On March 18, 1544, as the floodwaters at last seemed to be dropping, one of the royal officials, Cáceres, strongly "demanded" that the Spaniards abandon the entrada and return to Asunción. He was not willing to explore any further or stay at Puerto de los Reyes. With so many problems and the threat of death so clear, to keep going with such ill health, he feared, would lead to everyone's death and the loss of the province. To avoid disaster, they had to ready the ships and the canoes and evacuate the people.

Cáceres gave seven reasons in support of his demand. First, the company was not strong enough to explore again, and the local people were dangerous. To keep a garrison of eighty or ninety men there was risky, for they had to stay inside the stockade or be killed, yet not enough maize or flour could be left for them. They had to get food, but their enemies would not let them fish, and in recent days they had carried off five Spaniards and a number of the allies. Second, the Indians would burn the bergantinas and destroy the garrison. Water and sun already had damaged these boats, after only four months. Only God kept the Indians from resistance, he believed, for they knew that the Spaniards were in ever increasing danger, their supplies and strength diminishing.

Points three and four relied on the report of Francisco de Ribera. Although Cabeza de Vaca had found in it reasons for hope, Cáceres saw an ominous message there, for the hardships that he had described were reasons to quit. It would be very difficult and dangerous to follow his route, and for eighty or ninety leagues the land was empty. Undertaking such a great effort was likely to wear out the Spaniards, whose only food was now maize. They could expect at least twenty-five days of travel and would lose many people. If they made it, the Indians who had attacked Ribera would set upon them too, and there would be another fight. Then, if they got past those Indians, where were they going to find other people who had the food and other goods that they needed? Finally, the rain and high water were a danger to exploring, as Ribera had noted, and everyone might die of hunger. It was better to try again another time, he declared, when the waters were lower.

His fifth point was that the local people had decided to challenge the Spaniards and their allies. This plot had become known after it was confessed during the legal proceedings against them. They wanted to safeguard their fishing grounds and seize Guaraní canoes, he thought. Whoever went into the wilderness in the face of such unrest would come back tired and sick and would die at the hands of the neighboring Indians at Puerto de los Reyes. Besides, he was worried about what might happen to the few men who stayed there as a garrison.

Sixth, one had to think about the Guaranís. They, too, were weak and feeble, no longer wanting or willing to go into the interior; they had caught many slaves and were ready to return to their own land. A long journey away from the river would not suit them at all, but sending them home should strengthen their loyalty. After all, they had left their land in Spanish service and had been of benefit and value. In any case, he warned, they would very likely desert if not allowed to go, thereby causing much damage and death. Such a great injury to these allies would also be harmful to the Spaniards, so their interest in safeguarding the peace and safety of the Indians ought to be reason enough to send them back to Asunción. They should be kept "in peace and tranquility and love, being always regarded and befriended, as they are by the governor at present"—striking proof that even Cáceres admitted how effectively Cabeza de Vaca was carrying out his policy for the Guaraní Indians.

The seventh reason was the poor general health of the company. Winter was coming, and with it the cold. So many were weak and poorly clothed that each day would be harder for them. Get the ships ready and get out, he urged. Take the men where they can find good health and serve the king. To do so "is the duty of a Christian caballero, a friend and servant of God and his majesty." If the governor did not do as he urged, Cáceres warned, he would write to the king.[9]

Indeed, he was ready to do more than appeal to Spain. In 1564, as already noted, Pedro Fernández de la Torre, bishop of the province of the Río de la Plata, made an official inquiry into Cáceres' misdeeds. Among the charges against him were two involving Cabeza de Vaca. First, as was widely known, Cáceres had done "everything possible" to keep him from being received as governor. He had gone to Asunción via the river, trying to get there ahead of the governor, who came by land, to incite a rebellion against him by the residents. Later, Cáceres plotted to arrest or kill the governor in Puerto de los Reyes. He did not carry out that plan because of the decision to return to Asunción, where it seemed "that he could better put his evil intention into effect."[10] Even more than Domingo de Irala, perhaps, Cáceres was the chief of Cabeza de Vaca's enemies.

In January 1545 Hernández repeated the charge about the murder plot. The officials and captains greatly hated the governor, he wrote, because he was keeping the Spaniards away from the Indian women at Puerto de los Reyes. The explorers began to argue against an entrada, in order to obstruct the governor, "that he might not discover gold and silver, seeing that the land was good and there was so much gold and silver." If he did enter, they warned, that wealth would allow his government to survive, and then they would "have no influence in the land against him." His foes, including Irala and Cáceres, talked about killing him and setting fire to his dwelling but held back when he became sick. Then, Hernández said, Cáceres made his demand to go to Asunción, "to impede and obstruct the entrada and conquest."[11]

As yet unaware of danger, Cabeza de Vaca gave much thought to Cáceres's seven points. His answer, like the letter from Cáceres, opened with a review of the historical background. The province had seen many problems before his arrival to govern it, he said, and his success in exploring had offset them, in spite of the alarm that his plans had first aroused. Next, although Cáceres had used Francisco de Ribera's report to urge a retreat, the governor found in it reasons to advance. He hoped that God would be pleased to send them health, so that they might "enter the land and take out the gold and silver which there is in the land, and in great quantity." However, he agreed that he would put Cáceres's question "to the opinion of people of conscience and experience." Once again, he was ready to listen to the ideas of his men.

Advice came from a number of sources. Francisco de Ribera was encouraged by what he had seen while in the interior but believed that it was best for everyone's health to go first to Asunción and get well. Antonio Pasado and Julio Romero, on the other hand, wanted to wait at Puerto de los Reyes for a month and then look at the state of their health and the possibilities for exploring. Diego Barba urged Cabeza de Vaca to return to Asunción as quickly as possible. The people were sick, winter was near, and he feared that many would die from the cold. More people would survive if they went back, the ships would be kept sound, and there would be food. Nuflo de Chaves agreed with that viewpoint. Not only were almost all of them sick, but "the land is in itself sick." There was nothing to eat but maize, they would be cold, and the water would remain high for some time. Even the Indians who lived there retreated from their land at this time of the year. Hernando de Ribera had advice as well. Apparently he was still sick from his search for food. The people who lived inland had told him that illness always struck during the season of high water. Also, maize alone would not support those who were exploring, so he agreed that they should wait until meat and fish were again available.[12] Finally, there was the experience of the local Indians to ponder. The worst had not yet come, they warned, for the season of death, April through July, was still two months away.[13]

These opinions at last swayed the governor. He was ready, he said, to withdraw from Puerto de los Reyes for the health of the people. However, as soon as they regained good health, he intended to come back to extend the conquest. This retreat, he insisted, did not end his claim, made in the name of the king, to the land and its port.

Nevertheless, in spite of hope for the future, his days as an explorer were about to end. Before he could embark for Asunción, he faced another problem. The Spaniards, including officials and interpreters, had, as usual, collected a number of women—the daughters of the Indian chiefs—and wanted to take them along. Indeed, they tried to get Cabeza de Vaca to do the same, offering him several women. He refused to allow the women to be taken, "besides its wickedness being clear," because the king had ordered that no one could take any Indians away from their land. Only the Indians were pleased with this order. The Spaniards held the governor in "great hatred and enmity," and at this point Irala and Cabeza de Vaca's other rivals began plotting his death.

One duty remained before the Spaniards departed. The governor called the friendly local chiefs to speak kindly to them and give them presents. They learned why he was leaving and that he expected soon to be back. "Thus I left them in peace and concord." On March 23, 1544, the return to Asunción began. As weak and sick as these adventurers were, they had to fight their way down the river against the Guaxarapo Indians. Fortunately, the cannons on the bergantinas held off the attackers, while the Guaraní allies kept their canoes safely between the Spanish boats. On April 8, with few losses, they landed at Asunción.[14]

In 1546 Cabeza de Vaca reviewed his treatment of the Indians while at Puerto de los Reyes. Any warfare that happened in that land, he wrote, followed legal action related to the Indians' misdeeds. Among their crimes, they had killed many Spaniards and were continually making war. Before attacking, he had listened to the opinions of the officials, clergy, captains, and others. In these fights the Spaniards acted moderately, and there was no depopulation of towns, unless by choice of the Indians. Notwithstanding such wars, which were the Indians' fault, Cabeza de Vaca "tried always to attract them with good words to peace and friendship with the Christians." At Puerto de los Reyes, he stated, "he left the Indians very pacified and friends of the Christians."[15] In his mind, his Indian policies were both defensible and successful.

Liberty! Liberty!

The landing at Asunción on April 8 marked the end of Cabeza de Vaca's discoveries and career. "I arrived very weak and sick, at the point of death," he recalled, adding that all the people were the same. Usually he could not leave his bed, but once in a while strength had to be found to handle a pressing matter. In the dockyard, for example, was a caravel that his lieutenant, Captain Juan de Salazar, was building to carry reports to Spain. Let it be finished quickly, the governor said.[1] Pedro Dorantes believed that Cabeza de Vaca was harsh toward Salazar for some shortcomings in his work while he was lieutenant in Asunción. Perhaps later, when Salazar seemed less than eager to defend the governor, he was showing bitterness.

The Agaz Indians were still a serious problem. As soon as Cabeza de Vaca left Asunción for Puerto de los Reyes, they resumed their attempts to rob, kill, and enslave the Guaraní. Dorantes gave as one cause a Guaraní killing of two Agaz messengers, but this strife was ancient in origin.[2] On March 14 Salazar began a legal hearing against the Agaces and was ready to lead twenty thousand Indian allies to destroy them, but it is hard to say what success would have resulted. As it was, the governor returned before Salazar could begin. This struggle with the Agaces soon would be followed by another, and these Indians would cause the Spaniards worry for generations to come.[3]

Another story about Cabeza de Vaca is puzzling. According to a letter from

Felipe de Cáceres to the king, when the governor returned from Puerto de los Reyes, he terrorized both the Spaniards and the Indians.[4] Yet it is unclear how he could have been abusive to so many when he was so sick and too weak to defend himself against Cáceres and his fellow plotters.

The rebellion against Cabeza de Vaca erupted about two weeks after he entered Asunción. On Saturday night, the day of San Marcos (April 25), about thirty "Biscayans and Córdobans," with the royal officials and a few others, stormed into his house, the door opened by a Basque servant named Pedro de Oñate. With a great clamor they burst into the room and circled Cabeza de Vaca, screaming "Liberty! Liberty!" Jabbing swords, daggers, crossbows, and harquebuses at his chest, they shouted threats of death. He was too sick to stop them: "I could not stand on my feet." They grabbed him and paraded him through the streets in just a shirt, jeering and abusing him. "Now you'll pay for the injuries and harm you've done!" "Now you'll see how you dealt with gentlemen, Cabeza de Vaca!" "Now, you'll know how caballeros like us have to be treated, Alvar Núñez!"

The mob marched along after a drummer. "Tyrant!" yelled some. "Liberty! Liberty!" cried others. "Long live the king!" As townspeople were drawn to the outcry, the royal officials called out to them: "Señores, we have arrested this man to set you free, because he wanted to take everybody's property and have you as slaves." When they came to the dwellings of Garci Venegas and Alonso Cabrera, they shackled Cabeza de Vaca and set a guard. The governor and Hernández called the rebels *comuneros*, or "people of the community."[5] This label was sure to catch the eye of Charles I and bring to mind the dangerous revolt of the Spanish comuneros that had taken place from 1520 to 1521 in Castile. Perhaps he would also be aware that Cabeza de Vaca had fought for him against those earlier comuneros.

Several of Cabeza de Vaca's friends wrote about risks that they took to help him. Captain Ruy Díaz Melgarejo said in 1556 that when the governor was taken, "I was arrested also." He had gone with his arms to help and was charged with being a rioter. For months he had to hide, and he remained a fugitive for several years.[6] Francisco Ortiz de Vergara, later governor of Paraguay, also went out in support of the governor, but he and those with him were overcome, and he was held prisoner "for many days."[7] Alonso Riquelme de Guzmán, the governor's nephew, tried to help but was stopped by a group of armed men and a constable, who threatened to take him prisoner. Seeing that nothing could be done, he went to his house, but the rebels later seized him and other of the governor's kinsmen, holding them in prison for months and keeping them disarmed after their release.[8]

The leading names in the uprising are those of the royal officials: Cabrera, the overseer; Cáceres, the accountant; Venegas, the treasurer; and Dorantes, the factor (although his role is clouded by his later denials). Pero Díaz del Valle, the new alcalde mayor, took on an important position, and Martín de Orúe was again made notary, in place of Pero Hernández.[9] The part that these men played has allowed defenders of Domingo de Irala to obscure his blame.[10] Indeed, he did not join in the attack or arrest but stayed at home because of illness, or so it was said. As early as January 1545, when Cabeza de Vaca was still a prisoner, Hernández pointed to Irala as the chief actor.[11] The following December the governor stated the same idea, as one might well expect, for if he were ever to regain power, Irala had to be removed.[12]

What was Irala's role? He had good reason for using others to take power. If they failed, his puppets might be hanged instead of himself. The best evidence for blaming him, besides the words of Hernández and the governor, is a pardon offered to him by Captain Salazar. The background of this pardon is curious. Despite being held in prison, on January 23, 1545, Cabeza de Vaca signed a document that named Salazar as lieutenant governor and captain general. Only after the governor was on his way to Spain did Salazar try to use this authority. Then, trying vainly to win over the comuneros, on March 14 he offered a pardon to "whatever persons might have been, and are, guilty in [Cabeza de Vaca's] imprisonment, and might have been, and are, rebels and disobedient." One of those specified by name was "Captain Domingo de Irala, chief aggressor and guilty one in the said crime." This pardon, using the same words, went to Cáceres and to Dorantes.[13] These leaders were not impressed. Angrily, they seized Salazar and sent him to Spain.

Other evidence is found in the letters of witnesses. A year after the event, Francisco González Paniagua wrote that the principal leader was Irala, who was "confederated" with the royal officials, and "aspired to the government." Although not at the scene of the attack himself, Irala sent friends there and stayed with others at his "fortified house" to give aid if needed.[14] Gregorio de Acosta, writing long afterwards, was just as blunt about who was to blame. Working with the royal officials, Irala had Cabeza de Vaca seized. Thereafter, the land was "totally destroyed," as more than thirty thousand Indians died—"male and female, children and babes at the breast." This calamity came about because Irala, to keep himself in power, let the Spaniards rob the Indians and take their wives and daughters.[15] Martín González, a cleric, also believed that the royal officials would not have been able to subdue Cabeza de Vaca without Irala's encouragement, favor, and help.[16]

This rebellion was directed at Cabeza de Vaca's main policy. His enemies opposed any checks on the treatment of the Indians. Their call for liberty, according to Branislava Susnik, referred to the liberty of the individual, liberty for each conquistador to civilize the Indians in his own way. The result was the end of the initial bond formed between the Guaranís and the Spaniards that had been based on service through friendship. In deposing the governor, the liberty that each conquistador defended was that of controlling the Indians; it was the liberty to use violence to hold onto the labor force.[17]

The plot against the governor was born at Puerto de los Reyes. Hearing rumors of a mutiny, he was about to remove Irala as camp master for abusing his power but illness and the need to get back to Asunción kept him from acting quickly enough. A legal process was started against Irala "as chief mutineer," but Hernández, who as the notary was the first witness, became sick of fever and could not go on. Cabeza de Vaca also was ill. The overthrow, then, had to be carried out soon, for Irala would lose his office when the illness passed. Thus, the rebels nearly struck at Puerto de los Reyes. González Paniagua added that as they were about to act, someone pointed out that if the governor came to Asunción under arrest, then his appointed lieutenant, Captain Salazar, would hold the top position. If the governor were murdered, Salazar would succeed him. Since Irala wanted that title for himself, he had to allow authority to be switched again at Asunción, at least briefly, before taking it into his own hands.[18]

The spark set at Puerto de los Reyes had to be rekindled at Asunción. Irala recruited his fellow Biscayans and appealed to men from Córdoba to join in the attack. Pedro de Fuentes, like Cabeza de Vaca, was from Jerez de la Frontera, and he commented on how regional bonds affected these Spaniards. In March 1545 he wrote that all those who came from Jerez lost much by the governor's defeat, "because he loved and favored us greatly." He added that "we remain in factions: some are Aviles, and others Villavisencios."[19] Cabeza de Vaca and Hernández both spoke of Biscayans and Córdobans among the comuneros.[20] Local ties might not cause a rebellion, but if other stresses grew serious, it could make a difference when the Spaniards had to choose sides.

The governor later learned how Irala won his allies. Taking aside men he thought likely to follow him, he swore each to an oath of silence. Then he warned, "The governor has said, he swears to God that he has to hang you because you are a false traitor. I happened to be present, and I have said to him that you are an honest man; still, he was angry. Guard yourself from him, therefore, because he wished you evil." In this way he won over many people. Some of them asked Cabeza de Vaca why he wished them evil. He had no idea what they meant and denied the accusation, asking who had suggested such a thing. They did not answer, being sworn to secrecy, and so he did not discover that treason was spreading.

The other rebels worked the same way. Going to people they believed might be relied on, they enlisted them with threats or promises. "Señores," they said, "the governor wants to rob you and take your goods and Indian women—and have you for slaves! We, as officials of his majesty, wish to arrest him. We will be lords of the land and will be able to act for our friends, but it is necessary for you to help us with your arms." The Spaniards who could not be trusted were locked in their houses when the rebellion began. To make the uprising appear legal, the rebels read from the royal articles of instruction, Hernández recalled, using a "false understanding" to justify taking power.[21]

The comuneros also charged Cabeza de Vaca with cruelty. That word drew bitter irony and sarcasm from González Paniagua: "I say that he was cruel against himself, by being merciful with those who tried to destroy, dishonor and overwhelm him. This mercy, which he wished to use, brought him to the state in which he now is." If three or four heads had been cut off "when he was able and had power and legal cause for it, against those who he clearly saw and knew wanted to take away, steal and tyrannize his honor, property, and rank," then he would still be governor "and the land would be well run and in complete peace." Yet, González Paniagua did not know of even a single Spaniard being hanged by Cabeza de Vaca's order.[22]

Some of those in rebellion became frightened by their deed. As Cabeza de Vaca was led off to prison, they exclaimed that they had been tricked. "You're not examining him, but arresting him. Do you want to make us traitors against the king, arresting his governor?" For a moment sword clanged on sword, but doubts faded quickly before threats and greater strength. Then a number of Spaniards who were not part of the plot came from their houses to face the comuneros. Once again, threats or a promise to share power and goods kept Asunción in rebel hands. A curfew cleared the streets thereafter. Even so, the new rulers had to be on guard against counterrevolution, for Cabeza de Vaca had many friends.[23]

After the governor, the next victims were officials loyal to him. Among them was Hernández. With "great tumult and commotion," three of the leaders and many others came into his house "with swords drawn." Pointing them at his chest, they yelled "Liberty, Liberty!" and "Long live the king!" They said that Irala had sent them to get the documents drawn up against him by Cabeza de Vaca. Hernández, however, could not give them any papers, which were still at the governor's residence. In addition, the town officials of Asunción who had close ties to Cabeza de Vaca were ousted, and a number of them went to jail. Irala gave the order, charged Hernández. Some of the officials and constables were later set free,[24] but the mayor, Juan Pavón de Badajoz, complained of being locked up in Irala's house, "where I did not see the sun or moon in eleven months and eighteen days." Pavón was greatly mistreated, agreed Hernández and González Paniagua, and in a letter of 1556 Pavón recounted for the Council of the Indies his arrest and imprisonment. It ended with a cry of anger: "Lord, I call for justice! justice! justice!"[25]

Another target was Cabeza de Vaca's residence. There the leaders looked over papers both from the king and from Cabeza de Vaca's work in the Río de la Plata province. Among the records ready to go to Spain were legal cases against some of the rebels. They also looted his property, taking such goods as clothing, wine, oil, iron, and steel. He was never to see any of these items again. Whatever they did not want for themselves was left to their friends for "storing."[26] A document dated July 16, 1544, notes the deposit of his black slave, Juan Blanco, and some armor with Luis Ramírez, a partner of Dorantes. Later a listing of all stolen goods, including ten bergantinas, gave their value at more than 100,000 castellanos according to the prices in Asunción, for Cabeza de Vaca left Spain having spent much less than that amount.[27]

Irala took over much of this property. The reason, as noted when that governor made his will in 1556, was that several times he had borne the costs of conquest. For example, he had turned over several ships to Cabeza de Vaca when the governor arrived in Asunción. Then, when Irala first explored up to Puerto de los Reyes, it was at his own cost, as was the war that he fought against the Indian chief Tabaré.[28]

In Asunción the comuneros watched closely over the governor and the people. Keeping him in their hands was of the greatest importance. After he went to the dwelling that served as his prison, they kept him tightly bound. Besides shackles, he had full-time guards, one of them a man he had earlier jailed. Even shackles and armed guards were not enough for the new rulers. They fortified the chamber where he was held with a stockade, set deeply into the ground to block mining. Nearby buildings became barracks for approximately fifty men, who were to fight off any attempts at rescuing Cabeza de Vaca. For security, visitors entering this stronghold had to undergo a check. To cope with those opposing the regime, armed patrols and threats or beatings kept people off the streets and in their houses, as did the curfew.[29]

The new leaders tried to draw more people to their side. On the afternoon of April 26 they held a meeting in the public plaza near the doorway of Irala's house. Bartolomé González, a clerk, climbed onto a bench to read "a letter and libel defaming the governor, calling him a famous tyrant and a cruel person."[30] For González Paniagua, the speech was just another outrage. The speaker, he wrote, distorted whatever Cabeza de Vaca had done that might be twisted in a dishonest sense. "Since he was human, it would be impossible that there not be some such things," but "if ten truthful things were said, they invented two hundred lies and promoted as many other wicked and false testimonies."[31]

Other people heard the clerk's words quite differently. When he finished reading, they went into the house, and in the presence of the royal officials Irala was elected (or appointed) lieutenant governor and captain general of the province in place of Cabeza de Vaca.[32] Hernández repeated a comment by Alonso Cabrera to explain why the royal officials agreed on Irala. "He was the one of least rank of all, and he would always do as [Cabrera] directed him." For Ulrich Schmidt, on the other hand, Irala was appealing because he had earlier governed the colony, and "especially because most of the soldiers were satisfied with him."[33] If Schmidt is to be trusted on any point, it most likely would be as a spokesman for the other soldiers.

Nevertheless, the uprising against Cabeza de Vaca was not easy. On April 29, a few days after taking over, the new town officials in Asunción tried to seize and catalog his legal papers and effects. A clerk went to his house and wrote out the order in the company of Irala and his new mayor, Díaz del Valle. Both men were listed as officials of "his majesty," so they already sought to show that their rebellion was against Cabeza de Vaca, not the king. Among the items to be opened were two mailbags. The keys were said to be with the governor, so Díaz del Valle had a clerk demand the keys for the mayor. Cabeza de Vaca replied that he was not required to give the keys to anyone and that the mayor ought not interfere in this matter. When the clerk reported to Díaz del Valle, the mayor sent him back to demand the keys at once. Cabeza de Vaca refused to give in to his foes. Unless the mayor showed him a writ from the king or Council of the Indies, he was still governor, captain general, and adelantado of the province. Everyone living there had to obey his commands as if coming from the king, under threat of severe penalty. He then ordered the mayor, "one and two and three times," to set him free so that he could fulfill the king's commands. However, it would take more than words to snap those chains. This order was coupled with a plea about his own hardships. Although too sick to get out of bed, he was held in chains as a way to annoy him, and he wanted the chains taken off. The mayor answered that he was not the one who had arrested him; the royal officials had done so, and he would have to ask them about his freedom. Also, for the third time he demanded the keys. Cabeza de Vaca answered as before and added that he knew who had made him a prisoner and scolded the mayor for taking part and helping them. The mayor then decided not to open the mailbags until a more suitable time.[34]

Hernández was deeply involved in this matter too. Irala demanded of him, as the former notary, the records of the legal proceedings that Cabeza de Vaca had made against Irala and the royal officials. He wanted to get the key to the chest that held the papers, but Hernández did not have it.[35] In fact, he had only a few papers, for many had burned in the great fire of 1543.[36] Cabrera also tried to get Hernández to cooperate but did not succeed.[37] Eventually the key was found, and Díaz del Valle, in a letter of March 20, 1545, explained to the king that in the presence of witnesses the documents were taken from the chest and sent to Spain for his information.[38]

22

I Am the King and Ruler of This Land

The comuneros had power within their grasp. Now they had to hold on to it. Further, they knew that the change in command had to appear to be lawful. While revolts in Spain were not unknown during this era, Spaniards generally had a strong sense of loyalty to the crown.[1] In Asunción, most of the settlers clearly felt such a bond, so the new rulers had to find some excuse to justify their act of rebellion to the other colonists and to the government in Spain. Although the uprising resulted from Cabeza de Vaca's struggle to safeguard the Indians from harm, the rebels could not let Charles I suspect such a cause. One way to sidetrack the idea was to accuse the governor of mistreating the Indians. That point, however untrue it was, could alarm the king and arouse enough doubts for him to accept it without much proof. Even better was to accuse Cabeza de Vaca of disloyalty.

Their campaign to retain power began several weeks after the successful takeover. During the early summer of 1544 Cáceres, Cabrera, Dorantes, and Venegas, held two related legal hearings. The subject of the first and briefest was an instance of Cabeza de Vaca's use of his coat of arms "against the royal service and in dishonor of the royal coat of arms." While going up the Paraguay River to Puerto de los Reyes in 1543 he had put his personal coat of arms on his ship. Juan Velásquez, a painter, fashioned a copy of its design, which fifteen witnesses agreed was accurate. Here, for the king and the Council of the Indies, was a graphic display of an affront to the crown.[2]

In mid-July a second legal inquiry opened. This time the royal officials were looking into some of Cabeza de Vaca's "actions and words" that appeared dangerous to royal authority. Various witnesses were called to support three main charges to the effect that Cabeza de Vaca wanted to make himself king over the province. Their first charge dealt with a mark of royal sovereignty. In 1542 (actually early 1543) he had sent Irala to punish the Indian chief, Tabaré. Irala, as usual, had hanging from the mast of his boat a banner with the royal arms. When Cabeza de Vaca saw it, he ordered it down, scolded the sailor who had raised it, and had his own coat of arms put there. The second charge touched on royal orders. Many people, it stated, had spoken to the governor about ignoring the king's decrees and commands, and he answered them by saying, "Since swords and crossbows lost their strength past the equatorial line, it was no wonder that his majesty's decrees also lost theirs." The third charge concerned the royal sovereignty itself. He had often said: "I am the king and ruler of this land." Further, his officials and servants had called him "king, prince and natural lord."

Four dozen witnesses replied to the questions under oath. According to Enrique de Gandía, all were friends of the rebels or else answered under "harsh threats." Testimony began on July 17, 1544, and lasted for more than a month, although most of the witnesses were heard during the first week or so. Generally they agreed that the charges against Cabeza de Vaca were true or declared that they had heard that they were true. Nevertheless, the witnesses gave little detail about the words actually spoken, which became the basis of his rivals' case.

Among the witnesses, seven mentioned the ship and the banner. Most saw only the royal banner come down and the governor's go up in its place. More helpful was Jácome Luis, who had been on board at that moment and had taken part in what happened. He recalled that when Irala was ready to go after Tabaré, he set a royal banner from the mast as usual. Luis, who was the shipmaster, actually put up the banner. Other than that, even his knowledge was based on hearsay. He had heard that when the governor saw the royal arms, he wanted to know who had put it there, and demanded, "Have I not banners? Bring one of mine and take down that one." Pedro de Oñate, the governor's treacherous servant, testified that following Irala's attack on Tabaré he heard Cabeza de Vaca say, "The officials of his majesty and other people have told me that it seems to them I was wrong in taking down the banner . . . with his majesty's arms. I did nothing but what was right, because the officials . . . should not think that now is as long ago, when they were in the habit of doing those things. I am governor and king of this land, and my arms have to go where the ship goes." These words were voiced "with much anger and passion."[3]

In 1556 Martín González dismissed the furor over the banner as merely a pretext for taking power. He wrote to the king that the governor's enemies had charged "that he wanted to usurp this land," their proof being the story about taking the royal banner from a ship "and other things which, for being tedious and in themselves having little foundation, I will not state them." To his eyes what appeared important was "their falsity and cunning, and having rebelled to bring power to themselves."[4]

The second charge was that Cabeza de Vaca did not follow royal edicts. Six witnesses testified regarding Cabeza de Vaca's statement that he did not fulfill royal commands because "they lost force past the line." Some of the witnesses remembered hearing him use such words in the presence of many persons, while others repeated hearsay. Only Francisco de Palomino gave a clue about what the words meant. In the background was Alonso Cabrera's attempt to force the settlers to pay the revised and ruinous form of the quinto tax, which Cabeza de Vaca had stopped in 1542. Anger at this meddling brought Cabrera into the 1543 plot whereby the friars, Armenta and Lebrón, tried to flee to Spain with letters that were critical of the governor. After they were caught, Cabrera lost his post as overseer and was sent to the jail.

Later, Palomino asked that Cabrera's hardship in prison be eased. The governor's reply included the comment that Cabrera had mistakenly levied the quinto tax according to his own ideas instead of royal orders. Even so, it was not a serious matter, as "he who understood the orders had to give them their meaning." Indeed, the Council of the Indies did not know what occurred in the Indies. If its members did know, "they would apply them to suit what was needed—and that was not a marvel," he went on, "since swords and arms lost strength past the line here, it was no wonder that his majesty's orders lost theirs." That statement was not a rejection of royal authority. It was merely a proverb to show that royal commands had to be made to fit the local setting. Spanish viceroys later used a similar adage to evade undesired or misguided royal commands: "Obedezco pero no cumplo" ("I obey, but do not execute" an order).

The remaining charge was that Cabeza de Vaca said he was "king and lord of this land." Most of the witnesses heard him or his friends say something of this sort, and in rather different settings. One even had him being both king and pope. The number of stories suggests that he did say that he had the power of a king, but what he meant by those words is not easy to know. Luis Ramírez gave an example caused by stress at Puerto de los Reyes. Some soldiers were complaining about their burdens, when Cabeza de Vaca exploded at them, saying that he was the ruler of that land, and would "take their tongues out through the backs of their heads." Sebastián de Fuerte el Rey also linked Cabeza de Vaca's statements about kingship to displeasure when people disobeyed him.

A second example, however, did not reflect stress. Diego de Carabajal overheard Cabeza de Vaca and Gonzalo de Mendoza talking at Puerto de los Reyes. Mendoza declared that "it was good that the captains and men of repute be told of the things that he had to do, because if things went wrong, there would be so much blame charged to him." Cabeza de Vaca replied, "The King, is he not King of Spain?" He answered himself: "Yes, he is King, and he gives account to no one. Well, likewise, I am King of this land, and there is no one to whom I have to give account."[5] This retort was not a refusal to ask for his officials' advice. He often called for it. Nor was he asserting freedom from the rule of Spain. His point was that the king ruled Spain in the same way as he did as governor of the Río de la Plata province. He stated many times that he acted under the king's authority, and he depended on it to make his Indian policy work.

The comuneros made sure that their witnesses were all in agreement. Besides using bribery, threats, and even torture, they simply did not take down testimony that might help him. If a witness said anything favorable, according to Hernández, he was told, "They are not asking you that."[6] Irala and his people tried forcefully to stop any effort from being made on Cabeza de Vaca's behalf and allowed only what might harm him and profit themselves. Their desire was for the king to take Cabeza de Vaca's position away, so they had to send "false evidence" and agents to Spain with their case against him.[7] Historian Enrique de Gandía refuted these charges with sarcasm. If one believed the governor's enemies the only words that Cabeza de Vaca spoke in Paraguay were that he was the king and lord there. It was a slander invented by his enemies, and the idea came to them from some words uttered after his arrest.

Gandía's evidence is the "Relación" of January 28, 1545, by Pero Hernández. Cabeza de Vaca is quoted there as taunting his captors for their crimes: "Does it seem to you a just thing that each one of you wishes to be king of the land? Well, I want you to know that there is no other king, nor does one have to have another lord, but his majesty, and I in his name." Hernández added that with indirect arguments devised by Díaz del Valle, "they asserted that the governor had said that he was king." Further, they made up evidence about this charge and corrupted witnesses to affirm it. Gandía agreed with Hernández that this episode was the source of the false charges against the governor.[8]

Is there nothing more to the matter? Why did not Cabeza de Vaca or his supporters answer his enemies more clearly? Had he, perhaps, used words akin to what they stated, possibly when angered by strife with his men? The number of people who were willing to say under oath that he uttered shocking words and acted oddly makes the charges appear to be something more than bold lies. After all, he need not have imagined making himself king in his province. Perhaps he saw the role of adelantado and governor as being like that of a viceroy, a "king" for local matters, even if under the final, and far-off, authority of the king in Spain. As a viceroy he truly would have been a "vice" king, but the government of Spain did not wish to have adelantados as viceroys, and such ideas, however loyally held, could ignite distrust in Spain. Given the ways that most other adelantados of the Spanish conquest of America were ending their careers, his rivals had a good chance of success with their attacks against him.

Other evidence fits into the picture. As early as 1541 on the coast of Brazil Cabeza de Vaca had caused his coat of arms to be carved onto a large rock on the beach but not the arms of the king of Spain. Gandía called this action not only an error, but illegal.[9] Cabeza de Vaca clearly held that symbol of his rank in high regard, but pride need not infer treason.

Months passed before the legal case could be sent to the king. When it was finally ready, a number of other charges had been added. The comuneros had one great advantage. In Spain, Cabeza de Vaca would have only very limited means of disproving any charges.

23

No Man Was Safe from the Other

Cabeza de Vaca's final year in South America saw his Indian policy entirely overturned. The history of that reversal is disputed. Although his captors tried to keep all news from him in prison, he did learn something of events in the province. Later, in Madrid, he added to his knowledge, and on December 7, 1545, he wrote for the Council of the Indies a "Relación general" as a report.[1] Naturally, he focused on the crimes and misdeeds that he could tie to his enemies after they had taken power. Other sources also contributed to the story, including Pero Hernández's secret "Relación" written in Asunción in January 1545.[2] A decade later, these accounts were enlarged into the *Comentarios,* and they are similar in many ways.

The many clashes among the new rulers greatly interested the governor. These quarrels seemed to prove that a few selfish men held control over the others by bribery and terror. The bribes, used to win and hold the support of many Spaniards, either came from Cabeza de Vaca's own goods or were free Indians given out as slaves. Some of the new slaves had a special status among the leaders. The Indian chiefs had presented Cabeza de Vaca with a number of women, "freely, to serve." Domingo de Irala, his officials, and his friends took these women, an ancient symbol of a change in rulers. In general, the women suffered much harm. As the governor lamented, "They treated the Indian women of this land with great cruelty and blows; they gave them such bad treatment that they went to hang themselves." One Spaniard abused a woman and then took another one from "a servant of your majesty" (Cabeza de Vaca's words for any of the men loyal to him).

Before the governor had come to Asunción, these abuses were common. He had acted to stop them, however, and gave the victims to Spaniards who were willing to take better care of them. "Thus, they were treated well, and the Christians were served well."[3] Cabeza de Vaca and Hernández both compared the benefits of his rule against the many shortcomings of his rivals, showing that royal goals had succeeded much better under his leadership than under Irala and the comuneros. As Juan Friede observed, when Indians lost their independence, they had to look to the Spanish crown for protection.[4] In the Río de la Plata province, that protection was lost with the overthrow of Cabeza de Vaca.

Hernández had stories of his own about the rebels. After they seized power, he told the king, they began to remove the Indians from the villages, forcing them to build houses and clear woodlands without pay. The Spaniards took Indian wives and daughters against their will, selling or trading them for goods. They misused the women and girls sexually and gave no heed to complaints. Hernández reported case after case of the breakdown of peace and order, and his favorite targets were Irala's vices and jealousies.[5]

The stories of Cabeza de Vaca and Hernández might be doubted because of their self-interest. Yet other writers reported that such horrors continued for years afterward.[6] Even Spaniards faced abuse and injustice, as great disorder and uproar followed Cabeza de Vaca's overthrow. The province was being ruined, they grieved, because both the Indians and Spaniards were fleeing. One anonymous memorial related how Irala forced Bartolomé Salvador to go out with ten men to look for Indian women. Salvador's fear was justified, for the Indians killed him and most of the others and then attacked Asunción. When peace finally was made, Irala again demanded the wives and daughters from the Indians.[7]

A decade later the tally of abuses was far worse. In 1556 Martín González recalled that when the governor was overthrown, an edict had proclaimed that the uprising took place to give the people liberty, but he assured the king that the result was total ruin. After the rebel officials took over, "they decided to destroy the land to please their friends and defenders." Those they favored went throughout the region and, "like fire, wherever they went, they burned and scorched all the land." Among Indian women the loss was nearly beyond count. Beginning in 1544, approximately fifty thousand women were brought to Asunción; by 1556 only fifteen thousand remained among the Spaniards—the rest were dead. The mistreatment of the Indians had caused major uprisings, in which a great many of them died. Although a number like the fifty thousand might seem to be more for effect than an actual count, another letter of the era gave the same figure. In 1561 Captain Ruy Díaz Melgarejo told the king about the results of the rebellion, "It is very certain that from that time more than fifty thousand are dead."[8] One factor may have been smallpox, which had been unknown in the Río de la Plata province: an epidemic in 1559 killed more than ten thousand Indians.[9]

Juan Múñoz de Carvajal told the same story. He blamed the "passions and interests" of Irala and the royal officials for their actions. They began robbing and destroying the Indians, "taking their pregnant wives and those recently delivered of children, separating infants from their breasts and taking their children for their service." This terror had occurred only since Cabeza de Vaca's last day as governor.[10]

Even while the governor was still in prison, some of the rebel leaders began to have doubts. The king's officials, Cabeza de Vaca wrote, tried to settle matters with him and restore his freedom. Now they could see, they said, "the great mistake that had been done in the loss of the land and the disservice and contempt of his majesty." Perhaps the governor imagined more regret than really existed, hoping that they would flock to his side if Charles I returned him to power. Nevertheless, attracting such waverers and sending pleas to the monarch did not succeed.

Irala worked hard to keep command of the province. He made another entrada, following the lead of Cabeza de Vaca, who declared that Irala sought gold and silver in order to receive the government. Back in 1541, Cabeza de Vaca added, Irala had deserted Buenos Aires for gold and silver. Now that same greed caused him to overthrow an adelantado and governor. Hernández agreed that Irala sought gold and silver to send to Spain to win a pardon for the "crime" that he and his men had committed. Indeed, success in a conquest was often reckoned by the wealth it won, for the king had already embraced tainted conquistadores who gained riches.

To hold on to power, the comuneros struck at the loyalists again and again. Cabeza de Vaca's friends tried to free him until his enemies warned that they would kill him. Even so, rebel fears mounted. "Seeing two men meet," he said, "they arrested them, so the servants of his majesty had no liberty." They seized his allies in their sanctuaries or starved them out, stole from them, called them traitors, and threatened them. The rebels dreaded his escape. So afraid were they of losing their own heads that they swore an oath to cut off his head and throw it to the people if he was being freed. Every day, swords in hand, they threatened to kill Cabeza de Vaca if his friends did not keep the peace and stop trying to rescue him. Cabeza de Vaca told them to halt such efforts: it was better to go to the king under arrest, and he did not want "a single drop of blood" shed for him.[11]

Only once during his months in prison did he act against his foes. This attempt involved his lieutenant, Captain Juan de Salazar, who possibly could have given help but whose willingness to do so was uncertain. An anonymous relation, written sometime after 1558, reported that the governor's supporters met in secret while he was captive to discuss how he might transfer authority. As a result, he gave power to Salazar, who would then set Cabeza de Vaca free.[12] On January 23, 1545, Cabeza de Vaca signed a document that directed Hernández "to enact a power" for Salazar to govern the land in his place. It had a brief statement of his royal authority and described how the royal officials had arrested him and taken over, naming Cabrera, Cáceres, Dorantes, and Venegas but not Irala (the governor may still not have known Irala's role). Then Cabeza de Vaca "named and empowered" Salazar as lieutenant governor and captain general of the province.[13]

Seven weeks later this document became subject to much dispute. On March 13, a few days after Cabeza de Vaca embarked for Spain, Salazar obtained the document from a steward.[14] Perhaps Salazar did not know what to do with it or had decided to hold onto it as long as possible. According to the anonymous relation, Salazar did not want to use such power or even reveal that he had it until Cabeza de Vaca had been sent to Spain. Only then did he show his title to rule, so "he seemed to want to use the power for keeping himself in possession of the land."[15] Irala, of course, would not permit Cabeza de Vaca to be replaced by someone else. Although angry enough to kill Salazar, Irala agreed to send him to Spain.[16]

Salazar may have been blameless, but his ambition is clear. Historian Julio César Chaves surmised that in 1537 Salazar traveled from Asunción to Buenos Aires seeking to fill the power vacuum created by the imminent death of Pedro de Mendoza and by the disappearance of Juan de Ayolas.[17] As Cabeza de Vaca's appointed successor, Salazar may have hoped to wrest power from Irala, whose legal position was weak. Hernández wrote harshly about Salazar's refusal to act, claiming that Salazar could have prevented the governor's arrest and removal to Spain. Anger may have been a factor in Salazar's failure to act. According to Dorantes, Salazar may have been bitter because the governor treated him roughly after the settlers returned from Puerto de los Reyes. Dorantes also said that Salazar was warned about the overthrow of the governor and agreed to remain at home during the uprising. When Cabeza de Vaca's relatives went there that night, although it was still early, they were told that Salazar was sleeping.[18]

It is probable that very little could have been done for the governor, who repeatedly opposed plans to free him by force. If Salazar wanted seriously to challenge these men, he had to use violence, which not only went against his orders but would have imperiled himself and others as well. One voice, at least, spoke highly of him. A friar, also named Juan de Salazar, thought that he was "very loyal" and that his purpose was "to put the governor at his liberty if he could."[19]

The comuneros never did conquer their fears. Again and again they tried to win over Cabeza de Vaca's friends. With gifts and promises "they corrupted many other people," using the governor's property to do so. Hernández explained that part of this loot was the supplies stockpiled for the governor's next entrada or for building caravels to carry reports to Spain. Those who could not be bribed faced terror. Armed guards stripped men of their arms, barricaded and fortified the street by the prison, and ordered the people not to talk with each other. Anyone who went near the governor at night would be killed.

González Paniagua contended that Irala governed most of the people tyrannically. Rebel favoritism brought on beatings and stabbings, and every day there were many disturbances. Just thinking about these horrors grieved him. He wanted to shield his readers from such terrible events but could not hold his memories back. Likewise, Friar Salazar called Asunción "a town of more than five hundred men and more than five hundred thousand disorders, all in disservice to God and your majesty." He had good reason to speak of terror. Irala himself threatened Friar Salazar and González Paniagua because of their boldness against him. Cabeza de Vaca's magistrates were also harassed.[20]

The governor's friends were not alone in writing about this violence. Ulrich Schmidt wholly disliked Cabeza de Vaca, yet spoke frankly about the results of his fall from power: "There was discord among us Christians, and soon we fought day and night, so that any one would have thought that the devil governed among us; and no man was safe from the other." The cause of strife was clear to him. "We thus made war among ourselves for two whole years, the sending away Cabessa de Bacha being the occasion of it." He said also that the Indians under Tabaré revolted against Spanish control after the governor was gone but were once again defeated by Irala.[21] Spanish-Indian relations in the Río de la Plata province were dramatically undergoing a change that occurred elsewhere: a positive beginning followed by a breakdown.[22]

As his rivals struggled to hold on to power, the number of their victims grew. Many disliked the new rulers and fought them, despite the governor's words against violence. A priest, Luis de Miranda de Villafaña, spent months in prison for urging some Spaniards to free the governor.[23] Others tried to escape to the coast of Brazil and carry their tales of suffering to Spain. Cabeza de Vaca again called on them not to defy his enemies but to wait for the king to make his will known. This advice was misguided, however, for those who returned to Asunción were punished.[24]

Only supporters could journey freely to the coast of Brazil. When

Bernardo de Armenta and Alonso Lebrón had plotted such a trip in 1543, they were stopped. Four months after Cabeza de Vaca's arrest they were ready to go again. His defeat delighted them, as might be expected, and Cabeza de Vaca claimed that they preached what the new rulers wanted to hear, approving the rebellion. Some other clergy also took the side of his foes, but many supported him, a choice that cost them dearly.[25] Hernández charged that Armenta and Lebrón advised and helped the new rulers because the friars feared retribution for "the crimes they committed." Also, three priests and a friar defended the governor's arrest "because he rebuked them and made them live virtuously."[26]

This journey by those friars had the same goals as their first one. Armenta and Lebrón carried letters and dispatches, noted Cabeza de Vaca, "to explain to the king that I had done great disservice." They intended to use their religious standing to support the rebels' complaints and accounts of recent events.[27] Part of the plan was for Armenta to become bishop of the province. Dorantes later asked the king to send a clerical protector for the Indians.[28] If Armenta had not soon died, he might have been the kind of bishop and "protector" that the new rulers had in mind.

Some of the people in Asunción questioned the friars' journey, fearing that their absence would endanger the conquest, but Irala let the friars go. Again they took along women, forty or fifty in all. These "Christian women," daughters of important Indians, went by force, according to complaints, very much against their own will or that of the parents, and they had to be "tied and shackled at night so that they would not flee." Also, the friars traded free Indians with the comuneros as if they were slaves and used others as slaves.[29]

The memory of such misdeeds lived for decades. Francisco Ortiz de Vergara mentioned them in a report sent to the president of the Council of the Indies, Don Juan Ovando. Ortiz had come to the Río de la Plata province in 1540 with Cabeza de Vaca, acted as its governor (1558–65) not long after Irala's death, and called himself treasurer when he wrote this letter in 1573. As the two friars were leaving, he recalled, they professed to be taking the chiefs' children to catechize them, but it was "a thing that did not seem well to anybody, because it was to exile them from the land." He also thought that the trip was wrong because Cabeza de Vaca had earlier stopped Armenta and Lebrón from taking Indian girls on such a journey. As Ortiz told the outcome, "These friars came to an end on the coast of Brazil, and not so well, as in my opinion they would have been better in their monastery, because it was said they were much a part of the arrest of the governor."[30] According to Ricardo de Lafuente Machain, Armenta went to the island of Santa Catalina and died in 1546. Lebrón set out for Portugal but had not arrived a year later; it was assumed that he had been taken by a pirate.[31]

To Discredit Me with His Majesty

Power brought a dilemma for the rebels. Now that Cabeza de Vaca was in their hands, what was to be done with so dangerous a prisoner? Was he more dangerous dead or alive? After arresting him, possibly without thinking in their haste, they scuttled the ten bergantinas that had carried them from Puerto de los Reyes to Asunción and destroyed the caravel being built to carry a report to the king. Thus he could not be sent to Spain any time soon. Some of the rebels wanted to have Cabeza de Vaca dead. When several houses in Asunción caught fire, they blamed his friends and set ablaze the building where he was a prisoner. The new mayor of Asunción, Pero Díaz del Valle, said that the fires (he counted three) were part of a plot by the priest Luis de Miranda to overthrow the royal officials and restore Cabeza de Vaca as governor. Poison was another threat. Someone warned the governor that Irala wanted the cook to put realgar (arsenic sulfide) in his food. For many days he did not dare to eat meat or fish and lived on bread or fruit, which they could not poison.[1]

The comuneros wanted very much to keep Cabeza de Vaca away from his friends. Soon, however, the mayor learned that he was receiving news anyway. Cabeza de Vaca's Indian servant, Juan, went to the house where he was a prisoner and asked whether the man in charge of the guard was with him. If Cabeza de Vaca was alone, Juan tossed a piece of cane with letters inside through the tiny window. On July 16, 1544, somebody else was in the room when the cane sailed in, and despite a plea for secrecy and a promise of reward, betrayed the scheme. The chief suspects behind the messages were Captain Hernando de Ribera and Francisco González Paniagua.[2]

Nevertheless, the attempt to withhold news did not work. The Indian woman who brought Cabeza de Vaca's food smuggled in letters at great risk to herself. The guards were eager to find messages, "stripping her stark-naked, inspecting her mouth and ears, cutting her hair in order that she might not bring one amidst her hair, and examining everything possible"— including, the governor said, "her private parts." Yet such effort failed. Cabeza de Vaca was not kept entirely without information "because between her toes, in the hollow under her foot," she held a paper with news of what was happening, "wrapped in a little wax, very subtly fastened with cotton thread." In the same way, the governor sent messages to his friends.

These exchanges baffled the guards. Imagining treachery, they set spies on each other to find out how the news was being leaked. Four young men were picked "that they might be involved with the Indian woman." It was a task, in the words of Hernández, for which there was not much to do, "because by custom they are not sparing of their bodies, and hold it a great affront to refuse anyone who asks them for it. They say, what were we given it for but for that?" During the months that Cabeza de Vaca was in prison they gave the Indian woman many presents, but they could get no secret from her. As a Jesuit historian of Paraguay, Pierre François Xavier de Charlevoix (ca. 1682–1761), later observed, "though she easily gave up her chastity, she scrupulously preserved her integrity. On these occasions, women are more discreet than men."

That Cabeza de Vaca's life was spared is surprising. He believed that the vital efforts of his friends kept him alive. Otherwise, his foes would have ended their problem by murder. Throughout his arrest there were "great disruptions," he wrote, "and because of my imprisonment some were angry with others, and there were men's deaths." Popular unrest kept the rebels from killing him in the prison—they feared "the great disturbances and disruptions and clamor of the people. . . . The officials knew clearly that if they killed me in prison, then [his friends] would kill them." Indeed, whenever rumors of his death spread, the only way to calm the people was to have him sign letters.[3]

The royal officials eventually decided that the only way to resolve the impasse was to send Cabeza de Vaca to Spain. Seven months after taking power they rescued and repaired some of the ships they had earlier scuttled. The task was made harder because Cabeza de Vaca's shipbuilding supplies had been looted and were being used as doors, windows, and the like.[4] Also, the rebels had to prepare a defense for the king. Besides "official" reports on the arrest, Cabeza de Vaca said, they gave drafts of letters to their friends, "to write to Spain that I had done much damage and evil in that land, to discredit me with his majesty and everyone in general." Only letters that opposed him were to go. Any messages or legal papers that could help him were barred, for "the most principal thing that they want and are determined to get" was that the king take away his government.[5]

The royal officials met on March 5, 1545, to pick agents to go to Spain. After much discussion, they agreed to send Alonso Cabrera and Garci Venegas to guard Cabeza de Vaca and to defend the rebellion before the king. Martín de Orúe also went to help with the attack. Felipe de Cáceres and Pedro Dorantes stayed in the Río de la Plata province, "charged and entrusted with the good of the people, the peace of the land and the collection of royal finances."[6] They ignored other topics such as the legal charges Cabeza de Vaca had made against the friars and other rebels.[7]

25

He Was a Very Good Governor

Cabeza de Vaca's friends also sent documents to Spain, in spite of the efforts to prevent them from doing so. The carpenters who worked on the caravel to take him to Spain built a secret hiding place in a thick beam into which were put papers that might help him as well as letters to the king and Spanish officials. Their work was so well done that the comuneros never suspected the cache. One of the carpenters then passed on the secret to a sailor so that the papers would be found upon reaching Spain.[1] A number of letters supporting Cabeza de Vaca have been published during the past century. Although often impassioned, they express the ideas and experiences of major and minor actors in the settlement of the Río de la Plata. They also add support to the narrative in the previous two chapters, which is based heavily on the writings of Cabeza de Vaca and Pero Hernández.

Captain Hernando de Ribera, for example, wrote a vigorous defense of the governor. On February 25, 1545, he sent the king a general account of his adventures over many years. It told about the Indians and the Europeans, Buenos Aires when Pedro de Mendoza arrived, and Santa Catalina Island. Near its end, the letter came to the era of Cabeza de Vaca. Ulrich Schmidt had charged the governor with arresting Ribera and ordering him to be hanged on his return from exploring in early 1544. Ribera said nothing about this event but blamed the new rulers for bringing about much disturbance and disruption by overthrowing the governor. Ribera generally related the same story that Hernández and Cabeza de Vaca themselves were soon to tell. Streets and buildings were under guard, law courts corrupted, and the governor's goods stolen. The rebels had carried out legal proceedings against Cabeza de Vaca "with great cunning, falsehoods and bribes, presents and promises," so that the monarch might believe that he had done nothing good in that land. Their reports were untrue, Ribera declared, "because in all that was possible he has done what was suitable for the service of God and your majesty." The renegade officials had acted out of passion and personal interest. They had gone against God and king, ruining the land and endangering the conquest, for Indians and Europeans alike were fleeing from evil treatment and tyranny. Ribera begged the king not to believe those officials or their friends but to heal the harm done to the land and its people.[2]

Alonso Agudo, another of Cabeza de Vaca's friends, also wrote to Spain on February 25, 1545. A former official of the Inquisition in Granada, he reported the breakdown of religion and morals in the Río de la Plata region. This letter was not addressed to the king, but to the archbishop of Toledo and inquisitor general of Spain, Cardinal Don Juan Tavira. Agudo charged the Spaniards with disbelief, heresy, blasphemy, and immorality. Like other critics, he judged their sexual appetites to be more wicked than those of Muhammad's followers. Cabeza de Vaca had dared to check the worst lewdness and vice, and Agudo valued these reforms and saw the rebels as evil and malicious men who had illegally seized the king's justice for themselves. The people, he added, were treated badly under the new regime. Many Indians had fled or revolted, and the Spaniards fared little better. Bribery and terror reigned. The royal officials so abused their power that "we are tyrannized away from obedience to his majesty." Only force kept the new rulers in control. Because they had vowed to cut off the governor's head if a rescue attempt started, Agudo saw leaving Cabeza de Vaca to the mercy of God as being the safest course.[3]

On March 3, Francisco González Paniagua wrote a long defense of Cabeza de Vaca. If one compared his handling of the Indians with what had happened after his arrest, the loss became clear. While Cabeza de Vaca had power, noted the priest, "I never saw any Indian stabbed by Christians—an

Indian, I say, of our allies." Harming them had then meant punishment. Now there were so many stabbings, whippings, and other sorrows that he had lost count. From the beginning the governor had taken trade with the Indians into his own hands, but since his overthrow, everyone was trading for himself. As Branislava Susnik has argued, in economic terms the struggle against Cabeza de Vaca was a struggle on the part of his enemies for free trade. The Indians were upset, González Paniagua continued, complaining about Spaniards entering dwellings and taking things. "All this they have said, and say, to the credit of the governor, and condemn his arrest." Such disservice to God and injury to the crown, such disorder and breakdown, would lead to the loss of the people and the conquest.[4]

Another letter, dated March 1, 1545, was written by Francisco Galán, who wrote not to defend Cabeza de Vaca before the king but simply to send news to Rodrigo de Vera, alcalde of Zahara and apparently the governor's kinsman. Galán had promised to tell Vera about events in the Río de la Plata province and opened with an apology for several years of neglect. Trouble had started, he said, when Cabeza de Vaca stopped the royal officials from misusing the quinto tax. They struck back by sending Armenta and Lebrón to take protests to the coast of Brazil for passage to Spain. When that plan failed and the friars were arrested, the officials grew even more furious. They overthrew the governor amid great disorder and turmoil. Galán spoke also of the threats, violence, scorn, and other outrages that Hernández and Cabeza de Vaca themselves soon charged against the rebels. They had abused the governor, and his friends had tried to free him but had to give up when the danger made him order them to act with care.[5]

One letter from the colony went to a man of international fame, Pietro Aretino, an Italian Renaissance author who had as a secretary and friend a man who could fight as well as write, Ambrosio Eusebio (Ambrogio degli Eusebii), who may have come with Cabeza de Vaca to South America.[6] Eusebio's message is undated, but the text suggests that it was one of the flurry of letters composed in March 1545. The governor was then in prison, where the officials had put him "illegally," a deed done "with little justice, or better to say, without any; which I think has to be changed in paradise." As these words make clear, Eusebio thought highly of Cabeza de Vaca. Aretino himself was pressed to write to the emperor (for Charles was Holy Roman Emperor as well as king of Spain) about Cabeza de Vaca's "fidelity" and that his imprisonment was a result of the "envy and scorn" of his success for the "magnificence of his purposes." Eusebio wanted the king to make Cabeza de Vaca governor again, as a result of his having "worked so much in the service of the Catholic and Caesarean majesty."

Hernández later spoke about the high cost of Eusebio's loyalty. The rebels took him from church sanctuary because he had gone to the coast of Brazil to obtain help in warning the king about "the treason and revolt in this land." Eusebio said that he was held as a prisoner for four months, "with his neck in a stock and chains on his feet." He was even tortured and threatened with death for not going along with "the treasons or mutinies" that had happened. As Eusebio sarcastically told Aretino, "Do not think that one becomes indolent here."[7]

In later years Cabeza de Vaca's defenders continued to speak in his support. Enemies ruled the colony for a time, but many supporters survived, and some of them later mentioned him when they sent to Spain their claims of "merits and services" or simple relations of events. An anonymous relation written after 1558 discussed the governor and the royal officials' reasons for removing him. "They said that he said that Hernando Cortés had been a fool for not having usurped the land" and that "the provisions of his majesty lost force on passing the line. This I never heard, nor other things that were proclaimed." The writer also told of the deaths and mistreatment that followed Cabeza de Vaca's overthrow.[8]

Even colonists who never knew Cabeza de Vaca learned of his good work. Hernando de Montalvo, the royal treasurer in 1579, pointed out that those who had testified against the governor and judged him were the same ones who had overthrown him. However, many people "of good reputation" believed that they had arrested Cabeza de Vaca "without fault" and that "he was a very good governor."[9] Friar Pedro Fernández de la Torre, a newly arrived bishop, stated in 1557 that Cabeza de Vaca's arrest was without cause or reason and that "he was a good governor and had the land in justice and equity."[10] Even so, any praises must be kept in balance. Intense political struggles in the Río de la Plata province after 1545 meant that for many years the name of Cabeza de Vaca was a useful weapon against such rivals as Irala or Cáceres. It became easy, therefore, for Cabeza de Vaca's partisans to recall the good things that he had done while overlooking his pride, quirks, mistakes, or self-interest.

26

If He Were to Go on as He Began

The leaders of the new government stood at great risk. Their reports to the king had to be drafted carefully, for their hold on power could be secure only if they won support in Spain. Domingo de Irala was their chief, so one might expect him to explain and defend at length the shift in power. However, his letter of March 1, 1545, said little about the recent change in governors, dealing primarily with earlier events. Apparently it was more important to him to defend his failure in the futile search for Juan de Ayolas. The account of the rebellion against Cabeza de Vaca was brief: "It appearing to your majesty's officials and to all the people that he exceeded his authority in many areas that were suited to his service and the pacification of the land, and that he had not fulfilled what he had agreed with your majesty, they arrested him and carried him to prison."

Irala's explanation of why he now held power was not revealing: "They required me to accept the duty of lieutenant governor, as I used to have it from your majesty, until something contrary might be provided." A royal cedula, as noted earlier, allowed the colonists to fill vacancies until the king chose someone else. Irala implied that instead of leading the uprising, he was in the background, acting only as the other settlers wished. He remained, he said, "in your majesty's name," preparing to make an entrada, and he hoped "to come out with a great victory." Clearly he expected another entrada to succeed, even though one had just failed.[1]

An anonymous account written in Asunción on March 9, 1545, had a similar focus. Its author sought to provide a helpful report of Irala's efforts after 1537 to reach Ayolas and to point out Cabeza de Vaca's shortcomings. The latter section used unsupported charges, for the writer greatly favored life under Irala: "Everyone was well treated, and he was well-liked by all." Cabeza de Vaca had not really brought help to the colony, for the people who were already there had to supply the food and shelter. The trouble between the first colonists and the new ones emerges. A key problem was how the "old settlers" had been handled. "He never called us less than villains, tyrannizing the land and mistreating all the people by words and deeds." One remark exemplifies the writer's fears: "If [Cabeza de Vaca] were to go on as he began, it was to take from some their farms and from others dwellings and the service of the Indians and Indian women, so that we would come to lose everything."[2] The alarms aroused by Irala and the royal officials had worked well with this writer.

Pedro Dorantes, as royal factor, wrote several times to the king in 1545. Although he had come to the Río de la Plata province with the governor, the two men soon quarreled over policies. As early as 1543, Dorantes complained in a report that the officials had too small a role and that Cabeza de Vaca believed that if he had to consult with them about such matters, he would not be the governor. In 1545, after Dorantes helped to overthrow him, Cabeza de Vaca wrote of once having made a legal case against him for "transgressions."[3]

In a February 28, 1545, letter to the king, Dorantes cited other personal and official failings. The governor had said in public that the king's orders had lost their force. Dorantes also quoted Bernardo de Armenta's rebuke about Cabeza de Vaca's lack of fervor in converting the Indians, the friar's declared reason for trying to flee to the coast of Brazil. Dorantes was quite ready to believe the worst, as is seen in his hearsay "report" about the entrada to Puerto de los Reyes. He had returned to Asunción soon after the journey upriver began, so his account is based on the words of others. He could thus pass on distortions and lies about the governor in good conscience, supposing them to be true and in keeping with his own views. His standing as a man of good repute was useful to the other rebels.

Bitterness and bungling mark his story. Many Spaniards, for example, did not like Cabeza de Vaca's policies on trade with the Indians. He did not plan well and abused the Indian carriers. Worse, when the explorers grew short of food, the men he sent after supplies ravaged eight or nine Indian towns, killing many Indians and taking others captive. The Spaniards did the same to a village of Indians said to be cannibals. Dorantes commented at this point about his dislike for the rule against slave trading. Because the settlers were not allowed to buy from their allies their Indian captives, many more were killed than would be the case if they could be sold. Similar reasoning had earlier prevented medieval theologians in Europe from completely condemning the enslavement of prisoners of war.

Much of Dorantes's account dealt with the change in power. He had supported it because the governor was mistreating the Spaniards and Indians, especially by controlling trade. The colonists had become so upset that many were ready to escape to the coast of Brazil. There were other reasons as well, such as Cabeza de Vaca's remarks about royal orders losing force in America and his displacement of the royal banner on the ship with his own. To report everything that he had spoken or done would take a long time, so Dorantes and the other officials decided to prevent the loss of the colony through poor leadership and lack of wisdom. "Considering in our hearts that for the service of God and your majesty, and for the good of the people and the peace of the land which, by your orders, you entrusted to us, it was suitable to resolve ourselves to arrest him and remove him from the government of this land." [4]

A few days later, on March 5, Dorantes wrote a second letter to the king. His topic now was administrative reform, not the governor. Nevertheless, this letter shows some of the effects of the change in power. A hint of the plight of the Indians in the province can be seen in his advice to select a cleric as their protector. He may have guessed that when Cabeza de Vaca defended himself in Spain, he would stress his success in requiring good treatment and peaceful relations with the Indians. One way to ignore that record might be to argue that a new way of handling these people was needed, using religious rather than civil authority to protect them. Dorantes also restated his disagreement with the governor's ideas on slavery. The Indians went to war to get captives, he claimed, which they took to their villages to kill and eat, so it would be "a service to God and your majesty" if they could freely trade their slaves. As slaves, they would not be killed and eaten, the Spaniards might profit from the labor, and the king could tax the sales.

Two other problems reflect the change in government. First, the method used by the settlers to support themselves was "very harmful to our consciences" and to the Indian population. To sow the land, many Indian women, some of them "very close relatives," lived in the Spaniards' dwellings, and they were living together in such a way "that God must remedy it." This immorality also harmed the Indian men, who now lacked women for themselves and were "not reproducing." Indeed, the Guaraní women had quickly seen that there was an advantage of status from having mestizo rather than Indian children. (In another letter, written July 4, Dorantes warned that the Guaraní males were getting women from the Agaz Indians, their longstanding enemies. The reason for such an alliance was to kill the newcomers, for "they had to try to kill us in order to be left in liberty.") Besides sexual chaos, Dorantes admitted to the rebirth of another evil: the Indian women were being sold as if they were slaves. Although he wanted to use slavery as a cure for cannibalism, he opposed it when its purpose was sexual.

Dorantes argued that Cabeza de Vaca had been removed with the approval of almost all the people. Contrary to much evidence from other writers, he said that there had not been death or bloodshed in the months that the governor had been held "with some shackles in a dwelling of straw." It was true, he granted, that there might be some sorrow among Cabeza de Vaca's relatives or the people who had prospered under his government and perhaps among some idle folk, but the new rulers had support from nearly all the people.[5] In agreement with Dorantes, as expected, was Ulrich Schmidt, perhaps giving the soldiers' viewpoint. "There were some who had been the special friends of our aforesaid chief commander, Alburnunzo Cabessa de Bacha, who were not pleased. But we did not care for that."[6]

Soon, however, Dorantes wished to distance himself from the struggle against the governor. In 1548 he tried to get sworn testimony from witnesses that the overthrow "was not done by his will or advice, nor had he blame in it." Most of them, it turned out, were unwilling to support him.[7] Later, in 1551, Cabeza de Vaca himself excused Dorantes. He wrote to the Council of the Indies that, "having been informed that Pedro Dorantes, against whom I made complaint, was not at fault in my seizure nor for its consequences, . . . I withdraw the complaint and accusation lodged against him."[8] Dorantes's son, also named Pedro, asked for the same thing. In 1548 in Spain he persuaded both Cabeza de Vaca and Hernández to state that he had been too ill to take part in overthrowing the governor.[9]

The rebellion returned power to another former official, Pero Díaz del Valle, who had been mayor of Asunción before Cabeza de Vaca's arrival and recovered that title after his arrest. On March 5 Díaz del Valle drafted for the king another "official" account of events. His story is not clear and has only vague clues to what happened. The governor was arrested "for reasons that the officials of your majesty saw, which were suited to your royal service." Irala took over power because "the officials of your majesty," "the captains," "leading people," and "many others" accepted and obeyed him. The letter also spoke briefly of the loyalists. There were those who did not welcome the new government, it noted. Some still favored the jailed governor, others tried to flee to Brazil, and some wanted Captain Juan de Salazar as lieutenant governor rather than Irala. One of Díaz del Valle's ideas does show a religious outlook that is curious, but not likely unique. There was a great need for prelates to serve as examples of good living, because there were "many vices into which each day we fall." Few of the people were making confession and receiving the sacrament. He feared that "as we have blinded our consciences and understanding, God our Lord may blind to us the ways so that gold and silver cannot be found or discovered." The basis of human virtue, it seems, was the gold and silver that it might bring. At the end of his letter he looked to the Indians. They also needed a priest, "a person of good conscience," because it was important to keep them calm and peaceful as well as to assure their spiritual and physical health.[10] This plea was likely another effort to put in Armenta as protector.

The royal accountant, Felipe de Cáceres, drafted his report on March 7. Of all the hostile writers, he is to be trusted least, as he goes from half-truths to outright lies. His summary began with the root of the trouble, the quinto tax, which he and the officials had levied on goods that the other Spaniards needed for survival. That tax had been revoked to free the poor settlers from a heavy burden, a point that Cáceres did not reveal. Instead, he hinted that the governor somehow would keep the tax money for himself. Likewise, Cáceres would have Charles I believe that the governor's controls over trade between Spaniards and Indians were meant for Cabeza de Vaca's personal well-being.

Many Spaniards disliked Cabeza de Vaca's moral demands and his care for the Indians. Cáceres, nevertheless, said that the settlers were unhappy because of mistreatment, insults, and terror. He added that the governor had also robbed, killed, and enslaved Indians, destroyed their property, taken their women, and provoked them to rebel, no doubt interpreting the events at Puerto de los Reyes. Just a year earlier, in his letter of March 18, 1544, Cáceres had stated that Cabeza de Vaca wanted the Indians to be "regarded and befriended," but such words were not found in this report. He also did not repeat his earlier statement to the governor that the Indians whom the Spaniards attacked had been plotting an uprising.

The letter also brought together the other charges that the rebel leaders had made. It told about the governor's banner where the king's ought to have gone on the ship, his claim to be king or lord of the land, and the phrase about the king's words not carrying across the line of the equinox. Near the end of the letter the accountant aimed his treachery toward Irala. He asked the king to put the province under "a good Christian, zealous of your majesty and of God our Lord, and one very rich."[11] The phrase "very rich" would have excluded Irala, who did not meet that requirement, and suggests that Cáceres did not want him in power for long.[12]

The charges and countercharges between Cabeza de Vaca and his rivals make the truth hard to discover. Open-mindedness was rare when questions of self-interest challenged loyalty to king and religion. One conquistador, however, might be given some notice because he did not like either side. His viewpoint is one possible way of handling the biases found in the other letters of early 1545. Gerónimo Ochoa de Eizaguirre, a son-in-law of Martín de Orúe, wrote on March 8 to the Council of the Indies to denounce both the governor and his foes for their various shortcomings. While much about the Río de la Plata province displeased him, he wanted to share some ideas for making life there better.

Cabeza de Vaca, he stated, mistreated the Indians at Puerto de los Reyes. He had declared war without having been harmed by them at any time, which was a strange charge to make, for even the governor's enemies agreed that the Indians had been plotting and acting against the Spaniards. Also, the controls put on trade between Spaniards and Indians were annoying. Yet removing the governor did not bring relief. When Irala took power again, the Indians suffered even worse, as did Spaniards who were not in the ruling party: "Those people who have power have mistreated so much the ones who are able to do little." The conspirators and their friends were freed from all work and took "all the benefits from the land." One abuse was to buy goods from the Indians and sell them to the other Spaniards at ten times the cost, "whereby to have little comes to have nothing."

The new rulers did even worse things. They had divided the land among themselves, caused some of the people to perish, and would bring death to the rest. "There are so many chiefs among the few of us," he lamented, "and for them there is no lack of partiality." The rebels were taking property by force, so "one cannot expect anything but the total ruin of everybody." The new government had its own orders, controls, and bans against relations with the Indians (although for reasons quite unlike those of Cabeza de Vaca). The people were more like slaves to those who gave the orders "than are the blacks of Guinea to their masters."

The letter ended with an appeal to the king to send good leaders, both civil and religious. The clergy were not as bad as the men who had recently taken over, but even they lacked careful and effective control. In particular, the Indians needed a protector, especially for the women, who suffered abuse in both their labor and sexual roles.[13] Ochoa de Eizaguirre did not write to defend the governor, but his criticism of the royal officials fits well with what Cabeza de Vaca's supporters said.

27

A Completely Poor Caballero

When vessels were finally ready to take away Cabeza de Vaca, the comuneros moved quickly. His last hours in Asunción were naturally fixed into his memory. Near midnight on March 7, 1545, Garci Venegas, Alonso Cabrera, and Pedro Dorantes came to his prison to tell him that he was returning to Spain. Although he was then very sick, "the corpse candle almost in his hand," according to Hernández, two men pulled him out of bed and hauled him away. Seeing the sky for the first time in a year, he begged them to let him give thanks to God.

One last action of defiance was left. Seeing the comuneros in the street with harquebuses ready, he yelled to them to be witnesses that he appointed Captain Juan de Salazar to be lieutenant governor and captain general of the province. At the sound of these words Venegas rushed over, knife in hand, to muzzle Cabeza de Vaca, but again he named Salazar as his successor. Venegas clapped a hand over the governor's mouth, giving him a small wound and knocking down the men who carried him, but threats of harm drew only scorn. "I had not come to that province," he told Venegas, "for any other thing but to die for the service of God and his majesty." A few more shoves got him on board the caravel. Also bound for Spain were Juan Pavón, his long-suffering mayor of Asunción, and Pero Hernández. Although both

Hernández and Cabeza de Vaca stated that the priest Luis de Miranda also went along, historian Enrique de Gandía said that he stayed in America.[1]

A week after the caravel sailed, Salazar acted. On March 13 a servant gave him the document that Cabeza de Vaca had signed naming Salazar lieutenant governor. The next day his clerk, Alonso Gutiérrez, went to Irala's dwellings to read it, but many of the people there "furiously" blocked him.[2] Irala sent Dorantes to talk with Salazar, but Dorantes failed to persuade Salazar to avoid the trouble that would result from making a claim of authority. Both Dorantes and Díaz del Valle, the mayor, doubted that Salazar's document was genuine. The governor had been "in a chamber where he was not seen," Dorantes explained to the king, and the mayor agreed that he was under arrest when "the said authority" was given. Hernández, he added, was in sanctuary in the church.[3] They still did not know about the Indian woman who smuggled in notes.

This uprising was easily quelled. Friar Juan de Salazar declared that 120 friends were on the governor's side, and a list of about one hundred names exists.[4] However, Irala had many more supporters. Soon a mob of comuneros marched on Salazar's house. "Long live the king!" they shouted. "Punish whoever wishes to put the land in an uproar!" Salazar had to be arrested, Dorantes told the king, for if he were not sent away, great turmoil and many deaths would follow. He and the mayor stated that there was danger of murder or arson, but Antonio de Escalera wrote that the uproar and disturbance were caused by the royal officials, men "fearing neither God nor your majesty."[5]

Salazar, in chains, soon followed Cabeza de Vaca. He and the governor's cousin, Pedro de Estopiñán Cabeza de Vaca, were rowed on a bergantín two hundred leagues downriver, and on April 2 they boarded the governor's caravel as prisoners. Besides these two men, a few loyalists were expelled with Cabeza de Vaca. Otherwise, the rebels did not allow anyone to get to Spain who might defend the governor. Only his accusers were free to leave the Río de la Plata.

Danger attended Cabeza de Vaca even as he went toward the ocean. He and Hernández charged that realgar (arsenic sulfide) was put into his food, the second time that poison had been tried against him. Fortunately, he carried a remedy—"a jug of oil and a piece of unicorn." For four days he refused to eat what his enemies gave him until hunger forced it. He asked the guards why they wanted to poison him. One of them, Andrés Hernández el Romo, agreed that he was correct about the poison. Irala and the royal officials wanted him killed after being embarked, he stated, because they dared not do so among his supporters in Asunción. As proof for the king, Cabeza de Vaca added, he now had both the realgar and the letter that ordered his murder.

A great storm hit the ship after it reached the ocean. By the fourth day Garci Venegas and Alonso Cabrera were overcome by fear that God had sent the tempest to punish them for their "injuries and injustices" to the governor. Opening the cabin where he was chained, they freed him and begged his pardon, "saying that what they had done had been from ambition to command and to revenge him because he brought them to law." He was their governor, they said, and they promised to obey him and do as he commanded. When they set him free, wrote Hernández, "the waves and wind and tempest ceased."

This remorse was short-lived. To hide what they had done, recalled Captain Salazar, they began pleading with the governor to toss into the ocean any documents or letters that were on board and to go before the king only to seek help for the province without speaking about events there. They asked him to promise not to tell the king about their part in arresting him. To keep these secrets, those on the caravel would scatter as soon as they got to land. However, Cabeza de Vaca refused to agree. He intended "to give his majesty an account faithfully of what was happening." Other drastic ideas were rebuffed as well. They urged him to turn back to the Río de la Plata, but he thought it better to report to the king. They suggested landing in Portugal to ask the king there to intercede for them, but he would not go to a foreign ruler in place of his "king and natural lord" because he expected justice. After three months in extreme hunger because the storm had spoiled their food, they landed on July 16 at the Azores.[6]

The Azores meant safety and freedom for Cabeza de Vaca. His foes, naturally, grew increasingly fearful of what he might say to the king. As the island of Terceira drew near, they again begged him to join with them, and he again refused. He remained unwilling to sail back to the Río de la Plata, afraid now that his captors wanted to kill him. Accordingly, he decided to take another ship to Spain. The secret package of letters from his friends was already in his hands. While he was still a prisoner on the caravel someone passed him a note, and after he was freed he opened the hiding place and took out the papers. Venegas and Cabrera were greatly shocked to learn about these documents, having believed that only letters hostile to him were coming from the Río de la Plata province. In Hernández's *Comentarios,* the story ends abruptly. The governor's foes got to Spain first, he wrote, and spread lies about him. When he tried to have them arrested, the officials in Seville "did not think it proper." Both sides then went to Madrid, where they were ordered to stay within the jurisdiction of the court.[7] Cabeza de Vaca was to have a trial before the Royal Council of the Indies.

A worse time to defend oneself in Spain for protecting the Indians from abuse cannot be imagined. In a major attempt at reform, Charles I had approved the New Laws in 1542 "for the government of the Indies and good treatment and preservation of the Indians." The checks imposed on the Spaniards in America, especially regarding the *encomienda* system of Indian labor, proved unenforceable. In New Spain strong opposition caused the New Laws to be suspended in part, while in Peru they helped to bring on a civil war that lasted until 1548. The king yielded. By late 1545 and early 1546 he revoked the most unpopular of these laws.[8] Although the Río de la Plata province did not formally have the encomienda system yet, in many ways the overthrow of Cabeza de Vaca looked to be part of the wider struggle between those who would protect Indians and those who would exploit them. The Council of the Indies was in the midst of this crisis when it took the governor's case.

Meanwhile the governor worked steadily on his legal defense. The "Relación general," went to the Council of the Indies signed and dated December 7, 1545. It may have been based on a memoir that he was able to bring back to Spain.[9] On January 20, 1546, the council presented the charges drawn up against him.

The *fiscal* (prosecutor), Marcelo de Villalobos, accused Cabeza de Vaca of robbing Canary Islanders on his way to America; looting two ships at the Cape Verde Islands; not allowing trade with the Indians on the trip from Santa Catalina Island to Asunción; abandoning thirteen people during that trip; robbing Indians of provisions during that trip; giving the Guaranís twenty-five friendly Indians to eat; having Aracaré hanged; using a medal engraved with a cow's head to summon Indians; allowing free Indian girls to be sold; restricting trade with the Guaranís; setting prices so low that slaves were eaten instead of being sold; being guilty on other counts; wiping out four thousand Guaycurúes and nine villages; killing three thousand Socorinos and Los Reyes Indians; branding and selling six Indians as slaves; overloading Indian and Spanish carriers on his entrada; taking property without compensation; interfering with trade; taking the belongings of the deceased; coming to the province without enough supplies; putting his coat of arms in place of the king's; calling himself king and master of the land; engraving his coat of arms with the king's; preventing the royal officials from writing to the king; taking power from the royal officials; attempting to use torture to discover officials' writings; allowing the laws he imposed to be broken; and using royal tax laws for his own benefit.[10]

Between June and August 1546 Cabeza de Vaca had a number of witnesses give answers to seventy-six questions used as evidence on his behalf for the *promotor fiscal* (crown attorney) of the council.[11] In July, he also brought before the council charges against Venegas and Cabrera.[12] However, Cabeza de Vaca found it nearly impossible to defend himself. Evidence for his side was mostly hidden away in America, where it could not be brought before the council. Hostile witnesses outnumbered friendly ones, and in Spain there was little else to go on besides the volume of statements, whether or not they were true. Enrique de Gandía has analyzed and refuted some of these points, and Morris Bishop has related how Cabeza de Vaca denied or explained away most of the charges, but the governor could not match the number of witnesses sent against him and had to ask for more time to get his defense ready.[13]

Time did not help. Not only was Cabeza de Vaca unable to get evidence from America, but the Spanish government acted to replace him there. Juan de Sanabria, a cousin of Hernán Cortés, conqueror of Mexico, got a capitulation from the king on July 22, 1547, to become the next governor and captain general. This document said that "because of the differences and matters that were exhibited between Alvar Núñez Cabeza de Vaca and the people who were in the province, he was brought a prisoner to these kingdoms, and he is not to return again to the province because it is not suitable that he go back to it."[14] Thus, his future looked bleak. Soon thereafter Sanabria died, and his successor and son, Diego, was lost at sea, so Irala retained power while the court case remained unsettled. In 1555 he became the governor. Spain's interest in a land that produced neither mineral wealth nor export goods of value clearly was ebbing.[15]

In Spain, at least, Cabeza de Vaca's enemies came to bad ends. Garci Venegas died "a sudden and wretched death," without being able to tell what had happened in the Río de la Plata province. Alonso Cabrera "lost his senses" and later killed his wife. The two friars, Armenta and Lebrón, also died "suddenly and wretchedly," which, to Hernández, "seemed to prove the little blame" that Cabeza de Vaca had in this affair.[16]

The matter was not nearly as clear to others. Shortly after the return to Spain, Spanish historian Gonzalo Fernández de Oviedo y Valdés talked with people on both sides. Although he had a high regard for Cabeza de Vaca's earlier exploits in North America, his account of the Río de la Plata province followed the viewpoint of his rivals. "This relation the chronicler, Martín de Orúe himself, gave me, and afterwards Garci Venegas saw and approved it." The date was October 1547, the time for holding sessions of the royal councils of Castile and of the Indies. His sources, he admitted, were "rivals and enemies of the governor, Cabeza de Vaca."

The governor did get to see from Oviedo part of what Orúe had said to the government. Oviedo's summary of this report stressed mistreatment of the Indians. Although Cabeza de Vaca had supporters explain to Oviedo what really happened, the historian was not persuaded: "In some things they excused him, and he and they blamed their opponents for having caused rebellion and having him arrested; but at the end, what has happened is what is said." Certainly he doubted that adelantados might do much good, for he added to the story of Cabeza de Vaca and the Río de la Plata province (ch. 11) a tirade against their failures.[17] Thus, Oviedo's account, written in January 1549 and charging Cabeza de Vaca with several outrages against Indians, cannot be trusted without independent support. Not until after 1555, when *Comentarios* was published, did the governor's cause begin to win favor.

The Council of the Indies reached its decision on March 18, 1551. Cabeza de Vaca was condemned to the permanent loss of his position of governor and adelantado of the Río de la Plata province, its government, and all other offices. He also was condemned to permanent exile from all the Indies, under penalty of death, and to serve the king in Orán, North Africa, for five years with his arms and horses at his expense.[18] He quickly sent an appeal to the Council of the Indies. Reminding the officials of the length of time he had been held, he asked them to end his imprisonment. His appeal spoke also of great financial distress, given all that he had lost by seizure after his arrest in Asunción. He could offer no more security than an oath, for no one would bond him because of his poverty. On April 11 the council unanimously ordered that he serve the imprisonment.[19] Another appeal, on August 23, did bring a change. His exile to Orán was lifted and his banishment from all the Indies was limited to the Río de la Plata.[20]

The ending in *Comentarios* is briefer. It says, "After having held him a prisoner and detained him at the court eight years, they declared him free and he went away." However, he had lost his government, and a reason given was that "his opponents said that if he went back to the land, by punishing the guilty, there would be tumults and disturbances." Thus, he was dismissed "without repayment for the great amount that he had spent in the service that he did in going to help and to explore."[21]

His remaining years saw other appeals to the Council of the Indies. None succeeded, and time was running out. Gandía has cited a document that shows Cabeza de Vaca to be alive as late as 1556. Dated at Valladolid on September 15, it states that the king gave him twelve thousand maravedís, "for help to be cured of his illness." Perhaps it meant the end, for another document, written after 1559, states that "he died in Valladolid, a completely poor caballero."[22]

A conquistador in chains appears to be a contradiction in terms. Was Cabeza de Vaca so weak as to be defeated by those he sought to conquer, thus becoming no conquistador at all? Or was he chained by the government of Spain for treason or actions even more heinous than those of other conquistadores? Neither.

Cabeza de Vaca was unique among conquistadores. Although he held the ordinary understanding of *conquest* (to bring newly discovered peoples into subjection to Spain) and although he felt the standard motivations of religion, fame, and wealth that were common to his fellow conquistadores, his attitudes and methods were, for the most part, quite different. Forged by years of hardship in a harsh North American wilderness, Cabeza de Vaca's vision was refined so that he could see—as no other conquistador of his time did—the common humanity of conqueror and conquered. He dreamed of a humane conquest, and he tried to the best of his ability to conduct one in South America. Overthrown at last by fellow Spaniards who could not share his compassionate vision, he emerges from the sixteenth century as a single bright figure in a long night. His chains stand as a graphic indictment of his greed-struck compatriots. Those same chains frame the portrait of a man who tried to practice kindness and justice even in conquest.

Conclusion

"Alvar Núñez Cabeza de Vaca stands out as a truly noble and humane character. Nowhere in the lurid history of the Conquest does one find such integrity and devotion to Christian principles in the face of envy, malice, treachery, cruelty, lechery, and plain greed, as at early Asunción. The entire story . . . makes one sick at heart."[1] Samuel Eliot Morison said it well.

What made Cabeza de Vaca unique for his time? Why would that uniqueness make one of the most famous of twentieth-century North American historians "sick at heart"? The answers lie in the sixteenth-century context of Cabeza de Vaca's life, in his personal life-molding experiences in the land called Florida, in his administration in the Río de la Plata province, and in twentieth-century ideas about imperialism. A brief review of his story, with these questions in mind, can highlight the answers.

Cabeza de Vaca landed in Florida in 1528 to win the expected rewards of another Spanish conquest. As a royal official his chief task was to promote the success of the expedition and the survival of the men under his authority. According to his own account he did quite well, in spite of clashes with the leader of the entrada, Pánfilo de Narváez. Narváez made bad decisions, such as losing contact with his ships and provoking the Indians to war, and he finally deserted his men, leaving them to fend for themselves on the coast of

Texas. Cabeza de Vaca, as next in command, usually had to act to save the expedition, or so his report stated.

The first chapters of his narrative reveal no special interest in the Indians of America. Apart from their prowess as warriors, which aroused professional admiration as a soldier, and their impact on the entrada, he clearly saw them as a people entirely separate from his own. In spite of his responsibility as royal treasurer to have oversight about their treatment, "liberties," and religious instruction, his words and actions were not intended for their benefit. Indeed, he fought the Indians when they merely looked hostile and led the military occupation of the town of Apalache. Such neglect of the Indians' interests, such violence against them, and even the theft of their supplies, of course, were not uncommon among conquistadores, including those holding official positions. Yet the radical change that was soon to come in Cabeza de Vaca is highlighted by the lack of any initial interest in his royal orders about the Indians.

Only the failure of the entrada altered his outlook about the Indians. Shipwrecked and staring starvation and death in the face, Cabeza de Vaca and the other survivors suddenly had their relationship with the Indians entirely reversed. No longer did they take food from defeated or fleeing Indians. Now they begged for it as helpless dependents, accepted it as charity, or worked for it as slaves. The inferior members in such an alliance may well hold on to attitudes of hostility and scorn. For Cabeza de Vaca the truly beneficial outcome was his gradual change of opinion about the Indians. At first, sharing Spanish fears of a sacrificial death, he felt great relief at discovering the obvious pity of the Indians for the wretched seafarers who had been capsized on their island. Thus, he decided to ask for their help, and they agreed to give his men housing and food. Trust slowly began to replace the fear that he had learned while among the Indians of Florida.

It was an unforeseen and modest beginning. During the years in Texas, Cabeza de Vaca's respect for the Indians grew. His life with them, the good and bad parts alike, brought him to a realistic understanding of their culture and humanity. Yet unlike some Spaniards of his era who lived among free Indians and "went native" (Bernal Díaz del Castillo reported the example of Gonzalo Guerrero in Yucatán, and Francisco González Paniagua referred to a pilot who did so in South America),[2] Cabeza de Vaca looked to his own culture and, especially, religion to hold on to his identity.

The key to his changed outlook toward the Indians was the degree of personal growth in Cabeza de Vaca's own religion. Despite the great suffering and danger that they sometimes caused him, even making him a slave, as he was forced to become like them in his way of life, he discovered a bond of common humanity with these people who at first seemed so different from himself. The vital link was their shared need for divine help. He had come to depend on God for his survival, for the cures that were made on the Indians, for the hope that he might escape and return to Spanish territory, and for the understanding that his captivity had some ultimate purpose. Eventually he saw from the torments of Mala-Cosa that the Indians had the same need. Only belief in God and becoming Christians, he believed, could protect them from such demonic attacks. In the most basic of their needs they were like him. It is significant that his long years of distress did not simply make him formally religious in outlook or cause him to seek a religious vocation. His religious growth was that of a layman who had a genuine concern for the Indians. Unlike Christopher Columbus, who (according to Felipe Fernández-Armesto) was able to hold an attitude toward the Indians that was religious but not humane,[3] Cabeza de Vaca's religious insight was much more complete—a new understanding of God and of the American Indians.

During his journey toward New Spain, Cabeza de Vaca began to take charge of the physical welfare of the Indians. Besides healing them, he looked to their feeding. In time he tried to teach them about the Christian religion. Finally, encouraged by the example of a zealous royal official, Melchior Díaz, he came to believe that the best way to bring to the Indians spiritual and material blessings and the values of his civilization and culture was by a conquest that would ensure them liberty and justice. His words to the king were "God our Lord, by His infinite mercy, is willing in the days of your majesty and under your power and dominion, that these peoples come to be truly and with entire goodwill subjects of the true Lord Who created them and redeemed them . . . One sees clearly that to lead all these peoples to be Christians and to submission to the imperial majesty, they have to be brought with good treatment. This way is very certain. Any other way is not."[4] To bring about such a result, Cabeza de Vaca refused Viceroy Antonio de Mendoza's plan to return to Florida and sailed back to Spain to share his ideas with King Charles I.

Fortunately, Cabeza de Vaca was not alone in holding such ideas. Although apparently independent in origin, they were often in agreement with those of the influential Bartolomé de las Casas, who also conceived principles for Christian missions based in part on personal experience in America. During the 1530s Casas wrote *Del único modo,* which advocated persuasion and condemned force in converting the Indians. Later, he used Cabeza de Vaca's *Relación* in his *Apologética historia sumaria* to argue that some of the North American Indians did not engage in idolatry or human sacrifice. Another important parallel was their reluctance regarding Indian slavery. However, while Casas eventually concluded that the wars against Indians were so unjust as to prevent enslavement of them, Cabeza de Vaca ultimately resorted to what he saw as just warfare and allowed some enslavement. Another difference was that Casas understood the grounds for Indian self-defense, unlike Cabeza de Vaca, who could not see that they had a right to make war for freedom or that a Spanish conquest might bring them greater harm than would result from leaving them free.

Thanks to Casas and others, Charles I was aware of the moral focus that Cabeza de Vaca had just learned. He also had need of a man of his ability and experience. Although Hernando de Soto had stepped ahead of him in line to get Florida, an entrada in the Río de la Plata was suffering nearly as badly as the one that Narváez had lost. Cabeza de Vaca's background and ideas about good treatment for the Indians made him a fitting choice to succeed Pedro de Mendoza.

After careful preparation, Cabeza de Vaca and his settlers crossed the Atlantic Ocean. Meeting with the Indians at the Island of Santa Catalina, he applied his ideas about how to manage them while keeping the Spaniards under control. His achievement proved to be unique, and the journey overland to Asunción was a spectacular success. One problem, a portent of future trouble, was the conflict between how he wanted the Indians to be treated and how some of the settlers were treating them. Many Spaniards clearly expected to gain some benefit from the Indians and grew angry with the governor and his policies of separation and fairness. In Asunción the colonists had already learned to survive by depending on the Indians. The Spaniards there became divided, some growing unhappy with his policies while others supported him. Too many of the settlers saw their interests obstructed by Cabeza de Vaca, none more so than the royal officials, who had benefited by exploiting both the Guaraní and Europeans, until the arrival of a royal governor suddenly cut back their hard-won political power.

Cabeza de Vaca's policies shocked the Spaniards and at times the Guaraní too. He decreed that the Indians be treated well and not be harmed, injured, or forced to do the settlers' bidding. They were to be paid for their work, and their belongings were not to be taken. His edicts of April 1542 spoke directly to his goals for Spanish-Indian relations, especially affecting trade. Another important problem was the way that many Spaniards had become joined to the Indian women through kinship, sex, and work, although the governor approached this area with some caution. Adding to the unpopularity of his policies was a degree of pride and arrogance that Spanish settlers might have overlooked or even admired if they had found his ideas more congenial.[5]

Indians also came under Cabeza de Vaca's authority. Many of them showed their trust by appealing to him for justice and safety. At the same time, he expected them to obey Spanish law. An important example was cannibalism, and in April 1542 he ordered the Guaraní to stop the practice. Also, after his peacemaking efforts had clearly failed, hostile Indians could expect to be met with military force, and those who did not keep their agreements with him might be enslaved or even hanged. These sanctions were within his understanding of the exercise of Spanish law.

The loss of the quinto taxes united the royal officials against the governor, and there was no turning back for them until they ousted him from power. First they plotted with the two Franciscans to smuggle letters to the king. When that attempt failed, they discussed assassinating him during the entrada to Puerto de los Reyes. After returning to Asunción, they coaxed a number of other Spaniards to join a rebellion and seized—or retook—power for themselves.

A significant point in that contest was that many of the settlers supported the governor. Some of them, and not only the clergy, shared his moral outrage at Spanish misconduct and agreed with his goals for reform. Others supported him because of loyalties based on regional origins and kinship ties. Many had experienced, suffered, or feared the abuses of power during Domingo de Irala's first governorship. However, they failed to overcome the clever planning and skillful tactics used to overthrow Cabeza de Vaca, although at least they kept him alive and ensured his safe return to Spain. His policies and their effective enforcement struck at the self-interests of too many Spaniards. Appeals to moral and religious values that had become real to him during his years in North America did not win enough of a response to bring success for his policies in the Río de la Plata province. The primary conflict arose from the differences between his reasons for a Spanish conquest and those of the colonists who joined with the royal officials to overthrow him.

Silver and gold were the great lures that brought settlers to the Río de la Plata province. When it began to appear that the region was misnamed, the Spaniards who remained there had to find other attractions and means of survival. To maintain a Spanish community where mineral wealth was not to be found required making use of Guaraní kinship, labor, and sexual customs. For Cabeza de Vaca, each of these violated in some way the vision that he had for the settlement. Labor was to be paid for, not used to create ties between Spanish and Guaraní chiefs. Kinship and sexual relations were to follow Spanish and Christian customs, not those of the Indians. Altogether, whether or not he understood the forces that had grown in the colony before his arrival, he was seeking to adjust and reform the foundations of a society that initially was based on the self-interest of both Spaniards and Guaraní Indians.

The Spaniards in the Río de la Plata province expected to control the Guaraní Indians. Their model was the peasants (or Muslim captives) in contemporary Spain. Settlers came to the New World hoping to become landowners and perhaps even to rise to the level of hidalgo. This goal required the labor of a peasant-type population. Cabeza de Vaca himself saw political, economic, and social relations between the settlers and Indians in these terms. The idea of forming something other than the hierarchical structure of Spanish society, as it existed in Spain or America did not enter his mind. As a man of his era, he could hardly be expected to think in any other terms. To safeguard the North American Indians who came to him for protection from Spanish slavers, he had already taken on the role of a kind of lord. What he tried to do in South America was to ensure for the Indians the protection provided by Spanish legal and social structures and the Christian religion.

Spaniards in the Río de la Plata province escaped many of the social and religious restraints that existed in Spain. They had not usually experienced and thus did not share very much of Cabeza de Vaca's vision of a Christian and humane conquest or his goals of upholding justice within the bonds of a human society. Thus, they resented and opposed his interference in their efforts to apply the exploitative methods of Spanish control, learned in part during the Reconquista, to the Indians. Their requirements of labor and service, the social and political submission, and the sexual abuses all were made easier to impose because they were similar to customs of the Guaraní Indians. Irala and his partners did not need to work hard to organize their conspiracy. They had already spent several years creating the society they wanted, only to have their interests frustrated after Cabeza de Vaca arrived. Even some of the people who came to Paraguay with the governor favored the old, unreformed ways rather than his system.

That Cabeza de Vaca was overthrown should surprise no one. His ideas and policies went against the clear self-interest of many of the Spaniards who were attracted to America in the first place. It is significant that he was able to inspire and hold a strong group of defenders among the Spanish colonists in America and that they remained loyal to him during his time in prison and after his return to Spain. His overthrow affected the region for decades, as his enemies and defenders formed parties that struggled for influence and created a legacy for their followers. Although the governor lost his position, support for him remained strong among those writing letters to Spain during the next generation. That rehabilitation is beyond this study, but his memory clearly was honored by many of those who did not directly benefit from his arrest and exile. Despite the short time that he held power, Cabeza de Vaca did make an important difference. For those who shared his concerns, the brief era of his administration was inspiring. On a larger scale, publication of *Comentarios* (and *Naufragios*) in 1555 allowed him to make an effective statement of his philosophy about how to treat the American Indians: their destruction violated the laws of Spain and the teachings of Christianity.

One question, however, cannot presently be answered. Would Cabeza de Vaca's ideas have succeeded if he had won the favor of more of the Spaniards in the Río de la Plata province? Or, was the whole idea of a just conquest simply absurd? This question rocked sixteenth-century Spain and America, beginning with Kings Charles I and Philip II, provoking debates, treatises, legislation, lawsuits, and rebellion. Yet late-twentieth-century observers find it difficult to sympathize with Cabeza de Vaca's approach to cultural domination despite his concern for justice and legality or his gifts for working with Indian peoples at different stages of development. More time is needed before imperialism can be treated with enough dispassion for that kind of analysis. For the conquered, a just conquest is no less a conquest—not the worst type, perhaps, but still to be avoided.

INTRODUCTION

1. Cabeza de Vaca, *Relación de los naufragios y comentarios,* ed. Serrano y Sanz, 1: chs. 1, 38. Translations from Spanish into English are by the author.

2. "Probanza de méritos y servicios del Factor y Oficial Real Pedro Dorantes," in *Correspondencia de los oficiales reales,* ed. Levillier, 1:237 (hereafter *COR*). For other testimony about Cabeza de Vaca's age, see "[Información levantada a pedido de Gonzalo de Acosta para justificar sus servicios en el Río de la Plata]," in *Documentos históricos y geográficos,* ed. Torre Revello, 5:237 (hereafter *DHG*).

3. Gandía, *De la torre del oro a las Indias,* 95–129; Bishop, *The Odyssey of Cabeza de Vaca,* 3–10; Cabeza de Vaca, *Castaways,* 130–32. For the lighter side of Cabeza de Vaca's connection with the Duke of Medina Sidonia, see Cabeza de Vaca, *Naufragios,* ed. Maura, 22–25. For a brief look at the revolt of the *comuneros,* see Lynch, *Spain under the Hapsburgs,* 1:36–45. For a longer study, see Haliczer, *The Comuneros of Castile.* For a portrait thought to be of Cabeza de Vaca, see Cabeza de Vaca, *Castaways,* 2.

1. SEEING THE POORNESS OF THE LAND

1. Most of what is known of Cabeza de Vaca in North America is from Serrano y Sanz, ed., *Relación,* vol. 1, which includes Cabeza de Vaca's narrative of the years in North America. Other editions of this account are Cabeza de Vaca's *La relación de los naufragios de Alvar Núñez Cabeza de Vaca,* ed. Favata and Fernández; *Naufragios,* ed. Pupo-Walker; *Naufragios y comentarios; Naufragios,* ed. Maura. Translations of this work include *Relation of Nuñez Cabeza de Vaca;* "The Narrative of Alvar Nuñez Cabeza de Vaca"; *Cabeza de Vaca's Adventures in the Unknown Interior of America; Castaways: The narrative*

of Alvar Núñez Cabeza de Vaca; and *The Account: Alvar Núñez Cabeza de Vaca's* Relación.

In addition, Cabeza de Vaca and two other survivors made a brief report of events, which is now lost but was used by a Spanish historian, Gonzalo Fernández de Oviedo y Valdés (1478–1557), in *Historia general y natural de las Indias,* vol. 3 (bk. 35, chs. 1–7). English translations of this report appear in Cabeza de Vaca, *The Narrative of Alvar Núñez Cabeza de Vaca,* and in Quinn, ed., *New American World,* 2:15–59, 59–89.

Also, a brief, undated summary of events prior to Cabeza de Vaca's landing at Texas exists: "Relación de Cabeza de Vaca, tesorero que fué en la conquista," in *Colección de documentos inéditos,* ed. Pacheco, Cárdenas, and Torres de Mendoza, 14:269–79.

2. Oviedo, *Historia general,* 3 (bk. 35, ch. 4):602. For an English translation, see Quinn, ed., *New American World,* 2:77.

3. "Capitulations between Charles V and Pánfilo de Narváez," in *New American World,* ed. Quinn, 2:4–10; "Petitions of Narváez to the King of Spain, with Notes of Concessions Made to Him by the Council of Indias for the Conquest of Florida," in Cabeza de Vaca, *Relation of Nuñez Cabeza de Vaca,* 207–11. For Narváez in Jamaica and Cuba, see Casas, *Historia de las Indias,* vol. 2. For Narváez and Cortés, see Díaz del Castillo, *Historia verdadera de la conquista de la Nueva España,* chs. 58–75.

4. "Instructions Given to Cabeza de Vaca for His Observance as Treasurer to the King of Spain in the Army of Narváez for the Conquest of Florida," in Cabeza de Vaca, *Relation of Nuñez Cabeza de Vaca,* 221. For what seems to be an early draft, see "Relacion del viaje de Pánfilo de Narváez al Río de las Palmas hasta la punta de la Florida, hecha por el tesorero Cabeza de Vaca" (1527), in *Colección de documentos inéditos,* ed. Pacheco, Cárdenas, and Torres de Mendoza, 14:265–69.

5. Cabeza de Vaca, *Relación,* chs. 1–3; Parry, *The Spanish Seaborne Empire,* 95. For the debate about the landing site, see Marrinan, Scarry, and Majors, "Prelude to de Soto," 73. For evidence that the landing occurred near Tampa Bay and a brief look at the geographical and cultural background in Florida, see Mitchem, "Initial Spanish-Indian Contact in West Peninsular

Florida," 49–50, 52, 54, and Milanich, "The European Entrada into La Florida," 5–7.

6. Cabeza de Vaca, *Cabeza de Vaca's Adventures,* 15.

7. For a summary of the North American Indian cultures related to Cabeza de Vaca's travels, see Cabeza de Vaca, *Castaways,* appendix B.

8. Cabeza de Vaca, *Relación,* ch. 3. For these Indians, likely to be Timucuans, see Dobyns, *Their Number Become Thinned,* 148–211. See also Swanton, *The Indians of the Southeastern United States,* 37, 193–94; plates 42, 51, 53, 55, 57, 81, 82, 87, 97, 98, and 106.

9. "Instructions Given to Cabeza de Vaca," in Cabeza de Vaca, *Relation of Nuñez Cabeza de Vaca,* 221.

10. Fernández, *Alvar Núñez Cabeza de Vaca,* 121.

11. Cabeza de Vaca, *Relación,* ch. 4; Milanich, "European Entrada," 11. For the Spanish obsession with gold, see McAlister, *Spain and Portugal,* 80–81.

12. Arciniegas, *Latin America,* 84.

13. Cabeza de Vaca, *Relación,* chs. 4–5. For the *entrada,* see McAlister, *Spain and Portugal,* 96–100.

14. Hann, *Apalachee,* 5, 24–26; Marrinan, Scarry, and Majors, "Prelude to de Soto," 74–76. See also Milanich and Hudson, *Hernando de Soto and the Indians of Florida,* 226–28. For the Apalache Indians, see Swanton, *Indians of the Southeastern United States,* 89–91.

15. Cabeza de Vaca, *Relación,* chs. 5–7. For Cabeza de Vaca's anthropological merit, see Pupo-Walker, "Los *Naufragios* de Alvar Núñez Cabeza de Vaca," 765.

16. Fernández, *Alvar Núñez Cabeza de Vaca,* 121.

17. For archaeological analysis of possible sites of Aute, see Marrinan, Scarry, and Majors, "Prelude to de Soto," 76–77; Mitchem, "Artifacts of Exploration," 101, 103.

18. Cabeza de Vaca, *Relación,* chs. 7–8. For the site of the Bay of Horses boat works on Apalachee Bay and the impact of the Narváez quest on the Indians, see Marrinan, Scarry, and Majors, "Prelude to de Soto," 75, 78–79. For identifications of possible diseases, see Dobyns, *Their Number Become Thinned,* 262, 270.

19. Cabeza de Vaca, *Relación,* chs. 9–10. For the landing site, see Campbell and Campbell, *Historic Indian Groups,* 3.

20. Cabeza de Vaca, *Relación,* chs. 15, 17.

2. SO MISERABLE AN EXISTENCE

1. For the twenty-three Indian groups of Texas named in Cabeza de Vaca's book, see Campbell and Campbell, *Historic Indian Groups,* 9–40. For the Indians of Texas and the Southwest, including northern Mexico, see also Hinton, "Southern Periphery: West," 315–28; Griffen, "Southern Periphery: East," 329–42; Campbell, "Coahuiltecans and Their Neighbors," 343–58; and Newcomb, "Karankawa," 359–67.

2. Newcomb, "Karankawa," 359–60, 362–65; Aten, *Indians of the Upper Texas Coast,* 28–30. For nonsedentary Indian characteristics, see Lockhart and Schwartz, *Early Latin America,* 34–36.

3. Cabeza de Vaca, *Relación,* ch. 12.

4. Ibid., chs. 14–15. For an analysis of how the Spanish survivors adapted and used Indian practices, see Pupo-Walker, "Los *Naufragios,*" 768ff, and Adorno, "The Negotiation of Fear," 163ff.

5. Cabeza de Vaca, *Relación,* ch. 14. For discussion of possible causes of these deaths, see Dobyns, *Their Number Become Thinned,* 261, and Ashburn, *The Ranks of Death,* 160.

6. Campbell and Campbell, *Historic Indian Groups,* 32–33; map, 2.

7. Cabeza de Vaca, *Relación,* chs. 13, 15–16.

8. Campbell and Campbell, *Historic Indian Groups,* 11.

9. Cabeza de Vaca, *Relación,* chs. 16–17, 19, 38. For the debate about whether Estebanico was an African or an Arab, see Weber, *The Spanish Frontier in North America,* 277, n. 53.

10. Krieger, "The Travels of Alvar Núñez Cabeza de Vaca in Texas and Mexico," 460, 466; Campbell, "Coahuiltecans," 351–52; Campbell and Campbell, *Historic Indian Groups,* 6, 13–23.

11. For the Avavares Indians, see Campbell and Campbell, *Historic Indian Groups,* 24–27. For the debate about Cabeza de Vaca's route, see Chipman, "In Search of Cabeza de Vaca's Route Across Texas." For the most reliable

tracing of that route (according to Chipman), see Krieger, "Travels of Alvar Núñez Cabeza de Vaca," as adjusted by Campbell and Campbell, *Historic Indian Groups,* 6–7.

12. Oviedo, *Historia general,* 3 (bk. 35, ch. 4), 602; Quinn, ed., *New American World,* 2:77.

13. Cabeza de Vaca, *Relación,* chs. 19–22.

14. Pupo-Walker, "Los *Naufragios,*" 767. For the debate later caused by this healing, see Lafaye, "Los 'milagros' de Alvar Núñez Cabeza de Vaca," 76–84.

15. Cabeza de Vaca, *Relación,* chs. 22, 31; Acosta, *Historia natural y moral de las Indias,* 372.

16. Oviedo, *Historia general,* 3 (bk. 35, ch. 6), 610; Quinn, ed., *New American World,* 2:84.

17. Vega, *Historia de la Florida,* bk. 5, pt. 1, ch. 2. For English translations, see Vega, *The Florida of the Inca;* or *La Florida,* in *The De Soto Chronicles,* ed. Clayton, Knight, and Moore, vol. 2. For doubts about the reliability of Vega, see Henige, "The Context, Content, and Credibility of *La Florida del Ynca.*"

18. For Espejo, see "Relacion del viage," in *Colección de documentos inéditos,* ed. Pacheco, Cárdenas, and Torres de Mendoza, 15:107. For an English translation, see Quinn, ed., *New American World,* 5:377–78; see also Krieger, "Travels of Alvar Núñez Cabeza de Vaca," 468, n. 7.

19. "Letter from a Missionary to the Provincial of New Spain Respecting the Arrival of Indians in Cinaloa from the Pimeria Baja, in Quest of Friends Who Eighty Years before Had Followed Alvar Nuñez and His Comrades," in Cabeza de Vaca, *Relation of Nuñez Cabeza de Vaca,* 223–25.

3. WE LEFT THE WHOLE LAND IN PEACE

1. Cabeza de Vaca, *Relación,* ch. 22. For Cabeza de Vaca's nakedness, see Pastor Bodmer, *The Armature of Conquest,* 137, 139–40; and Pupo-Walker, "Pesquisas para una nueva lectura de los *Naufragios,*" 529–30.

2. Cabeza de Vaca, *Relación,* chs. 28–29.

3. For Cabeza de Vaca's role as the first anthropological observer of the American Indians, see Pastor Bodmer, *The Armature of Conquest,* 142.

4. Cabeza de Vaca, *Relación,* ch. 25.

5. For a careful analysis of the Indian societies that Cabeza de Vaca visited, see Campbell and Campbell, *Historic Indian Groups,* 10–40.

6. Cabeza de Vaca, *Relación,* chs. 24–25.

7. For these Indian groups, see Campbell and Campbell, *Historic Indian Groups,* 29–30, 38–40.

8. Cabeza de Vaca, *Relación,* ch. 28; Krieger, "Travels of Alvar Núñez Cabeza de Vaca," 461–67, 470–71.

9. Griffen, "Southern Periphery," 330, 334; map, 329.

10. Cabeza de Vaca, *Relación,* chs. 27–28.

11. Ibid., ch. 15.

12. Ibid., ch. 29.

13. Ibid., chs. 27–28. For the importance of such "looting" to Cabeza de Vaca's journey, see Adorno, "Negotiation of Fear," 178–79.

14. Cabeza de Vaca, *Relación,* ch. 28.

15. Ibid., chs. 24, 26.

16. Ibid., ch. 30.

17. Ibid., chs. 30–31; Krieger, "Travels of Alvar Núñez Cabeza de Vaca," 468–69, n. 7.

18. For the Jumanos Indians, see Griffen, "Southern Periphery," 329–42. For Espejo, see Pacheco, Cárdenas, and Torres de Mendoza, eds., *Colección de documentos inéditos,* 15:107.

19. Cabeza de Vaca, *Relación,* ch. 31. For the location of Corazones, see Krieger, "Travels of Alvar Núñez Cabeza de Vaca," 472; and Hedrick, "The Location of Corazones."

20. Cabeza de Vaca, *Relación,* ch. 31. For an analysis of the Indians' fear of the men, see Adorno, "Negotiation of Fear," 172–88.

4. TO LEAD ALL THESE PEOPLES TO BE CHRISTIANS

1. Cabeza de Vaca, *Relación,* ch. 32; Oviedo, *Historia general,* 3 (bk. 35, ch. 6), 611.

2. For the religious conversion of Casas, see his *Historia de las Indias,* bk. 3, ch. 79. For an English translation, see Casas, *History of the Indies,* 208–11.

3. Bartolomé de las Casas, "De unico vocationis modo omnium gen-

tium ad veram religionem," published in Spanish as *Del único modo de atraer todos los pueblos a la verdadera religión*. For an introduction and translation into English, see Casas, *The Only Way*. Chapter titles in part 2, "False Evangelization," show his viewpoint: "Wars of conversion contradict the human way," "Wars contradict the way of Christ," "Wars contradict the way of the missioner," "Wars contradict the way of the Christian," "The brutal missionary," and "Papal condemnation of armed oppression." For cases where Casas did concede a right of military action (as against cannibalism), see Carro, "The Spanish Theological-Juridical Renaissance," 270, 272.

4. Fernández, *Alvar Núñez Cabeza de Vaca,* 122.

5. Friede, "Las Casas and Indigenism in the Sixteenth Century," 146, 149–53, 165.

6. Casas, *Apologética historia sumaria,* bk. 3, chs. 74, 168 (also chs. 205, 206, 210); Giménez Fernández, "Fray Bartolomé de Las Casas," 86–89, 107–12; Keen, Introduction, 5. For Casas's use of Cabeza de Vaca's writings, see Adorno, "The Discursive Encounter of Spain and America," 220–27.

7. "Instructions Given to Cabeza de Vaca," in Cabeza de Vaca, *Relation of Nuñez Cabeza de Vaca,* 221.

8. Cabeza de Vaca, *Relación,* ch. 32.

9. Ibid., ch. 33; Oviedo, *Historia general,* 3 (bk. 35, ch. 6), 612; Cabeza de Vaca, *Cabeza de Vaca's Adventures,* 129; Krieger, "Travels of Alvar Núñez Cabeza de Vaca," 473.

10. Cabeza de Vaca, *Relación,* ch. 34.

11. Krieger, "Travels of Alvar Núñez Cabeza de Vaca," 473. For the location of Culiacán, see Brand, "Erroneous Location."

12. Cabeza de Vaca, *Relación,* ch. 35. For the *Requerimiento,* see Hanke, "The Requirement and its Interpreters"; Hanke, "The Development of Regulations for Conquistadores"; and Parry and Keith, eds., *New Iberian World,* 1:386–88. For Casas's use of Aguar, see his *Apologética historia sumaria,* bk. 3, ch. 74.

13. Cabeza de Vaca, *Relación,* ch. 35.

14. Adorno, "Negotiation of Fear," 191.

15. For the location of San Miguel, see Krieger, "Travels of Alvar Núñez Cabeza de Vaca," 473.

16. Cabeza de Vaca, *Relación,* ch. 36. For Cabeza de Vaca's ideology of empire, see Adorno, "Negotiation of Fear," 188–91. A league was about three statute miles (Parry and Keith, eds., *New Iberian World,* 5:xii).

17. Casas, *Apologética historia sumaria,* bk. 3, ch. 74.

5. NOT TO GO UNDER ANOTHER'S BANNER

1. Krieger, "Travels of Alvar Núñez Cabeza de Vaca," 473. See also Brand, "Erroneous Location," 193–201.

2. Krieger, "Travels of Alvar Núñez Cabeza de Vaca," 460–61.

3. Cabeza de Vaca, *Relación,* ch. 36.

4. Tello, *Libro segundo de la crónica miscelánea,* 229; González de Barcia Carballido y Zúñiga, *Ensayo cronológico para la historia general de la Florida,* 20. For an English translation, see González de Barcia Carballido y Zúñiga, *Barcia's Chronological History of the Continent of Florida.*

5. "Carta de D. Antonio de Mendoza á la emperatriz," México, Feb. 11, 1537, in Pacheco, Cárdenas, and Torres de Mendoza, eds., *Colección de documentos inéditos,* 14:235.

6. Cabeza de Vaca, *Relación,* ch. 37.

7. "Carta a Su Majestad de los ofyciales de la Contratacion de Sevilla," Sevilla, Nov. 8, 1537, in Pacheco, Cárdenas, and Torres de Mendoza, eds., *Colección de documentos inéditos,* 42:530. For the Casa de Contratación, see Haring, *The Spanish Empire in America,* 297–300.

8. "Concession Made by the King of Spain to Hernando de Soto of the Government of Cuba and the Conquest of Florida, with the Title of Adelantado," in *The De Soto Chronicles,* ed. Clayton, Knight, and Moore, 1:359–65. Also in Quinn, ed., *New American World,* 2:93–96. See also Milanich and Hudson, *Hernando de Soto,* 26–35.

9. "The Account by a Gentleman of Elvas," in *The De Soto Chronicles,* ed. Clayton, Knight, and Moore, vol. 1, ch. 2; Quinn, ed., *New American World,* vol. 2.

10. "The Account by a Gentleman of Elvas," in *The De Soto Chronicles,* ed. Clayton, Knight, and Moore, ch. 1; Hoffman, "Hernando De Soto," in *The De Soto Chronicles,* 1:427–34, 447. For Soto's marriage to a daughter of Pedrarias, see 449–50.

11. Oviedo, *Historia general,* 1:547, 566–67.

12. Casas, *Tratados de Fray Bartolomé de las Casas,* 1:157. For an English translation, see Casas, *The Devastation of the Indies.*

13. "The Account by a Gentleman of Elvas," in *The De Soto Chronicles,* ed. Clayton, Knight, and Moore, ch. 14.

14. Ibid., ch. 2.

15. Cabeza de Vaca, *Relación,* ch. 32.

16. "The Account by a Gentleman of Elvas," in *The De Soto Chronicles,* ed. Clayton, Knight, and Moore, ch. 2.

17. Ibid., ch. 35.

18. Cabeza de Vaca, *Relación,* chs. 31–32.

6. TO CONQUER AND PACIFY AND POPULATE THE LANDS

1. "Letter from Joao Fernando Lagarto to John the Third, King of Portugal," in *A Collection of Documents Relating to Jacques Cartier and the Sieur de Roberval,* ed. Biggar, 81. Also in Quinn, ed., *New American World,* 1:330.

2. Métraux, "The Guaraní," 3:75–76. See also Métraux, "Tribes of the Eastern Slopes of the Bolivian Andes," 3:465–66.

3. Susnik, *El rol de los indígenas,* 1:39, 42.

4. Schmidt, "The Voyage of Ulrich Schmidt to the Rivers La Plata and Paraguai," in *The Conquest of the River Plate,* ed. Dominguez, 6–12. For these Indians, see Lothrop, "Indians of the Paraná Delta and La Plata Littoral."

5. Parry, *The Discovery of South America,* 242–54.

6. "[Instrucción que el adelantado don Pedro de Mendoza dejó a nombre de Juan de Ayolas]," Buenos Aires, Apr. 21, 1537, in *DHG,* 2:190–92; "Testimonio de la provisión de don Pedro de Mendoza nombrando teniente de gobernador á Juan de Ayolas," Buenos Aires, Apr. 20, 1537, in *Anales de la Biblioteca,* 8:145–52; "Traslado de las instrucciones que dejó don Pedro de Mendoza, gobernador del Río de la Plata, á Juan de Ayolas su lugar teniente," Buenos Aires, Apr. 21, 1537, in *Anales de la Biblioteca,* 8:152–56; "Provisión de Don Pedro de Mendoza nombramiento teniente de gobernador a Juan de Ayolas," Buenos Aires, Apr. 20, 1537, in *Archivo colonial,* 1:184–91; and "Traslado sacado de una instrucción que Don Pedro de Mendoza dejó a Juan

de Ayolas, su lugarteniente de gobernador, al tiempo que se embarcó para España," Buenos Aires, Apr. 21, 1537, in *Archivo colonial,* 1:192–96.

7. "Carta de Domingo de Irala, al Emperador," Mar. 1, 1545, in *DHG,* 2:419. Also in Lafuente Machain, *El gobernador Domingo Martínez de Irala,* document L; and Serrano y Sanz, ed., *Relación,* 2:379–95. For an English translation, see Parry and Keith, eds., *New Iberian World,* 5:265–70.

8. "[Información de los servicios prestados por Gonzalo de Acosta en el Río de la Plata]," Asunción, Jan. 12, 1545, in *DHG,* 5:204–5; "[Información levantada a pedido de Gonzalo de Acosta para justificar sus servicios en el Río de la Plata]," Madrid, Jan. 20, 22, 1546, in *DHG,* 5:237; Groussac, *Mendoza y Garay,* 198–99; Lafuente Machain, *Conquistadores del Río de la Plata,* 27–28. For Acosta's career, see Medina, *El Portugués.*

9. Herrera y Tordesillas, *Historia general,* dec. 7, bk. 2, ch. 8. For an English translation, see idem., *The General History.*

10. "The Account of a Gentleman of Elvas," in *The De Soto Chronicles,* ed. Clayton, Knight, and Moore, ch. 14.

11. *DHG,* 2:267–72; 5:51–141, 197–98; Gandía, *Historia de Alonso Cabrera,* 61–65, 191–92.

12. "Capitulación que se tomó con Alvar Núñez Cabeza de Vaca," Madrid, Mar. 18, 1540, in *Colección de documentos inéditos,* ed. Pacheco, Cárdenas, and Torres de Mendoza, 23:10; and "Capitulación del Rey con Alvar Núñez Cabeza de Vaca," Madrid, Mar. [1]8, 1540, in *Archivo colonial,* 1:338. For the debate raised in Spain at this time about the treatment of the American Indians, see Friede, "Las Casas and Indigenism," 151–53. For the Spanish coinage system, see Davies, *The Golden Century of Spain,* 295–96.

13. Parry, *Spanish Seaborne Empire,* 98. For the position of *adelantado,* see Haring, *Spanish Empire,* 19–22.

14. Pacheco, Cárdenas, and Torres de Mendoza, eds., *Colección de documentos inéditos,* 23:8–33; *Archivo colonial,* 1:337–45; Tau Anzoátegui, ed., *Libros registros-cedularios,* 70–71. For background, see Madero, *Historia del puerto de Buenos Aires,* 180; Rubio, *Exploración y conquista del Río de la Plata,* 161–62; and Sierra, *Historia de la Argentina,* 1:239–40. For biographical sketches of the Europeans in the early Río de la Plata province, see Lafuente Machain, *Conquistadores.*

15. "R. P. para que en virtud de lo capitulado con Alvar Nuñez Cabeza de Vaca, se le de licencia para conquistar en las provincias del Río de la Plata desde el dicho río hasta la mar del Sur, con mas 200 leguas en la dicha costa que comienzan desde donde termina la gobernación encomendada a don Diego de Almagro hasta el estrecho de Magallanes," Madrid, Apr. 15, 1540, in *Anales de la Biblioteca*, 8:301–3.

16. Tau Anzoátegui, *Libros registros-cedularios*, 70–72.

17. Hanke, "Development of Regulations," 74–79. For an English translation of the 1526 cedula, see Quinn, ed., *New American World*, 2:6–10, note on 96.

18. Hanke, *The Spanish Struggle*, 72–77, 80; Brading, *The First America*, 64–65, 84–85; Parry, *Spanish Seaborne Empire*, 183; and Pagden, *The Fall of Natural Man*. For an English translation of *Sublimis Deus*, see Quinn, ed., *New Iberian World*, 1:386–88. For an English translation of Vitoria's lecture, "On the American Indians," see Vitoria, *Political Writings*, 233–92.

19. "R. P. para que, sequn lo tiene suplicado Alvar Nuñez Cabeza de Vaca, no pueda pasar al Río de la Plata ningun procurador ni abogado, para excusar pleitos y debates entre pobladores y conquistadores, por diez años á contar desde la fecha," Madrid, July 1, 1540, in *Anales de la Biblioteca*, 8:304.

20. Díaz del Castillo, *Historia verdadera*, ch. 159.

21. "Concessions made by the King of Spain to Hernando de Soto," in *The De Soto Chronicles*, ed. Clayton, Knight, and Moore, 1:363. Also in Quinn, ed., *New American World*, 2:95.

22. "Provanza hecha por parte de Albar Nuñez Caveza de Baca para el pleyto que sigue con el fiscal de S. M. sobre los cargos y acusaciones que le tiene puestos," Xerez de la Frontera, July 28, 1546, in *Relación*, ed. Serrano y Sanz, 2:109–12, 115–16; Tao Anzoátegui, ed., *Libros registros-cedularios*, 71, 74.

23. Susnik, *El indio colonial del Paraguay*, 1:13–17. See also Susnik, *El rol de los indígenas*, 1:72.

24. "R. C. al gobernador del Río de la Plata para que haga diligencias del paradero del factor don Carlos de Guevara, y si éste hubiese fallecido acaten y reconozan en dicho cargo á Pedro Dorantes," Madrid, Mar. 16, 1540, in *Anales de la Biblioteca*, 8:299–300; *COR*, 1:151. For feudalism, señorialism, and clientage in Spain, see McAlister, *Spain and Portugal*, 28–29 (n. 10), 38–40.

25. Serrano y Sanz, ed., *Relación,* 2:3, 111–12, 115–16, 138, 150, 195, 204, 246–47; Hernández and Cabeza de Vaca, *Comentarios de Alvar Núñez Cabeza de Vaca,* in *Relación,* ed Serrano y Sanz, 1: ch. 1 (hereafter *Comentarios*). See also Service, *Spanish-Guarani Relations,* 20–21, 24. For the titles of royal cedulas dealing with Cabeza de Vaca's outfitting, see Tao Anzoátegui, ed., *Libros registros-cedularios,* 70–78; and Molina, *Misiones argentinas,* 394–97.

26. Friede, "Las Casas and Indigenism," 135–36.

27. Cabeza de Vaca, "Relación general," in *Relación,* ed. Serrano y Sanz, 2:1–98.

28. *Comentarios,* 1:145–368. For an English translation, see "Commentaries of Alvar Núñez Cabeza de Vaca, governor of the Río de la Plata," in *The Conquest of the River Plate,* ed. Dominguez, 95–262. Cabeza de Vaca, "Prohemio," in *Relación,* ed. Serrano y Sanz, 1:148. For another piece of the official version of these events, see the letter from Hernández to the king, "Relación de las cosas sucedidas en el Río de la Plata," Asunción, Jan. 28, 1545, in *Relación,* ed. Serrano y Sanz, 2:307–58; in *DHG,* 2:393–409; and in *Archivo colonial,* 2:14–48. For a partial English translation with a brief evaluation, see Parry and Keith, eds., *New Iberian World,* 5:282–84. For the veracity of Hernández, see also Gandía, *Historia de la conquista,* 60, n. 17.

29. Serrano y Sanz, ed., *Relación,* 1:xxi; Rubio, *Exploración y conquista,* 166–67.

7. TO LOOK FOR A WAY THROUGH THE CONTINENT

1. *Comentarios,* chs. 1–3; Serrano y Sanz, ed., *Relación,* 2:3; Gandía, *Historia de la conquista,* 97, n. 9.

2. Hemming, *Red Gold,* 244–45, 264, 491–93 (map, 3); Susnik, *El rol de los indígenas,* 1:50 (map, 72); and Métraux, "The Guaraní," 69–70.

3. Susnik, *El rol de los indígenas,* 1:32–56 (map, 72); Susnik, *Los aborígenes del Paraguay,* 2:45–46 (map, 172), and for the pre-conquest Guaraní background, see part 1.

4. Métraux, "The Guaraní," 69–70.

5. Serrano y Sanz, ed., *Relación,* 2:4.

6. *Comentarios,* ch. 3.

7. *DHG,* 5:205–6, 214–15, and testimony for Acosta, 208–23; Medina, *El Portugués,* 87–89; Serrano y Sanz, ed., *Relación,* 2:8.

8. Córdoba, *La orden franciscana,* ch. 3; Córdoba, *Los franciscanos,* 12–24; Mateos, "El primer concilio," 278, 286; Lafuente Machain, *Conquistadores,* 66–67, 350.

9. *Comentarios,* ch. 3; Serrano y Sanz, ed., *Relación,* 2:4–5.

10. *Comentarios,* ch. 4; Serrano y Sanz, ed., *Relación,* 2:5–7, 113. For the Payaguáes and the death of Ayolas, see Susnik, *El rol de los indígenas,* 2:137.

11. *Comentarios,* chs. 3, 5; Serrano y Sanz, ed., *Relación,* 2:4–5, 8; *DHG,* 2:430–31, 5:205–19; "Albar Nuñez Cabeza de Vaca en su reemplazo á Hernando de Alvarado en el puerto de Vera," in *El archivo nacional de la Asunción,* 121–22; Gandía, *Historia de la conquista,* 98–99, n. 12.

12. "Carta del Factor del Río de la Plata, D. Pedro de Orantes, al Rey," Asunción, 1543[?], in *COR,* 1:60.

13. *Comentarios,* ch. 5; Serrano y Sanz, ed., *Relación,* 2:7.

14. [Letter of Fray Bernardo de Armenta to Charles I, Paraguay, Oct. 10, 1544], in Millé, *Crónica de la orden Franciscana,* 117.

15. Nowell, "Aleixo Garcia and the White King"; Susnik, *Los aborígenes,* 2:47–48; Susnik, *El rol de los indígenas,* 1:38–39, 42–43; Métraux, "Tribes of the Eastern Slopes," 465–66; Warren, *Paraguay,* 36. For Cabeza de Vaca's effort in 1543 to trace Garcia's Paraguay River route, see *Comentarios,* ch. 50.

16. *COR,* 1:59–61, 151, 153, 161–63; *Comentarios,* ch. 5; Serrano y Sanz, ed., *Relación,* 2:7–8; *DHG,* 5:206; Medina, *El Portugués,* 89–90; "Relación del piloto Juan Sánchez de Vizcaya," Río de la Plata, [1554], in *Archivo colonial,* 2:118; Lafuente Machain, *Conquistadores,* 191–93, 616–17.

17. *Comentarios,* chs. 4–5; Serrano y Sanz, ed., *Relación,* 2:5, 113.

18. "Petición de don Andrés Montalvo," Valladolid, May 23, 1557, in *Archivo colonial,* 2:203, 206, 209, 212; Lafuente Machain, *Conquistadores,* 431–33.

19. *Comentarios,* chs. 6–7; Serrano y Sanz, ed., *Relación,* 2:9, 14.

8. THE GOOD TREATMENT THAT WAS DONE TO THEM

1. *Comentarios,* ch. 6; Serrano y Sanz, ed., *Relación,* 2:9; *DHG,* 2:431; *COR,* 1:61.

2. *Comentarios,* chs. 6–7, 10–11, 37; Serrano y Sanz, ed., *Relación,* 2:9–12, 113–14; *DHG,* 5:206–7; Medina, *El Portugués,* 90–91.

3. Susnik, *El indio colonial,* 1:17–18; Susnik, *Los aborígenes,* 2:50–51; Susnik, *El rol de los indígenas,* 1:72.

4. Hanke, *Spanish Struggle for Justice,* chs. 5–6; Biermann, "Bartolomé de las Casas and Vera Paz," 443–84.

5. *Comentarios,* chs. 7, 10–11; Serrano y Sanz, ed., *Relación,* 2:12–14, 322–23; Gandía, *Historia de la conquista,* 103, n. 27.

6. *Comentarios,* chs. 6–12; Serrano y Sanz, ed., *Relación,* 2:15–16, 31, 248–49; Cabeza de Vaca, *Relación,* ch. 32; Susnik, *El rol de los indígenas,* 1:15–16; Métraux, "The Guaraní," 80; Service, *Spanish-Guarani Relations,* 14–15.

7. Casas, *Apologética historia sumaria,* bk. 3, chs. 59–60.

8. *Comentarios,* ch. 9; Serrano y Sanz, ed., *Relación,* 2:13, 327; *DHG,* 2:431; Lockhart and Schwartz, *Early Latin America,* 10; Gandía, *Historia de la conquista,* 101–2, n. 26; Millé, *Crónica,* 117–18; Mateos, "El primer concilio," 286–87.

9. *COR,* 1:60–62, 163, 193.

10. *Comentarios,* ch. 11; Serrano y Sanz, ed., *Relación,* 2:16–18, 322; *DHG,* 5:207; Medina, *El Portugués,* 91–92; *COR,* 1:62. For the use of body painting as a defense against evil spirits and feathers as charms in battle, see Karsten, *The Civilization of the South American Indians,* 3–6, 93–95. For Guaraní use of paint and ornaments, see Métraux, "The Guaraní," 83.

11. *Comentarios,* chs. 10, 12; Serrano y Sanz, *Relación,* 2:5, 115, 223–25, 250–51; *DHG,* 5:206–7; Medina, *El Portugués,* 91; Morison, *The European Discovery of America,* 549–50, 560. For Cabeza de Vaca's construction of ten bergantinas, see *Comentarios,* ch. 36.

9. AS WAS CUSTOMARY IN THE KINGDOM OF SPAIN

1. For the background to Spanish settlement of the Río de la Plata, see Gandía, *Historia de la conquista;* Gandía, *Historia de Alonso Cabrera;* Lafuente Machain, *El gobernador Domingo Martínez de Irala;* Chaves, *Descubrimiento;* Warren, *Paraguay.*

2. Susnik, *El rol de los indígenas,* 1:71.

3. "[Información de méritos y servicios del capitán Gonzalo de Mendoza]," Asunción, Feb. 15–Mar. 3, 1545, in *DHG,* 5:246–47; *Anales de la Biblioteca,* 8:359–60; Lafuente Machain, *Conquistadores,* 594–98; Bishop, *Odyssey of Cabeza de Vaca,* 184.

4. Schmidt, "The Voyage of Ulrich Schmidt," 22; Huffines, "The

Original Manuscript of Ulrich Schmidl"; Lafuente Machain, *Conquistadores,* 628.

5. "Carta de Francisco de Villalta," June 22, 1556, in Schmidel [Schmidt], *Viaje al Río de la Plata,* 312–13. For an English translation of Villalta's letter, see Parry and Keith, eds., *New Iberian World,* 5:257–63. See also Lafuente Machain, *Conquistadores,* 686–87.

6. Lafuente Machain, *Conquistadores,* 324–38. For a biography of Irala, see Lafuente Machain, *El gobernador Domingo Martínez de Irala.*

7. "[R. C. por la que se concede el título de veedor de las provincias del Río de la Plata, a Alonso de Cabrera]," in *DHG,* 2:150–52; Lafuente Machain, *Conquistadores,* 110–12. For a biography of Cabrera, see Gandía, *Historia de Alonso Cabrera.*

8. "[R. C. en donde se determina que, por falta de gobernador del Río de la Plata, los pobladores pueden elegir libremente quien lo sustituya]," Valladolid, Sept. 12, 1537, in *DHG,* 2:149–50. Also in *Anales de la Biblioteca,* 8:178–80. See also Rivarola, *La ciudad de la Asunción,* 1:30–32.

9. López, *The Revolt of the Comuneros,* 7.

10. "Declaración y sentencia del veedor Alonso de Cabrera," Buenos Aires, Dec. 20, 1538–Jan. 10, 1539, in *Archivo colonial,* 1:272; "Las diligencias q hizo [en el puerto de Nuestra Señora de Buen Aire] El S^(or.) capitan alonso cabrera]," Buenos Aires, Dec. 20, 1538–Jan. 10, 1539, in *DHG,* 2:255–57.

11. "[Instrucción dejada por don Pedro de Mendoza al capitán Francisco Ruiz Galán]," Apr. 20, 1537, in *DHG,* 5:336. Related documents appear in *Anales de la Biblioteca,* vol. 8 and in *Archivo colonial,* 1: documents 46, 48, 52. See also Lafuente Machain, *Conquistadores,* 579–81.

12. Schmidel, *Viaje,* 314–15; "[Relación anónima de algunos sucesos ocurridos en la conquista del Río de la Plata]," Asunción, Mar. 9, 1545, in *DHG,* 2:455–56; "Relación anónima sobre los sucesos ocurridos en el Río de la Plata," Asunción, Mar. 9, 1545, in *Anales de la Biblioteca,* 8:305–14. For an English translation of this work, see Parry and Keith, eds., *New Iberian World,* 5:270–74. See also Serrano y Sanz, ed., *Relación,* 2:311; *Comentarios,* ch. 75.

13. "Proceso hecho por orden del gobernador del Río de la Plata, Alvar

Núñez Cabeza de Vaca," Asunción, June 11–July 3, 1543, in Gandía, *Historia de Alonso Cabrera,* 335–68.

14. "Notificación por Alonso Cabrera, á los oficiales reales del Río de la Plata," Buenos Aires, Nov. 18, 1538, in *Anales de la Biblioteca,* 8:213–73; "Información de cierta fuerza que hizo Francisco Ruiz Galán," Buenos Aires, Feb. 25, 1539, in *Archivo colonial,* 1:285ff; *DHG,* 2:251–57, 273–89; Serrano y Sanz, ed., *Relación,* 2:312; Lafuente Machain, *El gobernador,* ch. 7; "Requerimiento del Capitan Domingo de Irala al veedor Cabrera," Asunción, June 20, 1539, 377–81. For suggested sites of Candelaria between present-day Coimbra and Corumbá, Brazil, see Parry and Keith, eds., *New Iberian World,* 5:287, n. 2; Hemming, *Red Gold,* 241 (map, 3–4); Gott, *Land without Evil,* 74 (map, [303]); and Morison, *European Discovery of America,* 576 (map, 551). For the Jesuit Candelaria, located near modern Posadas, Argentina, see Warren, *Paraguay,* 90 (map, 91).

15. *DHG,* 2:273–88; Lafuente Machain, *El gobernador,* document B.

16. "[Expediente relacionado con el requerimiento hecho por Alonso de Cabrera, veedor]," Apr. 10–16, 1541, in *DHG,* 2:295–99. Also in Lafuente Machain, *El gobernador,* documents C, D; *Archivo colonial,* 1: document 55; and Serrano y Sanz, ed., *Relación,* 2:368–77. See also Chaves, *Descubrimiento y conquista,* 138, n. 263.

17. "La relación q. dexo domingo minez deyrala en buenos ayres al tpo q. la despoblo," [1541], in *DHG,* 2:299–302; Lafuente Machain, *El gobernador,* document D; Serrano y Sanz, ed., *Relación,* 2:361–68. For an English translation, see Parry and Keith, eds., *New Iberian World,* 5:274–76.

18. Serrano y Sanz, ed., *Relación,* 2:251–52, 315–16.

19. "Fragmento de la información hecha in Valladolid," Jan. 21, 1558, in Gandía, *Historia de Alonso Cabrera,* 415.

20. "[Información mandada levantar por el adelantado, Alvar Núñez Cabeza de Vaca, para dar cuenta al Rey]," Aug. 22–Sept. 11, 1543 (misdated 1544 by the editor), in *DHG,* 2:361–62; "[Escrito de Alvar Núñez Cabeza de Vaca elevado a los miembros del Consejo Real de las Indias]," Madrid, July 15, 1546, in *DHG,* 2:479. For these charges, see also the legal testimony given in June and July 1543, in Gandía, *Historia de Alonso Cabrera,* 335–68.

21. Gandía, *Historia de la conquista,* 95–96, n. 3; Serrano y Sanz, ed., *Relación,* 2:67.

22. Sánchez Quell, *Estructura y función del Paraguay colonial,* 60; Lafuente Machain, *El gobernador,* 76, 80, 83.

23. "Carta de doña Isabel de Guevara á la princesa gobernadora doña Juana," July 2, 1556, in *Cartas de Indias,* 2:619–21. For an English translation, see Parry and Keith, eds., *New Iberian World,* 5:264–68.

24. *DHG,* 2:299; Parry and Keith, eds., *New Iberian World,* 5:274.

25. "Fundación de la ciudad de N. S. de la Asunción del Paraguay," Asunción, Sept. 16, 1541, document 4, in Aguirre, "Diario," 2:238–42; López, *Revolt of the Comuneros,* 8.

26. For the lack of gold or silver for use as money, see "Creación de monedas," Asunción, Oct. 3, 1541, document 5, in Aguirre, "Diario," 2:243–44. See also Lafuente Machain, *El gobernador,* 415–16. For an English translation, see Parry and Keith, eds., *New Iberian World,* 5:307–8.

27. Pastore, "Introducción a la historia política del Paraguay," 107, 109; Lafuente Machain, *El gobernador,* 115.

28. "Relación de las cosas sucedidas en el Río de la Plata," Jan. 28, 1545, in Serrano y Sanz, ed., *Relación,* 2:312–22; *DHG,* 2:395–97.

29. *Comentarios,* ch. 13; Serrano y Sanz, ed., *Relación,* 2:18–19, 114–16, 225–26, 250–52, 322–23; *DHG,* 2:458; *Anales de la Biblioteca,* 8:312; Gandía, *Historia de la conquista,* 106–7, n. 40.

30. *Comentarios,* ch. 14; Serrano y Sanz, *Relación,* 2:22.

31. Millé, *Crónica,* 118; *COR,* 1:62–63; Serrano y Sanz, ed., *Relación,* 2:22; Schmidt, "Voyage of Ulrich Schmidt," 35.

32. "Información hecha en Xerez," Jerez de la Frontera, Sept. 30–Oct. 7, 1545, in Serrano y Sanz, ed., *Relación,* 2:9, 295; *Comentarios,* ch. 6. For the importance of regional bonds, see Kicza, "Patterns in Early Spanish Overseas Expansion," 250.

33. *DHG,* 2:431.

34. Serrano y Sanz, ed., *Relación,* 2:295–96; *Comentarios,* ch. 37.

35. *Comentarios,* ch. 34; Serrano y Sanz, ed., *Relación,* 2:20; Gandía, *Historia de la conquista,* 110, n. 48.

36. *DHG*, 5:248–49; *Anales de la Biblioteca*, 8:364.

37. *Comentarios*, ch. 37; Serrano y Sanz, ed., *Relación*, 2:31.

10. THE PARADISE OF MUHAMMAD

1. *Comentarios*, ch. 15.

2. Serrano y Sanz, ed., *Relación*, 2:22–23, 116, 324.

3. Ibid., 2:116, 143, 181, 197–98, 227, 253; Millé, *Crónica*, 118.

4. Susnik, *El indio colonial*, 1:9–10, 187; Susnik, *Los aborígenes*, 2:47–49; Susnik, *El rol de los indígenas*, 1:35–36, 69–71; Métraux, "Tribes of Eastern Bolivia and Madeira," 3:437.

5. Service, *Spanish-Guarani Relations*, 7, 20. For estimates of the Indian and Spanish populations of Paraguay, see Bertoni and Gorham, "The People of Paraguay," 109–19.

6. *DHG*, 2:299; Parry and Keith, eds., *New Iberian World*, 5:274.

7. Cardozo, *El Paraguay colonial*, 64–65.

8. Service, *Spanish-Guarani Relations*, 20 (see also 16, 19, 35–37); Service, "The *Encomienda* in Paraguay," 233–34.

9. Susnik, *Los aborígenes*, 2:49–50; Susnik, *El rol de los indígenas*, 1:27–28, 73–74; Susnik, *El indio colonial*, 1:10–11.

10. Salas, *Crónica florida del mestizaje de las Indias*, 183; Service, *Spanish-Guarani Relations*, 34–35.

11. Schmidt, "Voyage of Ulrich Schmidt," 20, 22.

12. Susnik, *El indio colonial*, 1:10–11.

13. Service, *Spanish-Guarani Relations*, 17, 20, 27–30.

14. Warren, *Paraguay*, 132.

15. For a discussion of affinity and its most celebrated sixteenth-century case, see Scarisbrick, *Henry VIII*, ch. 7, esp. 183–86.

16. Serrano y Sanz, ed., *Relación*, 2:28–30, 298, 323. For the status of Indian women and changes resulting from the Spanish conquest, see Susnik, *El indio colonial*, 1:13–14; and Susnik, *El rol de los indígenas*, 1:79–80, 85.

17. "Carta a Don Juan Tavira, arzobispo de Toledo, de Alonso Agudo," Feb. 25, 1545, in Gandía, *Luis de Miranda*, 90–91; Davies, *Golden Century of Spain*, 36.

18. *DHG*, 2:449.

19. "[Carta de Gerónimo Ochoa de Eizaguirre, dirigida a los miembros del Consejo Real de las Indias]," Mar. 8, 1545, in *DHG*, 2:453–54; Lafuente Machain, *Conquistadores*, 459–60.

20. Serrano y Sanz, ed., *Relación*, 2:289; Lafuente Machain, *Conquistadores*, 546–47.

21. *COR*, 1:122–23.

22. "[Carta del presbítero Francisco de Andrada, dirigida al Consejo Real de las Indias]," Mar. 1, 1545, in *DHG*, 2:417; Lafuente Machain, *Conquistadores*, 49.

23. Millé, *Crónica*, 121.

24. Susnik, *El rol de los indígenas*, 1:88.

25. "Carta de Domingo Martínez al Emperador Don Carlos," July 2, 1556, Asunción, in *Cartas de Indias*, 2:623. For an English translation, see Parry and Keith, eds., *New Iberian World*, 5:313.

26. Susnik, *El rol de los indígenas*, 1:73–74.

27. "Estatutos y ordenanzas que mandó publicar el Gobernador D. Alvar Núñez Cabeza de Vaca, sobre el trato y gobierno de los indios," Apr. 5, 1542, in García Santillán, *Legislación*, 347–54; "Decretos del adelantado Alvar Núñez Cabeza de Vaca," Apr. 5 and 16, 1542, in Fitte, *Hambre y desnudeces en la conquista*, 293–96; Service, *Spanish-Guarani Relations*, 38; Zavala, *Orígenes*, 82, 119, n. 161; Susnik, *El rol de los indígenas*, 1:78–79.

28. "Carta del Contador y Oficial Real, Felipe de Caceres á S. M.," Asunción, Mar. 7, 1545, in *COR*, 1:86.

29. "Carta del Factor Don Pedro de Orantes, al Rey," Asunción, Feb. 28, 1545, in *COR*, 1:77.

30. Friede, "Las Casas and Indigenism," 168–70. For an English translation of the New Laws, see Parry and Keith, eds., *New Iberian World*, 1:348–59.

31. Serrano y Sanz, ed., *Relación*, 2:37, 324; *DHG*, 2:367–68; Lafuente Machain, *Conquistadores*, 140.

32. *DHG*, 2:446.

33. Serrano y Sanz, ed., *Relación*, 2:143, 293.

34. "Carta de Martín González, clérigo, al Emperador Don Carlos," June 25, 1556, in *Cartas de Indias*, 2:609; Lafuente Machain, *Conquistadores*, 277.

1. Serrano y Sanz, ed., *Relación,* 2:8, 23–24, 116, 323–24; *Comentarios,* ch. 16; *DHG,* 2:397; Gandía, *Indios y conquistadores en el Paraguay,* 33. For Guaraní cannibalism, see Métraux, "The Guaraní," 88; and Métraux, "Warfare, Cannibalism, and Human Trophies," 5:400–406; Susnik, *El rol de los indígenas,* 1:52–53. For Old World interest in cannibalism, see Pagden, *Fall of Natural Man,* 80–93.

2. Cabeza de Vaca, *Relación,* ch. 14. For cannibalism among these Indians of Texas, see Newcomb, "Karankawa," 366.

3. "[Relación de la conquista del Río de la Plata hecha por Gregorio de Acosta]," [1572?], Río de la Plata, in *DHG,* 2:486. This document also appears in *Archivo colonial,* 175–84. For an English translation, see Parry and Keith, *New Iberian World,* 5:279. See also Schmidt, "Voyage of Ulrich Schmidt," 10; Lafuente Machain, *Conquistadores,* 28–29.

4. "[R. C. dirigida al gobernador y demás autoridades del Río de la Plata en donde concede perdón a los cristianos que, por necesidad, comieron carne humana]," Valladolid, Nov. 20, 1539, in *DHG,* 2:175–76.

5. Serrano y Sanz, ed., *Relación,* 2:36; Service, *Spanish-Guarani Relations,* 18.

6. *Comentarios,* ch. 16.

7. "Los religiosos requieren al gouernador que no consienta tener esclauos a los carios por que les meten la tierra adentro y los comen," Asunción, Sept. 28, 1542, in Millé, *Crónica,* 329–33; Zavala, *Orígenes de la colonización,* 85–87.

8. "Información hecha por Alvar Núñez Cabeza de Vaca," in Gandía, *Luis de Miranda,* 84.

9. *DHG,* 2:359–92 (misdated 1544 by the editor).

10. *Comentarios,* ch. 16.

11. Serrano y Sanz, ed., *Relación,* 2:78, 352; *Comentarios,* ch. 82; *DHG,* 2:480.

12. Métraux, "Ethnography of the Chaco," 1:224 (map, 198); Susnik, *Los aborígenes,* 1:93–97; Ganson, "The Evueví of Paraguay," 461, 466; Hemming, *Red Gold,* 395–402.

13. "[Carta de Hernando Ribera, al Emperador]," Asunción, Feb. 25, 1545, in *DHG*, 2:412; Serrano y Sanz, ed., *Relación*, 2:363. See also *DHG*, 2:300.

14. Chaves, *Descubrimiento y conquista*, 138–39, n. 263. For Cabeza de Vaca's account of this event, see Serrano y Sanz, ed., *Relación*, 2:36.

15. Lafuente Machain, *Conquistadores*, 114.

16. Serrano y Sanz, ed., *Relación*, 2:313–14; *DHG*, 2:394.

17. Métraux, "Ethnography of the Chaco," 214–25.

18. Schmidt, "Voyage of Ulrich Schmidt," 18–19, 23.

19. Serrano y Sanz, ed., *Relación*, 2:363; *DHG*, 2:300.

20. Serrano y Sanz, ed., *Relación*, 2:35.

21. *Comentarios*, ch. 17; Susnik, *Los aborígenes*, 1:98–99.

22. *Comentarios*, ch. 17; *COR*, 1:63, 66–67.

23. Susnik, *Los aborígenes*, 1:100–101.

24. See Métraux, "Ethnography of the Chaco," 214–15 (map, 198); Susnik, *El rol de los indígenas*, 1:12, 17; 2:94; Susnik, *Los aborígenes*, 1:63, 72, 88–92; Hemming, *Red Gold*, 386–95, 493.

25. *Comentarios*, chs. 19, 26. For the role of some Guaycurú women as a labor force in the later colonial era, see Saeger, "Eighteenth-Century Guaycuruan Missions in Paraguay," 66.

26. Susnik, *Los aborígenes*, 1:65.

27. *Comentarios*, ch. 20; *COR*, 1:63–64; Service, *Spanish-Guarani Relations*, 18; Métraux, "Ethnography of the Chaco," 215. For Guaycurú livelihood, see Susnik, *El rol de los indígenas*, 2:95ff, and Saeger, "Another View of the Mission as a Frontier Institution," 495–96. For Guaycurú warfare, see Ganson, "Evueví," 472–76.

28. Cabeza de Vaca, *Relación*, ch. 35.

29. *Comentarios*, chs. 20, 22, 25. For the exaggeration of numbers, see Susnik, *El indio colonial*, 1:19; Métraux, "Ethnography of the Chaco," 217.

30. *Comentarios*, chs. 20–21; Susnik, *El rol de los indígenas*, 1:79, 2:98.

31. *Comentarios*, ch. 24.

32. Velásquez, *Breve historia de la cultura*, 20–21.

33. Métraux, "Ethnography of the Chaco," 365. For shamanism, see ibid., 360–65; and Susnik, *El indio colonial*, 1:222–24.

34. Serrano y Sanz, ed., *Relación,* 2:25–26; *Comentarios,* ch. 24.

35. *Comentarios,* chs. 25–26.

36. Ibid., ch. 29.

37. Susnik, *Los aborígenes,* 1:80–81.

38. *Comentarios,* ch. 30; Métraux, "Ethnography of the Chaco," 312; for the status of slaves later in the colonial era among the Mbayá-Guaycurú people, see 307–8. See also Saeger, "Eighteenth-Century Guaycuruan Missions," 82, n. 48.

39. *Comentarios,* ch. 31; Serrano y Sanz, ed., *Relación,* 2:24–25, 327.

40. Susnik, *Los aborígenes,* 1:81–82, 96.

41. Saeger, "Eighteenth-Century Guaycuruan Missions," 80, n. 34.

42. Serrano y Sanz, ed., *Relación,* 2:24–25.

43. Métraux, "Ethnography of the Chaco," 227; Susnik, *Los aborígenes,* 1:63–69 (map, 114).

44. *Comentarios,* chs. 27, 32; Susnik, *Los aborígenes,* 1:101–2.

45. *Comentarios,* ch. 32; Bishop, *Odyssey of Cabeza de Vaca,* 215.

46. Susnik, *Los aborígenes,* 1:67.

47. *DHG,* 2:359–60 (misdated 1544 by the editor).

12. THEY WOULD GO FROM THE LAND AND LEAVE THEM FREE

1. *Comentarios,* ch. 28.

2. "Carta del Factor D. Pedro De Orantes al Rey, sobre guerra con los Indios" (1542?), in *COR,* 1:68.

3. *Comentarios,* ch. 33; Serrano y Sanz, ed., *Relación,* 2:35–37, 127–28; *COR,* 1:66–69.

4. *COR,* 1:68.

5. *Comentarios,* chs. 73–74; "Junta que celebró en su casa el teniente de gobernador Juan de Salazar de Espinosa," Asunción, Mar. 14, 1544–Aug. 29, 1545, in *Archivo colonial,* 1:436–68.

6. *Comentarios,* chs. 34–35; Serrano y Sanz, ed., *Relación,* 2:34–35, 128–30; Gandía, *Historia de la conquista,* 114, n. 63; Susnik, *El rol de los indígenas,* 1:81.

7. Serrano y Sanz, ed., *Relación,* 2:35, 37, 130, 379–95; *DHG,* 2:423; Lafuente Machain, *El gobernador,* 109 and document L; Parry and Keith, eds.,

New Iberian World, 5:265–70; *Comentarios,* ch. 37; *COR,* 1:64; Schmidt, "Voyage of Ulrich Schmidt," 37–38.

8. Susnik, *El indio colonial,* 1:19. For a discussion of the Guaraní failure to organize effective resistance against Spanish control, see 1:215ff.

9. Susnik, *El rol de los indígenas,* 1:43, 85; Susnik, *Los aborígenes,* 2:50–51.

10. *Comentarios,* ch. 37; Serrano y Sanz, ed., *Relación,* 2:127–30, 187–88, 200–201, 232–35, 265–66, 392.

11. For the *Requerimiento,* see Hanke, "The Requirement and Its Interpreters," 4–5. For Casas, see Martínez, "Las Casas on the Conquest of America," 323.

12. Moreno, *La ciudad de Asunción,* 78–83; Rubio, *Exploración y conquista,* 166–67. See also Gandía, *Historia de la conquista,* 116, n. 68.

13. Pacheco, Cárdenas, and Torres de Mendoza, eds., *Colección de documentos inéditos,* 23:16–17; *Archivo colonial,* 1:342–43; Susnik, *El rol de los indígenas,* 1:81.

14. *Comentarios,* ch. 39; "[Declaraciones hechas por diversos indígenas que fueron interrogados por el capitán Domingo Martínez de Irala]," Dec. 18, 1542–Jan. 25, 1543, in *DHG,* 2:314–20, 398. Also in *Anales de la biblioteca,* 8:339–52; and Lafuente Machain, *El gobernador,* 399–414. For a partial translation into English, see Parry and Keith, eds., *New Iberian World,* 5:443–45. Serrano y Sanz, ed., *Relación,* 2:32–33, 324–25; Nowell, "Aleixo Garcia," 450–66.

15. *Comentarios,* ch. 38; Serrano y Sanz, ed., *Relación,* 2:34, 42, 226; Zubizarreta, *Historia de mi ciudad,* 43–44.

16. *Comentarios,* ch. 40; Serrano y Sanz, ed., *Relación,* 2:201, 235–37. For Guaraní obligations regarding revenge, see Susnik, *El rol de los indígenas,* 1:81, and Susnik, *Los aborígenes,* 2:27–28, 55.

17. *Comentarios,* ch. 41; Serrano y Sanz, ed., *Relación,* 2:37–38.

18. Schmidt, "Voyage of Ulrich Schmidt," 38–39. For alternative casualty figures, see Díaz de Guzmán, "Argentina," bk. 2, ch. 2.

19. Susnik, *El rol de los indígenas,* 1:82.

20. *Comentarios,* ch. 42; Serrano y Sanz, ed., *Relación,* 2:37–38, 235–38, 392–93; Schmidt, "Voyage of Ulrich Schmidt," 39; for a later uprising by Tabaré, in 1546, see 58–61.

21. Schmidt, "Voyage of Ulrich Schmidt," 37–39, 41, 50–52; Morison, *European Discovery of America,* 583. For other opinions of Schmidt's reliability, see Huffines, "The Original Manuscript of Ulrich Schmidel," 206; Parry, *Discovery of South America,* 253; and Cunninghame Graham, *The Conquest of the River Plate,* 8. For the role of vengeance in Guaraní warfare, see Métraux, "Warfare, Cannibalism, and Human Trophies," 384.

22. Gandía, *Historia de la conquista,* 131–32.

23. "Información sumaria seguida ante el alcalde mayor Pedro de Valle," July 15–Aug. 21, 1544, in *Archivo colonial,* 1:360–61. For Pedro Dorantes's version, see *COR,* 1:85.

24. Susnik, *El indio colonial,* 1:221.

13. THAT THEY MIGHT BE THE GOVERNORS AND NOT HE

1. Zorraquín Becú, *La organización,* 87; Gandía, *Historia de Alonso Cabrera,* 142, 339; Lafuente Machain, *Conquistadores,* 110–12, 114–15, 677. For the four royal officials used in early colonial administration, see Haring, *Spanish Empire,* 279.

2. Serrano y Sanz, ed., *Relación,* 2:33; Lafuente Machain, *Conquistadores,* 309–10, 477–79.

3. "[R. C. por la que se designa contador de la provincia del Río de la Plata a Felipe de Cáceres], Madrid, Oct. 24, 1539," in *DHG,* 2:172–73; "[R. C. por la que se designa a Martín de Orue, escribano público]," Valladolid, Nov. 20, 1539, in *DHG,* 2:176–77; "[R. C. por la que se concede, al contador Felipe de Cáceres, título de regidor]," Valladolid, Nov. 20, 1539, in *DHG,* 2:178; Gandía, *Historia de la conquista,* 98, n. 11; 146, n. 132; Lafuente Machain, *Conquistadores,* 114–15, 477–79.

4. Serrano y Sanz, ed., *Relación,* 2:28, 311, 322, 325–26; *DHG,* 2:362, 393, 397–98; Gandía, *Historia de Alonso Cabrera,* 339, 342, 345, 347, 349–52, 354–55, 357, 359–60, 363, 365–66, 368. For the *quinto,* see Haring, *Spanish Empire,* 259–60. For the lack of gold or silver for money in 1541, see Aguirre, "Diario," 2:243–44. Lafuente Machain, *El gobernador,* 415–16; Parry and Keith, eds., *New Iberian World,* 5:307–8.

5. *Comentarios,* chs. 18, 43; Serrano y Sanz, ed., *Relación,* 2:28; Gandía, *Historia de Alonso Cabrera,* 339 and passim; Gandía, *Historia de la conquista,*

125, n. 86. For conflicts between governors and royal officials, see Haring, *Spanish Empire,* 281.

6. "Testimonio de los requerimientos que hicieron los Oficiales Reales al Gobernador Cabeza de Vaca para que se junte con ellos a deliberar y tratar en todo lo que convenía a la Gobernación del Río de la Plata," excerpts in Gandía, *Historia de la conquista,* 127–28, n. 90.

7. Serrano y Sanz, ed., *Relación,* 2:31–32.

8. *DHG,* 2:362–91; Gandía, *Historia de Alonso Cabrera,* 339, 360, 363, 365–66, 368.

9. *DHG,* 2:437; "Carta del clérigo presbítero Antonio de Escalera al Emperador Don Carlos," Apr. 25, 1556, in *Cartas de Indias,* 2:584f.

10. Díaz de Guzmán, "Argentina," bk. 2, ch. 3; Laconich, *Caudillos,* 37.

11. *COR,* 1:84–85.

12. "Información de Fray Po. Fernandez obispo de las provincias del Río de la Plata," Asunción, Aug.–Sept. 1564, in *Colección,* ed. Garay, 1:87–88, 93.

13. Lafuente Machain, *El gobernador,* 186–87.

14. Serrano y Sanz, ed., *Relación,* 2:39–41, 327–29; *DHG,* 2:399; *Comentarios,* ch. 43.

15. "Carta del Factor Pedro de Orantes, al Rey," Asunción, June 8, 1543, in *COR,* 1:70–71.

16. *Comentarios,* ch. 43; Zavala, *Orígenes de la colonización,* 50–53.

17. Garay, ed., *Colección,* 1:93–94; Lafuente Machain, *Conquistadores,* 210.

18. *Comentarios,* ch. 43; Serrano y Sanz, ed., *Relación,* 2:39–41.

19. Millé, *Crónica,* 118–19.

20. Serrano y Sanz, ed., *Relación,* 2:134–35, 148, 190, 211–12, 242–44; *COR,* 1:244–45.

21. *DHG,* 2:436.

22. "[Carta de fray Juan de Salazar, de la Orden de la Merced, dirigida al Emperador]," Apr. 13, 1546, in *DHG,* 2:467.

23. Serrano y Sanz, ed., *Relación,* 2:41–42, 329; *Comentarios,* chs. 18, 43; *DHG,* 2:399, 446; *COR,* 1:73–74; Gandía, *Historia de Alonso Cabrera,* 165–68, 335–68.

24. Zubizarreta, *Historia de mi ciudad,* 39; Lafuente Machain, *El gobernador,* 138; see also 96, 99, 103, 110–11, 126–27, 140.

25. For brief biographies of the settlers, see Lafuente Machain, *Conquistadores.*

14. BEFORE THEY AND THEIR SOULS ARE LOST

1. Pacheco, Cárdenas, and Torres de Mendoza, eds., *Colección de documentos inéditos,* 23:11–12; *Archivo colonial,* 1:339–40; Serrano y Sanz, ed., *Relación,* 2:117; Zorraquín Becú, *Organización política Argentina,* 87–88; Brading, *First America,* 51.

2. "[Información levantada por orden del adelantado y capitán general de la provincia del Río de la Plata, Alvar Núñez Cabeza de Vaca]," May–Sept. 1543, in *DHG,* 2:320–25; Serrano y Sanz, ed., *Relación,* 2:38–39, 326; Lafuente Machain, *Conquistadores,* 316, 593.

3. Gandía, *Luis de Miranda,* 74.

4. *DHG,* 2:325–29. Also in Gandía, *Luis de Miranda,* 75–82.

5. Zavala, *Orígenes de la colonización,* 50–52; Gandía, *Historia de la conquista,* 145, n. 131.

6. *Comentarios,* ch. 22; Serrano y Sanz, ed., *Relación,* 2:290.

7. *DHG,* 2:327–32.

8. Ibid., 2:329–30; Serrano y Sanz, ed., *Relación,* 2:58.

9. *DHG,* 2:332–36.

10. Ibid., 2:336–41.

11. *Comentarios,* ch. 39; Serrano y Sanz, ed., *Relación,* 2:39, 117.

15. TO SEE IF I COULD FIND THE GOLD AND SILVER

1. Pacheco, Cárdenas, and Torres de Mendoza, eds., *Colección de documentos inéditos,* 23:9; *Anales de la biblioteca,* 8:303.

2. *Comentarios,* ch. 53.

3. For Spanish economic development in the Río de la Plata province as a "fringe" area, see Lockhart and Schwartz, *Early Latin America,* 253–65.

4. Serrano y Sanz, ed., *Relación,* 2:56.

5. "[Instrucciones dadas por el adelantado, Alvar Núñez Cabeza de Vaca, al teniente de gobernador, capitán Juan de Salazar de Espinosa]," Sept. 8, 1543, in *DHG,* 2:341–44 (see also 2:339–40); Serrano y Sanz, ed., *Relación,* 2:38, 118.

6. *Comentarios,* chs. 44, 46; "Licencia del governador al factor para que

en su lugar nombrar a su hijo que sirva el oficio de factor atenta su enfermedad año 1543," Port of Ytaqui, Sept. 21, 1543, in *COR*, 1:229–31; "Poder que le dio al hijo para vsar el oficio año 1543," Port of Ytaqui, Sept. 21, 1543, in *COR*, 1:230–31; Gandía, *Historia de la conquista*, 39, n. 111.

7. *Comentarios*, chs. 36, 44–45; Serrano y Sanz, ed., *Relación*, 2:38–39, 42–43, 117; *DHG*, 5:207; Medina, *El Portugués*, 92; Susnik, "Una visión antropológica," 197–98; Susnik, *El indio colonial*, 1:217. For estimates of how many Indians took part, see Gandía, *Historia de la conquista*, 139, n. 110.

8. *Comentarios*, ch. 46; Schmidt, "Voyage of Ulrich Schmidt," 39.

9. *Comentarios*, ch. 49; Serrano y Sanz, ed., *Relación*, 2:5–7, 43–44; Gandía, *Historia de la conquista*, 63, 68, n. 44. For population estimates of the Payaguáes, see Hemming, *Red Gold*, 493; and Ganson, "Evueví," 468.

10. *DHG*, 2:420–21; Lafuente Machain, *El gobernador*, document L; Parry and Keith, eds., *New Iberian World*, 5:266–67; Chaves, *Descubrimiento y conquista*, 138, n. 263.

11. *Comentarios*, ch. 4; Serrano y Sanz, ed., *Relación*, 2:321–22; *DHG*, 2:397; Parry and Keith, eds., *New Iberian World*, 5:284.

12. *Comentarios*, ch. 49.

13. Warren, *Paraguay*, 46; *DHG*, 2:456–57; *Anales de la biblioteca*, 8:308–10; Parry and Keith, eds., *New Iberian World*, 5:271–72.

14. *DHG*, 2:420–21; Lafuente Machain, *El gobernador*, document L; Parry and Keith, eds., *New Iberian World*, 5:266–67.

15. Chaves, *Descubrimiento y conquista*, 119, 139.

16. *DHG*, 2:486; *Archivo colonial*, 1:175; Parry and Keith, eds., *New Iberian World*, 5:278–79. Lafuente Machain, *Conquistadores*, 28–29.

17. *Comentarios*, chs. 49–50; Serrano y Sanz, ed., *Relación*, 2:44; Susnik, *Los aborígenes*, 1:101–4.

18. Bishop, *Odyssey of Cabeza de Vaca*, 226.

19. *Comentarios*, ch. 50; Serrano y Sanz, ed., *Relación*, 2:45; *Anales de la biblioteca*, 8:352–65. Lafuente Machain, *Conquistadores*, 416–19.

16. A LAND THAT WAS NEWLY DISCOVERED

1. *Comentarios*, chs. 53, 54; Serrano y Sanz, ed., *Relación*, 2:45, 55, 117–18; Karsten, *Civilization of the South American Indians*, 103; Susnik, *Los aborígenes*, 1:24–27; Métraux, "Ethnography of the Chaco," 245. For possible

locations of Puerto de los Reyes, see Susnik, *El rol de los indígenas,* 1:79; Susnik, *Los aborígenes,* 1:24; Métraux, "Ethnography of the Chaco," 200–201; Hemming, *Red Gold,* 242; Morison, *European Discovery of America,* 576, 583 (map, 551); Bishop, *Odyssey of Cabeza de Vaca,* 228 (map, 175); Gott, *Land without Evil,* 114–16 (map, [302]).

2. *Comentarios,* ch. 54. On idols, see Susnik, *Los aborígenes,* 1:26. For Chaco Indian beliefs about demons, see Métraux, "Ethnography of the Chaco," 351–52.

3. Casas, *Historia de las Indias,* bk. 3, ch. 117.

4. "[Título expedido, por el adelantado, Alvar Núñez Cabeza de Vaca, de maese de campo y justicia mayor de la gente de su ejército a favor del capitán Domingo Martínez de Irala]," Nov. 10, 1543, in *DHG,* 2:344–45; Serrano y Sanz, ed., *Relación,* 2:45.

5. Serrano y Sanz, ed., *Relación,* 2:53–55.

6. *Comentarios,* chs. 56–59; Serrano y Sanz, ed., *Relación,* 2:46–48. For the Xarayes, see Susnik, *Los aborígenes,* 1:28–33 (map, 32); and Métraux, "Tribes of Eastern Bolivia and Madeira," 381–85, 394–95.

7. *Comentarios,* ch. 60; Serrano y Sanz, ed., *Relación,* 2:47; Métraux, "Ethnography of the Chaco," 200–201; Gandía, *Historia de la conquista,* 143, n. 125.

8. *Comentarios,* ch. 58; Serrano y Sanz, ed., *Relación,* 2:46, 53, 125–26; *DHG,* 2:438.

9. Susnik, *Los aborígenes,* 1:22–24 (map, 32); and Métraux, "Ethnography of the Chaco," 214, 225 (map, 198).

10. Serrano y Sanz, ed., *Relación,* 2:44, 46.

11. *Comentarios,* ch. 58; Morison, *European Discovery of America,* 576–77.

17. UNINHABITED AND UNINHABITABLE

1. *Comentarios,* ch. 61; Serrano y Sanz, ed., *Relación,* 2:47–48, 118, 330; Susnik, *Los aborígenes,* 1:54; Lafuente Machain, *Conquistadores,* 568–69.

2. Métraux, "Ethnography of the Chaco," 197–201; Warren, *Paraguay,* 36.

3. Chaves, *Descubrimiento y conquista,* 41 (map, 201).

4. Susnik, *Los aborígenes,* 1:47.

5. J. Valerie Fifer, *Bolivia,* 21–22, 204. For a twentieth-century journey

over this road, with a dramatic account of its hardships, see Duguid, *Green Hell.*

6. Weil, et al., *Bolivia,* 53, 55.

7. *Comentarios,* chs. 62–64; Serrano y Sanz, ed., *Relación,* 2:48–49, 330–31.

8. Gandía, *Luis de Miranda,* 92.

9. *Archivo colonial,* 1:369, 398; Gandía, *Historia de la conquista,* 145, n. 131; Bishop, *Odyssey of Cabeza de Vaca,* 231, n. 8.

10. *DHG,* 2:439, 466; Serrano y Sanz, ed., *Relación,* 2:290.

11. Serrano y Sanz, ed., *Relación,* 2:48.

12. *Comentarios,* chs. 63, 65; Serrano y Sanz, ed., *Relación,* 2:48–49, 118, 296, 330–31; *DHG,* 2:349.

18. EVERYONE WAS DYING OF HUNGER

1. *Comentarios,* chs. 63–66; Serrano y Sanz, ed., *Relación,* 2:49–50, 118–19.

2. *DHG,* 2:446; *Comentarios,* ch. 54. See also document listing persons who received goods, tunics, clothing, and munitions in Puerto de los Reyes, January 8 and 15, 1544, in Gandía, *Historia de la conquista,* 168, n. 174.

3. García Santillán, *Legislación sobre indios,* 354–56. For the value of the *castellano,* see Davies, *Golden Century of Spain,* 295–96.

4. *Comentarios,* ch. 66; Serrano y Sanz, ed., *Relación,* 2:118–19.

5. Susnik, *Los aborígenes,* 1:24–26 (map, 32).

6. *Comentarios,* chs. 67–68; Serrano y Sanz, ed., *Relación,* 2:49–50, 119–21; "[Instrucciones extendidas por el adelantado, Alvar Núñez Cabeza de Vaca, al capitán Gonzalo de Mendoza]," Dec. 16, 1543, in *DHG,* 2:345–46.

7. *Comentarios,* ch. 68; Serrano y Sanz, ed., *Relación,* 2:50, 331–32; Lafuente Machain, *Conquistadores,* 540–42.

19. ONLY WHAT WAS NEEDED

1. *Comentarios,* chs. 69–70; Serrano y Sanz, ed., *Relación,* 2:50–51, 131, 332–33; *DHG,* 2:349–50, 400, 440; Gandía, *Historia de la conquista,* 151–52, n. 140; Lafuente Machain, *Conquistadores,* 539–42. For the Tarapecosi Indians, see Métraux, "Tribes of Eastern Bolivia and Madeira," 383–88; and Susnik, *Los aborígenes,* 1:39–40 (map, 62).

2. *Comentarios,* ch. 71; Serrano y Sanz, ed., *Relación,* 2:333.

3. *Comentarios,* chs. 68, 71; Serrano y Sanz, ed., *Relación,* 2:52, 120–25. For the use of feathers and paint in warfare, see Métraux, "Ethnography of the Chaco," 314.

4. "[Requerimiento hecho por el contador, Felipe de Cáceres]," Puerto de los Reyes, Mar. 18, 1544, in *DHG,* 2:348–49.

5. *COR,* 1:87. For Gandía's refutation of this charge, see his *Historia de la conquista,* 150–52, n. 139.

6. Serrano y Sanz, ed., *Relación,* 2:119–25, 184, 272, 275–80.

7. Millé, *Crónica,* 119.

8. *DHG,* 2:441.

9. "[Información levantada por orden del adelantado, Alvar Núñez Cabeza de Vaca]," Jan. 22, 1544, in *DHG,* 2:347–48.

10. *Comentarios,* ch. 72.

11. "Relación de Hernando de Ribera," Asunción, Mar. 3, 1545, in *Relación,* ed. Serrano y Sanz, 1:368–78. Also in Cabeza de Vaca, *Naufragios y comentarios,* 227–33. For an English translation, see "Narrative of Hernando de Ribera," in *The Conquest of the River Plate,* ed. Dominguez, 263–70. See also "Razon sumaria de la journada que hizo hernando de rribera por los parayes," in *COR,* 1:112–14; and "[Carta de Hernando Ribera, al Emperador]," Asunción, Feb. 25, 1545, in *DHG,* 2:413–14; Parry, *Discovery of South America,* 268.

12. Serrano y Sanz, ed., *Relación,* 2:297–98; Schmidt, "Voyage of Ulrich Schmidt," 41–50.

13. *Comentarios,* ch. 72; Serrano y Sanz, ed., *Relación,* 2:333–34; *DHG,* 2:401.

14. Schmidt, "Voyage of Ulrich Schmidt," 43, 49.

15. Gandía, *Historia de la conquista,* 155, n. 148.

16. *DHG,* 2:414.

17. Serrano y Sanz, ed., *Relación,* 2:51; *Comentarios,* ch. 73.

20. THAT HE MIGHT NOT DISCOVER GOLD AND SILVER

1. Serrano y Sanz, ed., *Relación,* 2:58, 298; *Comentarios,* ch. 71; *DHG,* 2:442; *COR,* 1:87.

2. *Comentarios,* ch. 71; Serrano y Sanz, ed., *Relación,* 2:53, 127; Susnik, *Los aborígenes,* 1:24–25 (map, 32).

3. Serrano y Sanz, ed., *Relación,* 2:53–54, 126–27, 131–32, 331; *DHG,* 2:441–42; *Comentarios,* ch. 71; Susnik, *Los aborígenes,* 1:26–27; Gandía, *Historia de la conquista,* 161–62, n. 161.

4. *Comentarios,* ch. 71; Serrano y Sanz, ed., *Relación,* 2:125–28, 132–34, 331; *DHG,* 2:400, 441. For doubts about cannibalism in this case, see Susnik, *Los aborígenes del Paraguay,* 1:27. For causes, including cannibalism, that allowed enslavement under Spanish law, see Friede, "Las Casas and Indigenism," 146–53; Zavala, *Orígenes de la colonización,* 93–94; Zavala, *Ensayos sobre la colonización Española en América,* ch. 5. For an English translation, see Zavala, *New Viewpoints on the Spanish Colonization of America,* ch. 5. See also Villamarín and Villamarín, *Indian Labor,* 7–8.

5. *COR,* 1:77–78, 87–89; *DHG,* 2:446.

6. Schmidt, "Voyage of Ulrich Schmidt," 50–51.

7. Serrano y Sanz, ed., *Relación,* 2:132; Susnik, *Los aborígenes,* 1:25–26.

8. *DHG,* 2:441–42; *Comentarios,* ch. 73.

9. *DHG, Relación,* 2:348–53.

10. Garay, ed., *Colección de documentos,* 1:62–63.

11. Serrano y Sanz, ed., *Relación,* 2:334–36; *Cartas de Indias,* 2:585–86.

12. *DHG,* 2:353–58.

13. Serrano y Sanz, ed., *Relación,* 2:291.

14. Ibid., 2:56–59; *Comentarios,* ch. 73.

15. Serrano y Sanz, ed., *Relación,* 2:126–28, 131–34.

21. LIBERTY! LIBERTY!

1. *Comentarios,* ch. 73; Serrano y Sanz, ed., *Relación,* 2:58–59, 336; *DHG,* 2:402.

2. *COR,* 1:76–77; Cardozo, "La fundación de la ciudad," 183.

3. *Archivo colonial,* 1:436–54; *Comentarios,* ch. 73; Susnik, *Los aborígenes,* 1:96–103.

4. *COR,* 1:87–89.

5. Serrano y Sanz, ed., *Relación,* 2:60–65, 90, 337–38, 342–45; *DHG,*

2:402–5, 468; *Comentarios,* ch. 74. For another revolt using the name *comuneros* (in eighteenth-century Paraguay), see López, *Revolt of the Comuneros,* 12–13, 123, 163; pt. 3.

6. "Carta de Ruy Díaz Melgarejo al Emperador Don Carlos," Asunción, July 4, 1556, in *Cartas de Indias,* 2:629–30; "Carta al rey de Ruy Díaz Melgarejo," Asunción, July 4, 1561 [1556], in R. Cardozo, *Ruy Díaz Melgarejo,* 102–3; Lafuente Machain, *Conquistadores,* 183–86.

7. "Provanza de los meritos y servicios de Francisco Ortiz de Vergara," Ciudad de la Plata, June 7, 1567, in *Colección de documentos,* ed. Garay, 1:469–77; "Probanza de los méritos y los servicios de Francisco Ortiz de Vergara," 1567, in R. Cardozo, *Ruy Díaz Melgarejo,* 113.

8. Serrano y Sanz, ed., *Relación,* 2:292–93; "[Carta de Juan Bernalte Cabeza de Vaca, dirigida a su hermano, Hernán Ruiz Cabeza de Vaca]," Jan. 13, [1545], in *DHG,* 2:312.

9. Serrano y Sanz, ed., *Relación,* 2:60, 62, 337–41; *Comentarios,* ch. 75; *DHG,* 2:402–3, 442–44; "Escritura de poder a favor de Pero Díaz del Valle," Asunción, Apr. 28, 1544, in Lafuente Machain, *El gobernador,* document H; Schmidt, "Voyage of Ulrich Schmidt," 52.

10. Lafuente Machain, *El gobernador,* 152–55.

11. Serrano y Sanz, ed., *Relación,* 2:336, 338; *DHG,* 2:402.

12. Serrano y Sanz, ed., *Relación,* 2:59.

13. "Título y poder que Alvar Núñez Cabeza de Vaca confirió . . . al capitán Juan Salazar de Espinosa," Asunción, Mar. 17, 1545, in *Archivo colonial,* 2:52–53, 61–63.

14. *DHG,* 2:442–43.

15. Ibid., 2:486–87; *Archivo colonial,* 1:176; Parry and Keith, eds., *New Iberian World,* 5:279.

16. *Cartas de Indias,* 2:604.

17. Susnik, *El rol de los indígenas,* 1:82–83; Susnik, *Los aborígenes,* 2:56–57.

18. Serrano y Sanz, ed., *Relación,* 2:63, 335; *DHG,* 2:401, 442.

19. Serrano y Sanz, ed., *Relación,* 2:298–99.

20. Ibid., 2:60–61, 65, 67, 86, 90, 337; *DHG,* 2:402.

21. Serrano y Sanz, ed., *Relación,* 2:59–60, 336–37, 340–41; *Comentarios,* ch. 74; *DHG,* 2:402–3.

22. *DHG,* 2:446.

23. Serrano y Sanz, ed., *Relación,* 2:66, 68; *Comentarios,* ch. 74.

24. Serrano y Sanz, ed., *Relación,* 2:338–40; *DHG,* 2:402–3; *Comentarios,* ch. 74.

25. "Carta de Juan Pavon al licenciado Agreda, fiscal del Consejo de Indias," June 15, 1556, in *Cartas de Indias,* 2:593–94; *Comentarios,* ch. 74; Serrano y Sanz, ed., *Relación,* 2:90; *DHG,* 2:443; Lafuente Machain, *Conquistadores,* 492–93.

26. Serrano y Sanz, ed., *Relación,* 2:64, 343; *DHG,* 2:404.

27. *Comentarios,* ch. 74; "Deposito de un esclavo negro y una cota y zarahuel de malla de Alvar Núñez Cabeza de Vaca," July 16, 1544, in *El archivo nacional de la Asunción,* 401–7; Lafuente Machain, *Conquistadores,* 529.

28. "Testamento," Mar. 13, 1556, in Lafuente Machain, *El gobernador,* 556–59.

29. Serrano y Sanz, ed., *Relación,* 2:64, 345; *DHG,* 2:405.

30. *DHG,* 2:443; Serrano y Sanz, ed., *Relación,* 2:65, 342; *Comentarios,* ch. 73; *Cartas de Indias,* 586; Lafuente Machain, *Conquistadores,* 272–73.

31. *DHG,* 2:443.

32. Ibid., 2:404, 424, 459; Parry and Keith, eds., *New Iberian World,* 5:270, 274; Serrano y Sanz, ed., *Relación,* 2:65, 342; "Acuerdo de los oficiales reales para llevar á España al adelantado Alvar Núñez Cabeza de Vaca," Asunción, Mar. 5, 1545, in Aguirre, "Diario," 2:245–46; *Comentarios,* ch. 75; Cardozo, "La fundación de la ciudad," 183.

33. *Comentarios,* ch. 75; Schmidt, "Voyage of Ulrich Schmidt," 53.

34. "Embargo de los bienes de Alvar Núñez Cabeza de Vaca quien se halla preso con grillos," Apr. 29, 1544, in *El archivo nacional de la Asunción,* 382–88; Serrano y Sanz, ed., *Relación,* 2:62.

35. Serrano y Sanz, ed., *Relación,* 2:340, 342; *DHG,* 2:403–4.

36. "El Escribano Dn Martin de Orue pide le sea entregado el archivo que tiene en su poder el Escribano Pedro Fernandez," July 26, 1544, in *El archivo nacional de la Asunción,* 408.

37. Gandía, *Historia de la conquista,* 174–76, n. 184.

38. "Dos cartas al Rey, de Pero Díaz del Valle," Asunción, Mar. 20, 1545, in Gandía, *Luis de Miranda,* 123–24; "Los oficiales Reales piden al Consejo

de las Indias que se remitan los portacartas de Alvar Núñez Cabeza de Vaca," Mar. 16, 1545, in *El archivo nacional de la Asunción,* 449–50.

22. I AM THE KING AND RULER OF THIS LAND

1. For Spanish loyalty to the crown, see McAlister, *Spain and Portugal,* 36–39, 81–82.

2. "Presentación de los oficiales reales . . . de los excesos cometidos contra el real servicio por el adelantado Alvar Núñez Cabeza de Vaca," Asunción, June 21, 1544, in *Archivo colonial,* 1:412–23. For Cabeza de Vaca's efforts to protect the Indians by legislation (discussed in chapter 10), see documents in García Santillán, *Legislación sobre indios,* 347–48, 350, 354–55.

3. *Archivo colonial,* 1:359–403; *Comentarios,* ch. 41; Gandía, *Historia de la conquista,* 189.

4. *Cartas de Indias,* 2:605.

5. *Archivo colonial,* 1:359–403; Gandía, *Historia de Alonso Cabrera,* 166–68. For the *obedezco* formula, see MacLachlan, *Spain's Empire in the New World,* 22.

6. Serrano y Sanz, ed., *Relación,* 2:346, 355; *DHG,* 2:405, 408; Bishop, *Odyssey of Cabeza de Vaca,* 266.

7. Serrano y Sanz, ed., *Relación,* 2:83; *Comentarios,* ch. 83.

8. Hernández, "Relación de las cosas sucedidas en el Río de la Plata," Jan. 28, 1545, in *Relación,* ed. Serrano y Sanz, 2:346–47; *DHG,* 2:392–409; *Archivo colonial,* 2:14–48; Gandía, *Historia de la conquista,* 189–90, n. 18, 191.

9. Gandía, *Historia de la conquista,* 98, n. 11.

23. NO MAN WAS SAFE FROM THE OTHER

1. Serrano y Sanz, ed., *Relación,* 2:1–98.

2. Ibid., 2:307–58; *DHG,* 2:392–409; *Archivo colonial,* 2:14–48.

3. Serrano y Sanz, ed., *Relación,* 2:67–69.

4. Friede, "Las Casas and Indigenism," 139.

5. Serrano y Sanz, *Relación,* 2:343ff; *DHG,* 2:404ff; *Comentarios,* chs. 76, 78, 80.

6. "Relación hecha por Diego Telles de Escobar," 1546, in *Archivo colonial,* 2:72–73; Gandía, *Historia de la conquista,* 183, n. 10.

7. "Memorial de las cosas que han sucedido después que Cabeza de Vaca

fué traído de los provincias del Río de la Plata," 1556?, in *Archivo colonial*, 2:174–75; Lafuente Machain, *Conquistadores*, 600.

8. R. Cardozo, *Ruy Díaz Melgarejo*, 103; *Cartas de Indias*, 2:630.

9. López, *Revolt of the Comuneros*, 52; Alden and Miller, "Out of Africa," 199; Crosby, *The Columbian Exchange*, 40.

10. *Cartas de Indias*, 2:604–9; "Carta de Juan Muñoz de Carvajal al Emperador Don Carlos," June 15, 1556, in ibid., 2:597–98. For these Indian uprisings, see Susnik, *El indio colonial*, 1:219–22; and Susnik, *Los aborígenes*, 2:56–58.

11. Serrano y Sanz, ed., *Relación*, 2:66–67; *Comentarios*, chs. 75–76.

12. "Relación de lo que pasó en el Río de la Plata después de la prisión de Cabeza de Vaca," 1556?, in *Archivo colonial*, 2:163–64; "Rrelacion delas provincias del rrio dela Plata," in *Colección de documentos*, ed. Garay, 1:52–53; Cardozo, "La fundación de la ciudad," 184–86.

13. *Archivo colonial*, 2:49–56, 63–64; Serrano y Sanz, ed., *Relación*, 2:78.

14. Gandía, *Historia de la conquista*, 205, n. 55.

15. *Archivo colonial*, 2:163–64; Garay, ed., *Colección de documentos*, 1:52–53.

16. *Archivo colonial*, 2:72–73.

17. Chaves, *Descubrimiento y conquista*, 125, n. 245.

18. *COR*, 1:76–77, 92–93.

19. *DHG*, 2:468.

20. Serrano y Sanz, ed., *Relación*, 2:68–69, 82, 345–46, 348; *DHG*, 2:404–6, 443, 447, 468; *Cartas de Indias*, 2:605.

21. Schmidt, "Voyage of Ulrich Schmidt," 54–61.

22. Stern, "The Rise and Fall of Indian-White Alliances," 461.

23. "Carta al Rey del capellán Luis de Miranda," Cárcel de la Asunción, Mar. 25, 1545, in Gandía, *Luis de Miranda*, 133; Serrano y Sanz, ed., *Relación*, 2:79, 348; *DHG*, 2:406.

24. Gandía, *Luis de Miranda*, 118–19.

25. Serrano y Sanz, ed., *Relación*, 2:79–80; *Comentarios*, ch. 79.

26. Serrano y Sanz, ed., *Relación*, 2:343; *DHG*, 2:404.

27. Millé, *Crónica*, 120–21.

28. Serrano y Sanz, ed., *Relación*, 2:80; "Carta del Factor Pedro de Orantes, al Rey," Asunción, Mar. 5, 1545, in *COR*, 1:80–81.

29. Serrano y Sanz, ed., *Relación,* 2:80, 135, 243–44, 271–72; Gandía, *Historia de la conquista,* 194, n. 24.

30. Garay, ed., *Colección de documentos,* 1:469–77; "Relación del Tesorero Francisco Ortiz de Vergara al Presidente del Consejo de Indias, Don Juan Ovando," Río de la Plata, [May 7, 1569], in *COR,* 1:244–45, 254. Also in *DHG,* 1:115, and Garay, ed., *Colección de documentos,* 1:97–107.

31. Lafuente Machain, *Conquistadores,* 66–67, 350.

24. TO DISCREDIT ME WITH HIS MAJESTY

1. Serrano y Sanz, ed. *Relación,* 2:73–74, 82–83, 118, 229, 346; *Comentarios,* ch. 78; *DHG,* 2:405; Gandía, *Luis de Miranda,* ch. 4; ibid., "Informaçiones hechas de ofiçio en la provinçia del rrio de la plata," Asunción, May 1, 1544–Mar. 6, 1545, 99–116, and 117–29; Gandía, *Historia de la conquista,* 186–87, 196, n. 28.

2. "Declaraciones de testigos para la averiguacion de quien facilito una carta a Alvar Nuñez en su celda donde se encontrava preso," July 16, 1544, in *El archivo nacional de la Asunción,* 395–401.

3. *Comentarios,* chs. 77, 79; Serrano y Sanz, ed., *Relación,* 2:60, 65–66, 69–71, 76–78, 292; *DHG,* 2:468; Charlevoix, *The History of Paraguay,* 1:124; Cardozo, "La fundación de la ciudad," 185–86.

4. *Comentarios,* ch. 82; Serrano y Sanz, ed., *Relación,* 2:72–74, 76–77.

5. Serrano y Sanz, ed., *Relación,* 2:82–83, 346, 355; *DHG,* 2:405, 408; *Comentarios,* ch. 83; *Cartas de Indias,* 2:586–87; Gandía, *Historia de la conquista,* 204, n. 53.

6. Aguirre, "Diario," 2:245–46; Serrano y Sanz, ed., *Relación,* 2:351–52; *DHG,* 2:407.

7. Serrano y Sanz, ed., *Relación,* 2:83–84.

25. HE WAS A VERY GOOD GOVERNOR

1. *Comentarios,* ch. 83.

2. *DHG,* 2:409–14.

3. Gandía, *Luis de Miranda,* 89–97.

4. *DHG,* 2:443, 447; Susnik, *El indio colonial,* 1:16.

5. "Carta a Rodrigo de Vera, alcalde de Zahara," Asunción, Mar. 1, 1545, in Gandía, *Historia de Alonso Cabrera,* 407–9. Also in *DHG,* 2:424–29.

6. Roeder, *Man of the Renaissance,* 515.

7. Salas and Vázquez, eds., *Relación,* 128–29. For Eusebio's letter in Italian, see Marcolini, ed., *Lettere scritte a Pietro Aretino,* vol. 2, pt. 1:44–52; Serrano y Sanz, ed., *Relación,* 2:348; *DHG,* 2:405; Lafuente Machain, *Conquistadores,* 214.

8. *Archivo colonial,* 2:163–64; Garay, ed., *Colección de documentos,* 1:52–53.

9. "Carta del Tesorero Hernando de Montalvo á S. M.," Asunción, Nov. 15, 1579, in *COR,* 1:322–23.

10. "Carta del tesorero Hernando de Montalvo al Rey," Buenos Aires, Oct. 12, 1585, in *COR,* 1:368–69.

26. IF HE WERE TO GO ON AS HE BEGAN

1. *DHG,* 2:419–24; Lafuente Machain, *El gobernador,* document L; Parry and Keith, eds., *New Iberian World,* 5:265–70.

2. *DHG,* 2:455–59; *Anales de la biblioteca,* 8:305ff. For an English translation, see Parry and Keith, *New Iberian World,* 5:270–74.

3. *COR,* 1:64; Serrano y Sanz, ed., *Relación,* 2:63–64, 84.

4. *COR,* 1:73–79; Carro, "The Spanish Theological-Juridical Renaissance," 241; Métraux, "Warfare, Cannibalism, and Human Trophies," 399.

5. *COR,* 1:80–82; "Un memorial de avisos que dio de lo que se devia hacer en la conquista," Asunción, July 4, 1545, in *COR,* 1:116; Susnik, *El indio colonial,* 1:14. See also Susnik, *El rol de los indígenas,* 1:84–89; and Susnik, *Los aborígenes,* 2:58–59.

6. Schmidt, "Voyage of Ulrich Schmidt," 57.

7. "Probanza de méritos y servicios del Factor y Oficial Real Pedro Dorantes," in *COR,* 1:150–60. Also in Garay, ed., *Colección de documentos,* 1:149ff.

8. "Petition of Cabeza de Vaca, Governor of La Plata, to the Council of Indias," in Cabeza de Vaca, *Relation of Nuñez Cabeza de Vaca,* 231.

9. "Ynformación hecha en consejo año de 48 por el hijo de como sirvio algun tiempo," Valladolid, Aug. 28–Sept. 3, 1548, in *COR,* 1:232–38.

10. Gandía, *Luis de Miranda,* 121–22.

11. "Carta del Contador y Oficial Real, Felipe de Caceres á S. M.," Asunción, Mar. 7, 1545, in *COR,* 1:83–90; *DHG,* 2:350–52.

12. For Irala's will, see Lafuente Machain, *El gobernador,* 547–65.

13. *DHG,* 2:452–54.

27. A COMPLETELY POOR CABALLERO

1. Serrano y Sanz, ed., *Relación,* 2:84–85, 90; *Comentarios,* ch. 84; Gandía, *Luis de Miranda,* 63–66.

2. *Archivo colonial,* 2:64; *Comentarios,* ch. 83; Serrano y Sanz, ed., *Relación,* 2:92; Lafuente Machain, *Conquistadores,* 294.

3. "Carta del Factor Pedro de Orantes, al Rey," Asunción, Mar. 20, 1545, in *COR,* 1:91–94; Gandía, *Luis de Miranda,* 124–28; Gandía, *Historia de la conquista,* 205–11.

4. *DHG,* 2:469–70; *Archivo colonial,* 2:60–61.

5. *Comentarios,* ch. 83; *COR,* 1:93; *Cartas de Indias,* 2:586; Gandía, *Luis de Miranda,* 126–27.

6. Serrano y Sanz, ed., *Relación,* 2:89, 93–95; *Comentarios,* ch. 84; "Declaraciones prestadas en Madrid por Juan de Salazar y Pero Hernández, a petición del fiscal del Rey, en el proceso de Cabeza de Vaca contra los oficiales del Río de la Plata Garcí Venegas y Alonso de Cabrera," Madrid, Sept. 7, 1547, in Gandía, *Historia de Alonso Cabrera,* 418, 420–21.

7. *Comentarios,* ch. 84; Serrano y Sanz, ed., *Relación,* 2:95–98; Gandía, *Historia de Alonso Cabrera,* 419, 421; Gandía, *Historia de la conquista,* 214, n. 84.

8. Hanke, *Spanish Struggle for Justice,* 91–92, 96, 101.

9. Serrano y Sanz, ed., *Relación,* 2:1, 98; Gandía, *De la torre del oro,* 128.

10. Bishop, *Odyssey of Cabeza de Vaca,* 276–77.

11. Serrano y Sanz, ed., *Relación,* 2:99–281.

12. *DHG,* 2:479–80; Gandía, *Historia de Alonso Cabrera,* 417.

13. Gandía, *Historia de la conquista,* 216, n. 89; Bishop, *Odyssey of Cabeza de Vaca,* 275–80.

14. "Capitulacion que se tomo con Juan de Sanabria," Madrid, July 22, 1547, in *Colección de documentos inéditos,* ed. Pacheco, Cárdenas, and Torres de Mendoza, 23:118–19, 124.

15. Warren, *Paraguay,* 27, 75–77.

16. *Comentarios,* ch. 84.

17. Oviedo, *Historia general,* 2:206–8.

18. For a copy of the sentence, see Zubizarreta, *Capitanes de aventura,* 190–91. For an English translation, see Bishop, *Odyssey of Cabeza de Vaca,* 285.

19. "Petition of Cabeza de Vaca, Governor of La Plata, to the Council of Indias," in Cabeza de Vaca, *Relation of Nuñez Cabeza de Vaca,* 231–32.

20. Bishop, *Odyssey of Cabeza de Vaca,* 287.

21. *Comentarios,* ch. 84.

22. Gandía, *De la torre del oro,* 122–23, n. 5; "Verdadera relación de lo que sucedío al gobernador Jaime Rasquín en el viage que intentó para el Río de la Plata en el año de 1559 años, hecha por Alonso Gómez de Santoya," in *Colección de documentos inéditos,* ed. Pacheco, Cárdenas, and Torres de Mendoza, 4:148; Bishop, *Odyssey of Cabeza de Vaca,* 285–90.

CONCLUSION

1. Morison, *European Discovery of America,* 580.

2. Díaz del Castillo, *Historia verdadera,* ch. 27; *DHG,* 2:431.

3. Fernández-Armesto, *Columbus,* 138.

4. Cabeza de Vaca, *Relación,* chs. 32, 36.

5. For grievances of Cabeza de Vaca's enemies, see Lafuente Machain, *El gobernador,* chs. 9–10.

Bibliography

Acosta, José de. *Historia natural y moral de las Indias.* 2d ed. Mexico City: Fondo de Cultural Económica, 1962.

Adorno, Rolena. "The Discursive Encounter of Spain and America: The Authority of Eyewitness Testimony in the Writing of History." *William and Mary Quarterly,* 3d ser., 49 (1992): 210–28.

———. "The Negotiation of Fear in Cabeza de Vaca's *Naufragios.*" *Representations* 33 (1991): 163–99.

Aguirre, Juan Francisco. "Diario." *Revista de la Biblioteca Nacional* (Buenos Aires) 18 (1949): 238–46.

Alden, Dauril, and Joseph C. Miller. "Out of Africa: The Slave Trade and the Transmission of Smallpox to Brazil, 1560–1831." *Journal of Interdisciplinary History* 18 (1987): 195–224.

Anales de la biblioteca 8 (1912): 145–56, 178–80, 213–73, 299–314, 339–65.

Archivo colonial. 3 vols. Buenos Aires: Museo Mitre, 1914–16.

El archivo nacional de la Asunción. Asunción, 1900–1902.

Arciniegas, Germán. *Latin America: A Cultural History.* New York: Alfred A. Knopf, 1968.

Ashburn, Percy M. *The Ranks of Death: A Medical History of the Conquest of America.* New York, 1947. Reprint, Philadelphia: Porcupine Press, 1980.

Aten, Lawrence E. *Indians of the Upper Texas Coast.* New York: Academic Press, 1983.

Azara, Féliz de. *Descripción e historia del Paraguay y del Río de la Plata.* 2 vols. Madrid: Imprenta de Sanchiz, 1847.

Bertoni, Guillermo T., and J. Richard Gorham. "The People of Paraguay: Origin and Numbers." In *Paraguay: Ecological Essays,* ed. J. Richard Gorham, 109–19. Miami, Fla.: Academy of the Arts and Sciences of the Americas, 1973.

Biermann, Benno M. "Bartolomé de las Casas and Vera Paz." In *Bartolomé de las Casas in History,* ed. Juan Friede and Benjamin Keen, 443–84. Dekalb, Ill.: Northern Illinois University Press, 1971.

Biggar, H. P., ed. *A Collection of Documents Relating to Jacques Cartier and the Sieur de Roberval.* Ottawa: Public Archives of Canada, 1930.

Bishop, Morris. *The Odyssey of Cabeza de Vaca.* New York: The Century Company, 1933.

Brading, D. A. *The First America: The Spanish Monarchy, Creole Patriots, and the Liberal State, 1492–1867.* Cambridge: Cambridge University Press, 1991.

Brand, Donald D. "Erroneous Location of Two Sixteenth-Century Spanish Settlements in Western Nueva España." In *Across the Chichimec Sea,* ed. Basil C. Hedrick and Carroll L. Riley, 193–201. Carbondale, Ill.: Southern Illinois University Press, 1978.

Cabeza de Vaca, Alvar Núñez. *The Account: Alvar Núñez Cabeza de Vaca's Relación.* Trans. Martín A. Favata and José B. Fernández. Houston: Arte Público, 1993.

———. *Cabeza de Vaca's Adventures in the Unknown Interior of America.* Trans. and ed. Cyclone Covey. New York: Collier Books, 1961.

———. *Castaways: The Narrative of Alvar Núñez Cabeza de Vaca.* Ed. Enrique Pupo-Walker. Trans. Frances M. López-Morillas. Berkeley: University of California Press, 1993.

———. "Decretos del adelantado Alvar Núñez Cabeza de Vaca." In Ernesto J. Fitte, *Hambre y desnudeces en la conquista,* document 1, 293–96. Buenos Aires: Emécé Editores, 1963.

———. "Estatutos y ordenanzas que mandó publicar el Gobernador D. Alvar Núñez Cabeza de Vaca, sobre el trato y gobierno de los indios." In Juan Carlos García Santillán, *Legislación sobre indios del Río de la Plata en el siglo XVI,* 347–54. Madrid: Imprenta del Asilo de huérfanos del S.C. de Jesus, 1928.

———. *The Narrative of Alvar Núñez Cabeza de Vaca.* Trans. Fanny Bandelier. Barre, Mass.: The Imprint Society, 1972.

———. "The Narrative of Alvar Núñez Cabeza de Vaca." In *Spanish Explorers in the Southern United States, 1528–1543,* ed. Frederick W. Hodge. New York, 1907. Reprint, Austin: Texas State Historical Association, 1984.

———. *Naufragios.* Ed. Juan Francisco Maura. Madrid: Cátedra, 1989.

———. *Naufragios.* Ed. Enrique Pupo-Walker. Madrid: Editorial Castalia, 1992.

———. *Naufragios y comentarios.* 5th ed. Madrid: Espasa-Calpe, 1971.

———. *La relación de los naufragios de Alvar Núñez Cabeza de Vaca.* Ed. Martín A. Favata and José B. Fernández. Potomac, Md.: Scripta Humanística, 1986.

———. *Relation of Núñez Cabeza de Vaca.* Trans. Buckingham Smith. Ann Arbor, Mich.: University Microfilms, [1966]. Originally published New York, 1871.

———. "The *Relation* of Alvar Núñez Cabeza de Vaca." In *New American World,* ed. David B. Quinn, 2:15–59. New York: Arno Press, 1979.

Campbell, T. N. "Coahuiltecans and Their Neighbors." In *Handbook of North American Indians,* vol. 10, *Southwest,* ed. William C. Sturtevant and Alfonso Ortiz, 343–58. Washington, D.C.: Smithsonian Institution Press, 1983.

Campbell, T. N., and T. J. Campbell. *Historic Indian Groups of the Choke Canyon Reservoir and Surrounding Area, Southern Texas.* San Antonio: Center for Archeological Research, University of Texas at San Antonio, 1981.

"Capitulations between Charles V and Pánfilo de Narváez." In *New American World,* ed. David B. Quinn, 2:4–10. New York: Arno Press, 1979.

Cardozo, Efraím. "La fundación de la ciudad de Asunción en 1541." In *Anuario de historia Argentina, 1940,* 145–222. Buenos Aires: Sociedad de Historia Argentina, 1941.

———. *El Paraguay colonial: Las raíces de la nacionalidad.* Buenos Aires: Ediciones Nizza, 1959.

Cardozo, Ramón Indalecio. *Ruy Díaz Melgarejo.* Asunción, 1939.

Carro, Venancio D. "The Spanish Theological-Juridical Renaissance and the Ideology of Bartolomé de las Casas." In *Bartolomé de las Casas in History,* ed. Juan Friede and Benjamin Keen, 237–77. Dekalb, Ill.: Northern Illinois University Press, 1971.

Cartas de Indias. 3 vols. Madrid: Biblioteca de Autores Españoles, 1974.

Casas, Bartolomé de las. *Apologética historia: Obras escogidas de Fray Bartolomé de las Casas.* 5 vols. Madrid: Biblioteca de Autores Españoles, 1957–58.

———. *Apologética historia sumaria.* Ed. Edmundo O'Gorman. 2 vols. Mexico City: Instituto de Investigaciones Históricas, UNAM, 1967.

———. *Del único modo de atraer todos los pueblos a la verdadera religión.* Trans. Antenógenes Santamaría. Mexico City: Fondo de Cultura Económica, 1942.

———. *The Devastation of the Indies: A Brief Account.* Trans. Herma Briffault. Baltimore: Johns Hopkins University Press, 1992.

———. *Historia de las Indias.* 2d ed. 3 vols. Mexico City: Fondo de Cultura Económica, 1965.

———. *History of the Indies.* Trans. and ed. Andrée Collard. New York: Harper and Row, 1971.

———. *The Only Way.* Ed. Helen Rand Parish. Trans. Francis Patrick Sullivan. New York: Paulist Press, 1992.

———. *Tratados de Fray Bartolomé de las Casas.* 2 vols. Mexico City: Fondo de Cultura Económica, 1965.

Charlevoix, Pierre François Xavier de. *The History of Paraguay.* 2 vols. London: Lockyer Davis, 1769.

Chaves, Julio César. *Descubrimiento y conquista del Río de la Plata y el Paraguay.* Asunción: Ediciones Nizza, 1968.

Chipman, Donald E. "In Search of Cabeza de Vaca's Route across Texas: An Historiographical Survey." *Southwestern Historical Quarterly* 91 (1987): 127–48.

Clayton, Lawrence A., Vernon James Knight, Jr., and Edward C. Moore, eds. *The De Soto Chronicles: The Expedition of Hernando De Soto to North America in 1539–1543.* 2 vols. Tuscaloosa: University of Alabama Press, 1993.

Córdoba, Antonio S. C. *Los franciscanos en el Paraguay.* Buenos Aires: Imprenta López, 1937.

———. *La orden franciscana en las repúblicas del Plata.* Buenos Aires: Imprenta López, 1934.

Crosby, Alfred W. *The Columbian Exchange: Biological and Cultural Consequences of 1492.* Westport, Conn.: Greenwood Press, 1972.

Cunninghame Graham, R. B. *The Conquest of the River Plate.* New York, 1924. Reprint, Westport, Conn.: Greenwood Press, 1968.

Davies, R. Trevor. *The Golden Century of Spain, 1501–1621.* New York: Harper and Row, 1965.

Díaz de Guzmán, Ruy. "Argentina." In *Colección de obras y documentos relativos a la historia antigua y moderna de las provincias del Río de la Plata,* ed. Pedro de Angelis, vol. 1. Buenos Aires: Colmega, 1910.

Díaz del Castillo, Bernal. *Historia verdadera de la conquista de la Nueva España.* 2d ed. Madrid: Espasa-Calpe, 1968.

Dobyns, Henry F. *Their Number Become Thinned: Native American Population Dynamics in Eastern North America.* Knoxville: University of Tennessee Press, 1983.

Dominguez, Luis L., ed. *The Conquest of the River Plate.* London: Hakluyt Society, 1891.

Duguid, Julian. *Green Hell: Adventures in the Mysterious Jungles of Eastern Bolivia.* London: Jonathan Cape, 1931.

Fernández, José B. *Alvar Núñez Cabeza de Vaca, the Forgotten Chronicler.* Miami, Fla.: Ediciones Universal, 1975.

Fernández-Armesto, Felipe. *Columbus.* Oxford: Oxford University Press, 1992.

Fifer, J. Valerie. *Bolivia: Land, Location, and Politics since 1825.* Cambridge: Cambridge University Press, 1972.

Fitte, Ernesto J. *Hambre y desnudeces en la conquista.* Buenos Aires: Eméce Editores, 1963.

Friede, Juan. "Las Casas and Indigenism in the Sixteenth Century." In *Bartolomé de las Casas in History,* ed. Juan Friede and Benjamin Keen, 127–234. Dekalb: Northern Illinois University Press, 1971.

Friede, Juan, and Benjamin Keen, eds. *Bartolomé de las Casas in History.* Dekalb: Northern Illinois University Press, 1971.

Gandía, Enrique de. *De la torre del oro a las Indias.* Buenos Aires: Talleres Gráficos Argentinos L. J. Rosso, 1935.

———. *Historia de Alonso Cabrera y de la destrucción de Buenos Aires en 1541.* Buenos Aires: Librería Cervantes, de J. Suárez, 1936.

———. *Historia de la conquista del Río de la Plata y del Paraguay.* Buenos Aires: A. García Santos, 1932.

———. *Indios y conquistadores en el Paraguay.* Buenos Aires: A. García Santos, 1932.

———. *Luis de Miranda, primer poeta del Río de la Plata.* Buenos Aires: Librería y editorial "La Facultad," Bernabé y cía., 1936.

Ganson, Barbara. "The Evueví of Paraguay: Adaptive Strategies and Responses to Colonialism, 1528–1811." *The Americas* 45 (1989): 461–88.

Garay, Blas, ed. *Colección de documentos relativos a la historia de América y particularmente a la historia del Paraguay.* 2 vols. Asunción: H. Kraus, 1899.

García Santillán, Juan Carlos. *Legislación sobre indios del Río de la Plata en el siglo XVI.* Madrid: Imprenta del Asilo de Huértados del S.C. de Jesus, 1928.

Giménez Fernández, Manuel. "Fray Bartolomé de las Casas: A Biographical Sketch." In *Bartolomé de las Casas in History,* ed. Juan Friede and Benjamin Keen, 67–125. Dekalb: Northern Illinois University Press, 1971.

González de Barcia Carballido y Zúñiga, Andrés. *Barcia's Chronological History of the Continent of Florida.* Gainesville: University of Florida Press, 1951.

———. *Ensayo cronológico para la historia general de la Florida.* Madrid: En la Oficina Real, 1723.

Gott, Richard. *Land without Evil: Utopian Journeys across the South American Watershed.* London: Verso, 1993.

Griffen, William B. "Southern Periphery: East." In *Handbook of North American Indians,* vol. 10, *Southwest,* ed. William C. Sturtevant and Alfonso Ortiz, 329–42. Washington, D.C.: Smithsonian Institution Press, 1983.

Groussac, Paul. *Mendoza y Garay, las dos fundaciones de Buenos Aires, 1536–1580.* 2d ed. Buenos Aires: J. Menéndez, 1916.

Guevara, José. *Historia del Paraguay, Río de la Plata y Tucumán.* Ed. Paul Groussac. Buenos Aires: Anales de la Biblioteca Nacional, 1908.

Guía de los documentos microfotografiados por la unidad móvil de microfilm de la UNESCO. Mexico City: Instituto Panamericano de Geografía e Historia, 1963.

Haliczer, Stephen. *The Comuneros of Castile.* Madison: University of Wisconsin Press, 1981.

Hallenbeck, Cleve. *Alvar Núñez Cabeza de Vaca: The Journey and Route of the*

First *European to Cross the Continent of North America*. Glendale, Calif.: Arthur H. Clark Company, 1940.

Hanke, Lewis. "The Development of Regulations for Conquistadores." In *Contribuciones para el estudio de la historia de América: Homenage al Dr. Emilio Ravignani,* 71–88. Buenos Aires: Editores Peuser ltda., 1941.

———. "The Requirement and Its Interpreters." In *Selected Writings of Lewis Hanke on the History of Latin America,* 4–7. Tempe: Center for Latin American Studies, Arizona State University, 1979. Originally published in *Revista de Historia de América* 1 (1938): 25–34.

———. *The Spanish Struggle for Justice in the Conquest of America*. Boston: Little, Brown, 1965.

Hann, John H. *Apalachee: The Land between the Rivers.* Gainesville: University Press of Florida, 1988.

Haring, C. H. *The Spanish Empire in America*. New York: Harcourt, Brace, and World, 1963.

Hedrick, Basil C. "The Location of Corazones." In *Across the Chichimec Sea,* ed. Basil C. Hedrick and Carroll L. Riley, 228–32. Carbondale: Southern Illinois University Press, 1978.

Hedrick, Basil C., and Carroll L. Riley, eds. *Across the Chichimec Sea.* Carbondale: Southern Illinois University Press, 1978.

Hemming, John. *Red Gold: The Conquest of the Brazilian Indians, 1500–1760.* Cambridge: Harvard University Press, 1978.

Henige, David. "The Context, Content, and Credibility of *La Florida del Ynca*." *The Americas* 43 (1986): 1–23.

Hernández, Pero. "Relación de las cosas sucedidas en el Río de la Plata." In *Relación de los naufragios y comentarios,* ed. Manuel Serrano y Sanz, 2:307–58. Madrid: V. Suárez, 1906.

Herrera y Tordesillas, Antonio de. *The General History.* 2d ed. 6 vols. London, 1740. Reprint, New York, 1973.

———. *Historia general de los hechos de los Castellanos, en las islas y tierra-firme de el mar océano.* 10 vols. Asunción: Editorial Guaranía, 1944–47.

Hinton, Thomas B. "Southern Periphery: West." In *Handbook of North American Indians,* vol. 10, *Southwest,* ed. William C. Sturtevant and Alfonso Ortiz, 315–28. Washington, D.C.: Smithsonian Institution Press, 1983.

Hoffman, Paul E. "Hernando De Soto: A Brief Biography." In *The De Soto Chronicles: The Expedition of Hernando De Soto to North America in 1539–1543,* ed. Lawrence A. Clayton, Vernon James Knight, Jr., and Edward C. Moore, 1:421–59. Tuscaloosa: University of Alabama Press, 1993.

Huffines, Marion Lois. "The Original Manuscript of Ulrich Schmidl: German Conquistador and Chronicler." *The Americas* 34 (1977): 202–6.

Karsten, Rafael. *The Civilization of the South American Indians.* London: Dawsons, 1968.

Keen, Benjamin. Introduction to *Bartolomé de las Casas in History,* ed. Juan Friede and Benjamin Keen, 3–63. Dekalb: Northern Illinois University Press, 1971.

Kicza, John E. "Patterns in Early Spanish Overseas Expansion." *William and Mary Quarterly,* 3d ser., 49 (1992): 229–53.

Krieger, Alex D. "The Travels of Alvar Núñez Cabeza de Vaca in Texas and Mexico, 1534–1536." In *Homenaje a Pablo Martínez del Río en el vigésimo-quinto aniversario de la primera edición de* Los Orígenes Americanos, 459–74. Mexico City: Instituto Nacional de Antropología e Historia, 1961.

Laconich, Marco Antonio. *Caudillos de la conquista.* Buenos Aires: Ediciones Nizza, 1961.

Lafaye, Jacques. "Los 'milagros' de Alvar Núñez Cabeza de Vaca (1527–1536)." In *Mesías cruzada, utopías: El judeo-cristianismo en las sociedades ibéricas,* 65–84. Mexico City: Fondo de Cultura Económica, 1984.

Lafuente Machain, Ricardo de. *Conquistadores del Río de la Plata.* 2d ed. Buenos Aires: Editorial Ayacucho, 1943.

———. *El gobernador Domingo Martínez de Irala.* Buenos Aires: Librería y Editorial "La Facultad," Bernabé y cía., 1939.

Levillier, Roberto, ed. *Correspondencia de los oficiales reales de hacienda del Río de la Plata con los reyes de España.* Madrid: Sucesores de Rivadeneyra, 1915.

Lockhart, James, and Stuart B. Schwartz. *Early Latin America: A History of Colonial Spanish America and Brazil.* Cambridge: Cambridge University Press, 1983.

López, Adalberto. *The Revolt of the Comuneros.* Cambridge, Mass.: Schenkman Publishing Company, 1976.

Lothrop, S. K. "Indians of the Paraná Delta and La Plata Littoral." In *Hand-*

book of South American Indians, ed. Julian H. Steward, 1:177–96. New York: Cooper Square Publishers, 1963.

Lynch, John. *Spain under the Hapsburgs.* 2 vols. New York: Oxford University Press, 1964–69.

McAlister, Lyle N. *Spain and Portugal in the New World, 1492–1700.* Minneapolis: University of Minnesota Press, 1984.

MacLachlan, Colin M. *Spain's Empire in the New World: The Role of Ideas in Institutional and Social Change.* Berkeley: University of California Press, 1988.

Madero, Eduardo. *Historia del puerto de Buenos Aires.* 3d ed. Buenos Aires: Editores Buenos Aires, 1939.

Marcolini, Francesco, ed. *Lettere scritte a Pietro Aretino.* 2 vols. Bologna: Commissione per i Testi di Lingua, 1968.

Marrinan, Rochelle A., John F. Scarry, and Rhonda L. Majors. "Prelude to De Soto: The Expedition of Pánfilo de Narváez." In *Columbian Consequences,* vol. 2, *Archaeological and Historical Perspectives on the Spanish Borderlands East,* ed. David Hurst Thomas, 71–80. Washington, D.C.: Smithsonian Institution Press, 1990.

Martínez, Manuel M. "Las Casas on the Conquest of America." In *Bartolomé de las Casas in History,* ed. Juan Friede and Benjamin Keen, 309–49. Dekalb: Northern Illinois University Press, 1971.

Mateos, Francisco. "El primer concilio del Río de la Plata en Asunción." *Missionalia Hispánica* (Madrid) 26 (1969): 257–359.

Medina, José Toribio. *El Portugués, Gonzalo de Acosto, al servicio de España.* Santiago, Chile: Imprenta Elzevieriana, 1908.

Métraux, Alfred. "Ethnography of the Chaco." In *Handbook of South American Indians,* ed. Julian H. Steward, 1:197–370. New York: Cooper Square Publishers, 1963.

———. "The Guaraní." In *Handbook of South American Indians,* ed. Julian H. Steward, 3:69–94. New York: Cooper Square Publishers, 1963.

———. "Tribes of Eastern Bolivia and Madeira." In *Handbook of South American Indians,* ed. Julian H. Steward, 3:381–463. New York: Cooper Square Publishers, 1963.

———. "Tribes of the Eastern Slopes of the Bolivian Andes." In *Handbook of South American Indians,* ed. Julian H. Steward, 3:465–506. New York: Cooper Square Publishers, 1963.

———. "Warfare, Cannibalism, and Human Trophies." In *Handbook of South American Indians,* ed. Julian H. Steward, 5:383–409. New York: Cooper Square Publishers, 1963.

Milanich, Jerald T. "The European Entrada into La Florida: An Overview." In *Columbian Consequences,* vol. 2, *Archaeological and Historical Perspectives on the Spanish Borderlands East,* ed. David Hurst Thomas, 3–29. Washington, D.C.: Smithsonian Institution Press, 1990.

Milanich, Jerald T., and Charles Hudson. *Hernando De Soto and the Indians of Florida.* Gainesville: University Press of Florida, 1993.

Millé, Andrés. *Crónica de la orden Franciscana en la conquista del Perú, Paraguay y el Tucumán.* Buenos Aires, 1961.

Mitchem, Jeffrey M. "Artifacts of Exploration: Archeological Evidence from Florida." In *First Encounters: Spanish Explorations in the Caribbean and the United States, 1492–1570,* ed. Jerald T. Milanich and Susan Milbrath, 99–109. Gainesville: University Press of Florida, 1989.

———. "Initial Spanish-Indian Contact in West Peninsular Florida: The Archeological Evidence." In *Columbian Consequences,* vol. 2, *Archaeological and Historical Perspectives on the Spanish Borderlands East,* ed. David Hurst Thomas, 49–59. Washington, D.C.: Smithsonian Institution Press, 1990.

Molina, Raúl. *Misiones argentinas en los archivos europeos.* Mexico City: Instituto Panamericano de Geografía e Historia, 1968.

Moreno, Fulgencio R. *La ciudad de Asunción.* Asunción: Casa América-Moreno Hnos., 1969.

Morison, Samuel Eliot. *The European Discovery of America: The Southern Voyages.* New York: Oxford University Press, 1974.

Musso Ambrosi, Luis Alberto. *El Río de la Plata en el archivo general de Indias de Sevilla, guía para investigadores.* 2d ed. Montevideo: [s.n.], 1976.

Newcomb, W. W., Jr. "Karankawa." In *Handbook of North American Indians,* vol. 10, *Southwest,* ed. William C. Sturtevant and Alfonso Ortiz, 359–67. Washington, D.C.: Smithsonian Institution Press, 1983.

Nowell, Charles E. "Aleixo Garcia and the White King." *Hispanic American Historical Review* 26 (1946): 450–66.

Oviedo y Valdés, Gonzalo Fernández de. *Historia general y natural de las Indias.* 4 vols. Madrid: Impr. de la Real Academia de la Historia, 1851–55.

Pacheco, Joaquín F., Francisco de Cárdenas, and Luis Torres de Mendoza, eds. *Colección de documentos inéditos relativos al descubrimiento, conquista y colonización de las antiguas posesiones. españolas de América y Oceanía.* 42 vols. Madrid, 1864–84.

Pagden, Anthony. *The Fall of Natural Man: The American Indian and the Origins of Comparative Ethnology.* Cambridge: Cambridge University Press, 1982.

Parry, John H. *The Discovery of South America.* New York: Taplinger, 1979.

———. *The Spanish Seaborne Empire.* Berkeley: University of California Press, 1990.

Parry, John H., and Robert G. Keith, eds. *New Iberian World.* 5 vols. New York: Times Books, 1984.

Pastor Bodmer, Beatriz. *The Armature of Conquest: Spanish Accounts of the Discovery of America, 1492–1589.* Stanford: Stanford University Press, 1992.

Pastore, Carlos. "Introducción a la historia política del Paraguay." *Estudios Paraguayos* 4 (1976): 101–14.

Pilkington, William T. "The Journey of Cabeza de Vaca: An American Prototype." *South Dakota Review* 6 (1980): 73–82.

Pupo-Walker, Enrique. "Los *Naufragios* de Alvar Núñez Cabeza de Vaca: Notas sobre la relevancia antropológica del texto." *Revista de Indias* 47 (1987): 755–76.

———. "Pesquisas para una nueva lectura de los *Naufragios* de Alvar Núñez Cabeza de Vaca." *Revista Iberoamericana* 53 (1987): 517–39.

Quinn, David B., ed. *New American World.* 5 vols. New York: Ayer Company Publishers, 1979.

Rivarola, Juan Bautista. *La ciudad de la Asunción y la cédula real del 12 de setiembre de 1537.* Asunción: Impr. Militar, 1952.

Roeder, Ralph. *The Man of the Renaissance.* New York: Viking Press, 1933.

Rubio, Julián M. *Exploración y conquista del Río de la Plata, siglos XVI y XVII.* Buenos Aires: Salvat Editores, 1942.

Saeger, James S. "Another View of the Mission as a Frontier Institution: The Guaycuruan Reductions of Santa Fe, 1743–1810." *Hispanic American Historical Review* 65 (1985): 493–517.

———. "Eighteenth-Century Guaycuruan Missions in Paraguay." In *Indian-Religious Relations in Colonial Spanish America,* ed. Susan E. Ramírez, 55–86. Syracuse, N.Y.: Maxwell School of Citizenship and Public Affairs, Syracuse University, 1989.

Salas, Alberto M. *Crónica florida del mestizaje de las Indias.* Buenos Aires: Editorial Losada, 1960.

Salas, Alberto M., and Andrés Ramón Vásquez, eds. *Relación varia de hechos, hombres y cosas de estas Indias meridionales.* Buenos Aires: Editorial Losada, 1963.

Sánchez Quell, Hipólito. *Estructura y función del Paraguay colonial.* Asunción: Casa América, 1972.

Sauer, Carl. *Sixteenth-Century North America.* Berkeley: University of California Press, 1971.

Scarisbrick, J. J. *Henry VIII.* Berkeley: University of California Press, 1970.

Schmidel [Schmidt], Ulrich. *Viaje al Río de la Plata (1534–1554).* Ed. Samuel A. Lafone Quevedo. Buenos Aires: Cabaut y Cía., 1903.

Schmidt, Ulrich. "The Voyage of Ulrich Schmidt to the Rivers La Plata and Paraguai." In *The Conquest of the River Plate,* ed. Luis L. Dominguez, 1–91. London: Hakluyt Society, 1891.

Serrano y Sanz, Manuel, ed. *Relación de los naufragios y comentarios.* Supplementary sources. 2 vols. Madrid: V. Suárez, 1906.

Service, Elman R. "The *Encomienda* in Paraguay." *Hispanic American Historical Review* 31 (1951): 230–52.

———. *Spanish-Guarani Relations in Early Colonial Paraguay.* Ann Arbor, Mich., 1954. Reprint, Westport, Conn.: Greenwood Press, 1971.

Sevillano Colom, Francisco. "Lista del contenido de los volúmenes microfilmados del archivo nacional de Asunción." *Hispanic American Historical Review* 37 (1958): 60–120.

Sierra, Vicente D. *Historia de la Argentina.* 8 vols. Buenos Aires: Union de Editores Latinos, 1956–69.

Stern, Steve J. "The Rise and Fall of Indian-White Alliances: A Regional View of 'Conquest' History." *Hispanic American Historical Review* 61 (1981): 461–91.

Steward, Julian H., ed. *Handbook of South American Indians.* 6 vols. New York: Cooper Square Publishers, 1963.

Sturtevant, William C., and Alfonso Ortiz, eds. *Handbook of North American Indians.* Vol. 10, *Southwest.* Washington, D.C.: Smithsonian Institution Press, 1983.

Susnik, Branislava. *Los aborígenes del Paraguay.* 8 vols. Asunción: Museo Ethnográfico Andrés Barbera, 1978–87.

———. *El indio colonial del Paraguay.* 3 vols. Asunción: Instituto Paraguayo de Estudios Nacionales, 1965–71.

———. *El rol de los indígenas en la formación y en la vivencia del Paraguay.* 2 vols. Asunción: Instituto Paraguayo de Estudios Nacionales, 1982–83.

———. "Una visión antropológica del Paraguay colonial." *Historia Paraguaya* 21 (1984): 193–214.

Swanton, John R. *The Indians of the Southeastern United States.* New York: Greenwood Press, 1969. Originally published 1946.

Tao Anzoátegui, Victor. *Libros registros-cedularios del Río de la Plata (1534–1717): Catálogo I.* Buenos Aires: Instituto de Investigaciones de Historia del Derecho, 1984.

Tello, Antonio. *Libro segundo de la crónica miscelánea.* Guadalajara: Impr. de "La República Literaría" de C. L. de Guevara, 1891.

Thomas, David Hurst, ed. *Columbian Consequences,* vol 2., *Archeological and Historical Perspectives on the Spanish Borderlands East.* Washington, D.C.: Smithsonian Institution Press, 1990.

Torre Revello, José, ed. *Documentos históricos y geográficos relativos a la conquista y colonización Rioplatense.* 5 vols. Buenos Aires: Talleres Casa J. Peuser, 1941.

Vázquez de Espinosa, Antonio. *Compendium and Description of the West Indies.* Washington, D.C.: Smithsonian Institution Press, 1942.

Vega, Garcilaso de la. *The Florida of the Inca.* Trans. and ed. John Grier Varner and Jeannette Johnson Varner. Austin: University of Texas Press, 1951.

———. *Historia de la Florida: Obras completas del Inca Garcilaso de la Vega.* 4 vols. Madrid: Biblioteca de Autores Españoles, 1960.

Velásquez, Rafael Eladio. *Breve historia de la cultura en el Paraguay.* Asunción: [s.n.], 1965.

Villamarín, Juan A., and Judith E. Villamarín. *Indian Labor in Mainland Colonial Spanish America*. Newark: University of Delaware, 1975.

Vitoria, Francisco de. *Political Writings*. Trans. Jeremy Lawrence. Cambridge: Cambridge University Press, 1991.

Warren, Harris Gaylord. *Paraguay: An Informal History*. Norman: University of Oklahoma Press, 1949.

Weber, David J. *The Spanish Frontier in North America*. New Haven: Yale University Press, 1992.

Weddle, Robert S. *Spanish Sea: The Gulf of Mexico in North American Discovery, 1500–1685*. College Station: Texas A&M University Press, 1985.

Weil, Thomas E., et al. *Bolivia: A Country Study*. 2d ed. Washington, D.C.: U.S. Government Printing Office, 1985.

Zavala, Silvio. *Ensayos sobre la colonización Española en América*. Buenos Aires: Eméce Editores, 1944.

———. *New Viewpoints on the Spanish Colonization of America*. New York: Russell and Russell, 1968.

———. *Orígenes de la colonización en el Río de la Plata*. Mexico City: Editorial de El Colegio Nacional, 1978.

Zorraquín Becú, Ricardo. *La organización política Argentina en el período Hispánico*. Buenos Aires: Eméce Editores, 1959.

Zubizarreta, Carlos. *Capitanes de aventura: Cabeza de Vaca, el infortunado; Irala, el predestinado*. Madrid: Ediciones Cultura Hispánica, 1957.

———. *Historia de mi ciudad*. Asunción: Editorial EMASA, 1964.

Index

Fernández de la Torre, Bishop Pedro, 95, 143, 175
Francis I, King of France, 37
Friede, Juan, 43, 162
Fuentes, Pedro de, 63–64, 136, 150

Galán, Francisco, 174
Gandía, Enrique de, 1, 2, 39, 61, 90, 98, 101, 103, 119, 136, 156, 159, 160, 185, 188, 190
Garcia, Aleixo, 49, 88, 117, 121
González, Bartolomé, 153
González, Martín, 73, 149, 157, 162
González Paniagua, Francisco, 64, 69, 72, 94, 97, 98, 124, 127, 134–35, 138, 139, 140, 141, 149, 150, 151, 152, 153, 166, 170, 173–74, 194
Guerrero, Gonzalo, 194
Guevara, Isabel de, 61
Gutiérrez, Alonso, 185
Guzmán, Diego de, 15

Heredia, Pedro de, 134
Hernández, Pero (clerk and notary), 43, 44, 52, 60, 62, 75, 76, 77, 78, 79, 80, 81, 82, 89, 92, 93, 98, 110, 112, 113, 116, 118, 120, 123, 125, 128, 136, 138, 140, 143, 147, 148, 149, 150, 151, 152, 153, 154, 159, 161, 162, 163, 164, 165, 167, 170, 172, 173, 174, 175, 181, 184, 185, 186, 187, 189
Hernández el Romo, Andrés, 186
Herrera y Tordesillas, Antonio de, 39
Herrezuelo, Friar Luis de, 82, 101

Indians (North America): Apalaches, 6–8; Arbadaos, 18; Avavares, 12–13, 16–18, 30; Aztecs, 10; Capoques, 9; Charrucos, 10; Conchos, 18; Cuchendados, 18; Hans, 9; Iguases, 11; Jumanos, 14, 20; Karankawas, 9; Maliacones, 18; Mariames, 11; Pimas, 25; Timucuas, 4 (n. 8), 5–8; Tobosos, 18
Indians (South America): Agaces, 75–78, 84–86, 111, 139, 146, 180; Arrianicosies, 128–29, 132–34, 138; Carios (Carijó), 46, 77; Chanés, 115; Charruas, 38; Evueví, 77; Eyiguayegis, 78; Guarambarense, 85; Guaraníes, 38, 45–47, 49, 51–52, 54–56, 58–59, 61, 63, 66–68, 70, 74–89, 91, 107, 110–19, 121–22, 125, 127, 131, 133, 135, 138–40, 142, 145–46, 149, 180, 188, 196–98; Guaxarapos (Guachí), 119–20, 126, 132, 138, 140, 145; Guaycurúes, 76, 78–82, 84–86, 103, 188; Incas, 31, 33, 38, 49, 61, 66, 109, 121, Mbayá-Guaycurúes, 78; Mbiazás, 45; Orejones, 115; Payaguáes, 48, 76–77, 111–14, 119; Querandíes, 38; Sacocis, 115, 138, 140; Socorinos (Surucusis), 115, 138, 140, 188; Tarapecosis, 131; Timbúes, 38; Xaquetes (Xaqueses), 115, 138; Xarayes, 117–19, 129–30, 135; Yapirúes, 82–83
Irala, Captain Domingo Martínez de, 44, 59, 67–68, 70, 77, 80, 87, 89, 91, 98, 106, 109, 110, 115–16, 121, 151, 154, 156–57, 159, 161–65, 169, 176, 183, 185–86; death of Captain Juan de Ayolas, 111–13; exploration to Puerto de los Reyes, 85–86, 88, 90; 100–104; interim governor, Río de la Plata, 38, 60–63, 94–96, 153, 166–67, 177–78, 181–82, 189, 197; overthrow of Cabeza de Vaca, 124, 143, 145, 148–50, 152, 197
Isabella, Queen of Castile, 78
Isabella, Queen Regent of Spain, 59
Ivitachuco (Apalache), 6

About the Author

David A. Howard is Professor of History, Houghton College, Houghton, New York. He received his bachelor's degree from Gordon College, Wenham, Massachusetts, and his master's degree and doctorate from Duke University, Durham, North Carolina. His publications include *The Royal Indian Hospital of Mexico City* (1980).